Lost and Found in Translation

Lost and Found
in Translation

Contemporary Ethnic American

Writing and the Politics

of Language Diversity

MARTHA J. CUTTER

The University of North Carolina Press   Chapel Hill

© 2005 The University of North Carolina Press
Manufactured in the United States of America

Designed and typeset in Adobe Garamond by BW&A Books, Inc.

Chapter 1 has been reprinted in revised form from *Criticism* 39 (1997): 581–612, by permission of Wayne State University Press.

An excerpt from "Drowning in My Own Language" has been reprinted from Mitsuye Yamada, *Camp Notes and Other Writings*, © 1976, 1980, 1986, 1988, 1992 by Mitsuye Yamada, by permission of Rutgers University Press. "Querida Compañera" has been reprinted from Cherríe Moraga, *Loving in the War Years*, by permission of South End Press.

This book was published with the assistance of the Anniversary Endowment Fund of the University of North Carolina Press.

The paper in this book meets the guidelines for permanence and durability of the Committee on Production Guidelines for Book Longevity of the Council on Library Resources.

Library of Congress Cataloging-in-Publication Data
Cutter, Martha J.
Lost and found in translation : contemporary ethnic American writing and the politics of language diversity / Martha J. Cutter.
    p. cm.
Includes bibliographical references and index.
ISBN 0-8078-2977-3 (alk. paper)—ISBN 0-8078-5637-1 (pbk.: alk. paper)
1. American literature—Minority authors—History and criticism.
2. Language and languages—Political aspects—United States.
3. Minorities—United States—Intellectual life. 4. Pluralism (Social sciences) in literature. 5. Ethnic relations in literature. 6. Ethnic groups in literature. 7. United States—Languages. 8. Minorities in literature.
9. Ethnicity in literature. I. Title.
PS153.M56C88 2005
810.9'920693—dc22   2005016886

cloth   09 08 07 06 05   5 4 3 2 1
paper   09 08 07 06 05   5 4 3 2 1

Contents

Acknowledgments

I MUST BEGIN by thanking my students at Kent State University, who have for several years now been listening to me discuss my passionate obsession with the theme of translation in ethnic American literature. More to the point, they have often pointed out textual nuances I had not noticed, and this book would not have been what it is without their insights.

I also owe a large debt of gratitude to Françoise Massardier-Kenney and Fanny Arango-Keeth for allowing me to audit their translation theory seminar in the Department of Modern and Classical Language Studies at Kent State University. Françoise and Fanny generously listened to my ideas and shared their expertise with me in a way that gave real meaning to the term "community of scholars." I also thank Carol Maier for discussion of my ideas about Malinche, who plays a role in Chapter 5. Tim Morris offered helpful feedback on the introduction and general enthusiasm for the project. I am indebted to Betsy Huang for her thoughts on the role of translation in Chinese American literature and to Debby Rosenthal for helping me revise Chapter 5 on Chicano/a literature. Peter Ibarra discussed with me many of my ideas on Chicano/a literature and language and helped with some of the translations in Chapter 5. Terry Rowden's feedback on Chapter 4 and on the introduction and his general enthusiasm for the project have also been invaluable; I thank Terry as well for recommending that I read Derrida's *Monolingualism of the Other*, which plays a pivotal role in this book's conclusion. I thank Florence Dore for asking me some pointed questions about the project and for help in formulating my revision response letter. Tom Hines provided valuable suggestions about the title and about publishers. Werner Sollors, Bonnie Tu-Smith, and Keith Byerman also offered warm support for the project. To Carolyn Sorisio I owe a vast debt of gratitude; she has read many of my chapters and offered insightful criticism and intellectual and moral support for the project.

A special thanks also to my friends known as the "SBs": Robert Trogdon, Carol Harrison (in absentia), Gene Pendelton, Deborah Barnbaum, Susan Roxburgh, Jeff Kreidler, Linda Williams, Deb Smith, and Gina Zavota. The support of the SBs over the past ten years at Kent State has been crucial to my success as a scholar and my happiness as a human being. I also thank Xavier Brice, who discussed many of my ideas about translation theory with me, and Mayuri Deka, who helped with the proofreading of the manuscript. Walter Corbella spent a great deal of time and energy carefully checking citations and proofreading; he also helped with some difficult translations in Chapter 5, for which I am very grateful.

I thank the Division of Research and Graduate Studies at Kent State University for granting me research leaves in the spring of 2000 and the spring of 2003 to work on this book. Research and Graduate Studies also granted me money to pay permission fees and hire a research assistant to help with citation checking and the index. Over and over again RAGS (as the division is, rather ironically, known) has aided me in my research. Kent State University's English Department also granted me a sabbatical leave during the fall of 2001, during which I completed Chapters 4 and 5. I would not have been able to finish this project in a timely fashion were it not for this generous university and departmental support.

Finally, I owe a large debt of gratitude to my family and especially to my mother and father, Eve and Philip Cutter. They have always supported my efforts to be a scholar and offered me much moral support during difficult times. I am sure that this book would not have been possible without them.

This book is dedicated to all the writers of ethnic American literature that I have studied over the past fifteen years. Their cogent and articulate struggles with language have encouraged me to find my own voice as a scholar and a writer and to refuse to speak in "the master's tongue."

Lost and Found in Translation

Introduction

Translation as Transmigration

"IT IS NORMALLY supposed that something always gets lost in translation; I cling, obstinately, to the notion that something can always be gained," remarks Indian writer Salman Rushdie in *Imaginary Homelands* (17). The topic of cultural translation has been extensively assessed in postcolonial writing and criticism, yet few scholars have acknowledged that a wide variety of contemporary ethnic American writers from diverse time periods deploy questions of literary and cultural translation in their works. Although most of their texts are written in English and the ethnic language is most often transcribed into English words, ethnic American writers maintain a constant preoccupation with questions of cultural translation: Who can be a translator? What can be translated? When a second- or third-generation child no longer speaks the parent's ethnic tongue, what gets "lost" in translation? And what might be "found" in translation? Finally, as Gustavo Pérez Firmat phrases it in a clever linguistic wordplay, how might "translation [take us] to a place where cultures divide to conga" (*Life* 21–22)—where they mesh, mingle, and re-create themselves in a border zone or even border dance of linguistic and cultural free fall?

Through analysis of twenty works of fiction and autobiography written by contemporary ethnic writers, this book examines the simultaneous loss and gain of translation. I demonstrate that there is a trope of cultural and linguistic translation specific to this body of writing and distinguishable from the treatment of this topic in Anglo-American literature; this trope involves transcoding ethnicity, transmigrating the ethnic tongue into the English language, and renovating the language of hegemony. I contend that the trope of translation recurs in the twenty works of fiction and autobiography discussed in this book as well as in many other works of ethnic American literature because it presents a central methodology for reformulating and reconceptualizing the relationship between the American and the ethnic, the child and the parent, the dominant discourse and the marginalized one; translation typifies, then, a remaking of not only language but also racial, generational, and cultural identities.

Debates about translation in these texts often reflect questions about the feasibility of inhabiting multiple linguistic worlds and creating multiple ethnic cultures. An effective translator can creatively mesh languages and worldviews so that the spiritual, cultural, and social values of the original or parent culture are not lost as the translator moves into a new culture and language. For these writers, translation entails moving the ideas and values of one culture to a new context, but it also involves transplanting, transmigrating these ideas—making a new location for them in the new world and the new language they must inhabit. Literary and cultural translation also divides and unmakes separate languages to "conga" them—to both conquer and remake them; translation entwines these languages in a syncretic linguistic whole that is still marked by difference, that is still (and always) divided by conga. Pérez Firmat argues that over the past several decades in the United States, Cuba and America have been on a "collusion course"; the best products of this collision/collusion display "an intricate equilibrium between the claims of each culture" (*Life* 6). As he notes, however, equilibrium does not necessarily mean stasis—it also involves the "freedom to mix and match pieces from each culture" (7), to combine cultural and linguistic entities into balances that are more than the sum of the parts. The conga as a dance form can appropriate aspects of past and present, of Latin, Hispanic, and Anglo cultures; it can incorporate cultural forms and then evolve again into something new.[1] Similarly, I argue that the translator may achieve more than synthesis between cultures (A + B = AB); instead she or he may enable the emergence of new and unique cultural and linguistic formulations (A + B = C). I also hypothesize that there is a trope of translation specific to ethnic American literature that crosses boundaries of diverse ethnic identities and therefore may be considered "transethnic." In this trope a new mode of voice, language, or subjectivity may be formulated that meshes—but also exceeds—prior subjectivities or languages.

The parameters of this trope can be briefly elucidated through an example, discussed in more detail in the next chapter. Initially the translation conflict seems to center on language, with the protagonist of the work of ethnic literature refusing or resisting translation and seeking instead assimilation to the dominant norm, to the language of hegemony, English. There is also a concomitant rejection of the parent or ethnic culture. In Maxine Hong Kingston's *The Woman Warrior* (1976), the young protagonist's mother demands that she return some medicine that a pharmacist has erroneously sent her family—a bad omen in Chinese tradition that only candy (or "sweetness") can amend. The protagonist does not think she can translate this Chinese custom, and indeed she does not believe this custom is worthy of translation, of transmigration or relocation within a new context, as the following conversation with her mother reveals:

> "You say, 'You have tainted my house with sick medicine and must remove the curse with sweetness.' He'll understand."
> "They don't understand stuff like that. I won't be able to say it right. He'll call us beggars."
> "You just translate." She searched me to make sure I wasn't hiding any money. (170)

The protagonist's tone—calling the custom "stuff like that" which will mark her family as "beggars"—signifies a derogatory stance toward the ethnic culture of China, which is often depicted in Kingston's work as "alien" or "other." The custom itself appears to be well on its way to being lost in translation. So perhaps it is predictable that the protagonist then refuses even to attempt to translate this tradition to the druggist:

> "Mymotherseztagimmesomecandy," I said to the druggist.
> . . .
> "What? Speak up. Speak English," he said, big in his white druggist coat.

"Tatatagimme somecandy."
The druggist leaned way over the counter and frowned.
"Some free candy," I said. "Sample candy."
"We don't give sample candy, young lady," he said. (170)

The protagonist falls into child-speak ("tatatagimme somecandy")
or falsehoods ("sample candy") that elide the real significance of the
Chinese tradition. In the course of the work, however, Kingston's
autobiographical persona develops facility as a translator. As argued
in Chapter 1, she transmigrates her mother's language and customs
to a new context, but Kingston also transcodes the meaning of
her own ethnicity: it no longer functions as "baggage" she must
"discard" but as something that can give her "ancestral strength"
in the difficult world of America. So the work ends fittingly with
Kingston's re-creation of one of her mother's Chinese stories about
a woman translator and the following three words: "It translated
well." The trope of translation is fundamental to Kingston's ability to transcode ethnicity so that she can be *both* American and
ethnic; this trope also allows her to transmigrate Chinese language
and customs into the English language and into her new cultural
context. What appears to be "lost" in translation is finally "found"
through an act of metaphorical translation itself.

Kingston's text, for the most part, only rarely includes Chinese
words and their English translations, but it is nonetheless preoccupied with a series of translation dilemmas written into the English
language of the text. Other texts are more multilingual. Effective
translations are often created by a translator who moves between
different dialects, speaks several languages, blends languages, or
"codeswitches"—moves back and forth between different languages.
Therefore I also consider the role bilingualism, intralingual translation (translation within a language or between different codes or
dialects), codeswitching, multilingualism, and other related linguistic phenomena play in the trope of translation as it is presented
in these texts.

It should be emphasized that these struggles over translation
are often transcribed into English and only textually represented
—that is, a parent and child may have a debate in two languages
about which language one should speak in the home, yet within

the text itself this debate is transcribed *into* English by the author. In the above exchange from Kingston's text, for example, Kingston's mother speaks Chinese, as she does throughout the text, yet the Chinese language is not used to represent this conversation. The struggle over translation, then, is not represented lexically or linguistically in this passage but rather thematically. As I will demonstrate, often translation is not an actual lexical practice in these texts but rather a trope—a metaphorical construct utilized to constellate a series of questions about ethnic identities, language practices, and the way tongues from other cultures can (or cannot) be preserved within the linguistic domain of the English language.

Translation as trope also concerns a struggle to transcode the meaning of ethnicity itself so that one can be both ethnic and "American."[2] Historically, forgetting the parent language (whether it is Chinese, Dakota, Mexican Spanish, or African American Vernacular English) was sometimes understood as facilitating the assumption of an assimilated "American" identity. According to Werner Sollors, in the early history of this country some individuals believed that "'American' meant 'white'" ("National Identity" 93), and even today the "inclusive use of 'American' remains ambiguous" and does not include all languages and cultural traditions (115). Standard definitions present ethnicity as a form of bonding between peoples structured around languages, ancestry, and other symbolic elements: "An ethnic group is defined here as a collectivity within a larger society having real or putative common ancestry, memories of a shared historical past, and a cultural focus on one or more symbolic elements defined as the epitome of their peoplehood. Examples of such symbolic elements are: kinship patterns, physical contiguity, . . . religious affiliation, language or dialect forms, tribal affiliation, nationality, phenotypical features, or any combination of these" (Schermerhorn 12). However, as Stuart Hall notes, ethnicity is constructed culturally, historically, and politically through a politics of "difference." Hall and others suggest that in a discourse of racism, the "ethnic" was often set off against the "mainstream" group as the "other" who is *of* the nation but not quite *part* of the nation (162). Hall argues that we must "transcode" ethnicity—disarticulate the term from the discourse of racism. For the writers discussed in this book, the trope of translation is fundamental to their attempts to transcode ethnicity—to recuperate it so that it no longer signifies an "alien" or "excluded" other but rather a plurality of interarticulated subject positions *within* the discourse of the "American."

In the works I discuss, a refusal to translate is often allied with an attempt to assimilate into an identity as a white American and a corresponding refusal to transcode ethnicity and create an identity that is multicultural and multilinguistic. Still, I do not maintain that in these texts translation as trope resolves the tensions of multicultural and multilinguistic identities. Indeed, struggles over translation can be violent. White settlers, for example, used Native American translators to gain access to indigenous cultures of the United States. Once this access was acquired, they attempted to force their ideology, religion, language, and culture down the throats of Native Americans. Translators who resisted this imperative often suffered a dire fate: death or the silencing of their voices. But death does not always mean that the translator stops her rebellious translations and transmigrations, as argued in the discussion of Susan Power's *The Grass Dancer* (1994) in Chapter 3. Translation as trope often signifies a process of continual negotiation and renegotiation between languages and an ongoing struggle between conflicting and often clashing cultures and ideologies.

In some of the works discussed, however, translation creates a syncretic reconciliation between competing cultures, languages, and ideologies; translation, in other words, enables the coalescence of varying, often contradictory systems of language and culture into a new conglomerate that is itself (often) still marked by internal inconsistencies. The languages and cultures are not merely blended so that differences disappear or are washed away; in fact, differences between languages and cultures remain within the new linguistic and cultural formation. To use a metaphor, two different roses (a red one and a white one) might be hybridized in such a way that differences disappear (a pink rose is produced). Or they might be hybridized in such a way that differences remain (the red rose and the white rose produce a new type of flower that is red with white streaks, markings, or even dots). I argue that translation as trope, in its most radical moments, can produce a text in which differences remain or undergo change, but they do not disappear.

Translation as trope transcodes ethnicity, but it also transcodes the meaning of the ethnic tongue so that it is no longer a disenfranchised dialect but rather part of the very texture of American speech. Translation may also create a new mode of speech that exceeds the original dialects or codes of which it is comprised. Translation theorists have argued that a good translation is a new work of art that both embodies and surpasses the original text.[3] A successful translation takes account of the "source text" (the original world and language) but also re-creates this source text so that it admits of a new reality (the "target" world and culture).[4] A good translation of *Crime and Punishment*, it might be argued, is no longer purely English or Russian but both. Raskolnikov's and Sonya's names should not be transformed into "Ray" and "Sue," for example, because the translator must maintain a sense of another language's and culture's presence, even while writing in English, the target language. As a trope in the works discussed, translation evokes a crossing of borders, a permeation of barriers erected between what seem to be separate and disjunctive cultural and linguistic terrains (the ethnic and the American). Therefore in these texts, translation literally enables communication between the different generations, but more symbolically it produces a new intercultural, interlinguistic entity that ultimately transmigrates tongues and transcodes ethnicities.

Some of the characters who are translators, then, may achieve an ethnic identity and mode of voice that is more than the sum of their parts. As one linguist has recently suggested, codeswitching (the use of two languages within a single communicative episode) is emblematic of a dual identity (Poplack, "Contrasting Patterns" 237). But at times this dual identity and speech, this codeswitching, becomes integrative and syncretic.[5] In the example presented above from *The Woman Warrior*, initially the protagonist sees her mother's Chinese traditions as alien and refuses to translate them. But because she does not deny the contradictions between being Chinese and being American, she eventually creates a methodology of storytelling that goes beyond biculturalism and bilingualism. As illustrated in Chapter 1, Kingston's protagonist finds a creative syncretism that through collision and collusion enables the emergence of innovative forms of language and identity. In so doing she becomes more aware of how she can inhabit an identity as

Chinese American—in short, she transcodes herself. Similarly, in Leslie Marmon Silko's *Ceremony* (1977) the medicine man Betonie speaks English but gives certain words a distinct Native American meaning. For instance, Betonie speaks the word "comfortable" in English, but by the way he uses it, the protagonist Tayo knows that Betonie intends a distinct Native American meaning—the comfort of belonging to the land rather than the more Anglicized notion of the comfort material wealth can provide (117). Betonie does not simply move between the native tongue and English; instead, he transmigrates both tongues until "marginal" and "majority" discourse cannot be disentangled.

A transcoding of ethnicity and a transmigration of tongues can occur only when the protagonists of these texts become "writerly" translators who actively participate with the source text, struggle to understand its complexities, and refuse to take a passive and literal approach to its meaning.[6] A writerly translator is also willing to re-create the source text for a new audience and a new culture; such a translator does not deny the contradictions between worlds but rather uses them productively. These characters finally realize that it is precisely their divergent and often contradictory cultural/ linguistic heritages that engender the ability to produce new meanings, new stories, translations that break down binary oppositions, enriching and finally re-creating both cultural terrains. As Sherry Simon comments in a discussion of Canadian writing, translation represents difference both within and between languages—or "the play of equivalence and difference in cultural interchange." Translation therefore "permits communication without eliminating the grounds of [cultural] specificity" (159). Translation is a crucial trope for the theorization of ethnic literature, then, because it presents a methodology for the movement beyond binary thinking about "the Ethnic" and "the American"—a methodology that illustrates how these categories can enrich, interanimate, and finally re-create each other. By studying translation struggles, writers and readers learn how to "divide to conga"—how to renovate the dominant language by unearthing its hidden multilinguistic subtexts, how to re-create the language of hegemony by teaching the play of equivalence and difference, of conga-ing and conquering, it contains.

Not all the authors considered in this book, however, deploy the trope of translation to create transcoded ethnicities and trans-migrated tongues. A number of the writers discussed (such as N. Scott Momaday) stress the failure of translation, its inability to mesh worlds—in other words, what is irrevocably lost in transla-tion. And several of the writers (such as Sherman Alexie or Richard Rodriguez) sometimes argue that actual translation is unnecessary —one can preserve the world without the word, the culture with-out the language. And there are many ethnic writers who do not believe that speaking a particular language is a key to an "authen-tic" identity. As such writers as Ien Ang have argued, *not speaking* a particular language (such as Chinese) is still a political and social positioning of ethnic identity (553). Yet individuals from a wide va-riety of ethnic cultures must contend with the fact that they are expected to be bilingual and to translate. Thus the "imperative to translate" shapes their sense of linguistic and social identity, even when they remain uninterested in the ethnic language. In this book I examine this set of expectations. In all the works discussed, trans-lation as trope is a significant metaphor for the negotiation between cultural and linguistic identities, between words and worlds, that is at the center of contemporary ethnic American literatures. Trans-lation represents one methodology for depicting power struggles within language and culture but also for reconfiguring these power struggles, so it is not surprising that it is foregrounded in ethnic literature.

Furthermore, there is a trope of translation distinctive to eth-nic American literature—one that is transethnic because it crosses the boundaries of groups normally kept separate. However, to date, few critical studies have provided discussion of the significance of this trope. Pioneering books such as Mary Dearborn's *Pocahontas's Daughters* (1986), Werner Sollors's *Beyond Ethnicity* (1986), and Bonnie TuSmith's *All My Relatives* (1993) consider a wide range of ethnic writers but not how often such writers refer to linguistic or cultural translation. Explication of the trope of translation is infrequent even within discussions of specific ethnic traditions. I have found only one discussion of translation in Chinese American literature and no treatment of it in Japanese American literature.[7] And while there have certainly been considerations of the oral and vernacular roots of African American literature, no critic has explored the trope of translation that is often present in these works. When literary scholars such as Alfred Arteaga and Juan Bruce-Novoa have discussed Chicano/a (Mexican American) literature as bilingual or "interlingual" (between languages), they have failed to notice how often this interlingualism is broached through the metaphor of translation. Finally, one more recent collection of essays— *Multilingual America: Transnationalism, Ethnicity, and the Languages of American Literature* (1998), edited by Werner Sollors,—considers the multiple languages of American literature but not translation as a trope in ethnic literature as a whole.[8]

The translation of Native American literature and translation in Native American literature, on the other hand, have received some critical attention.[9] Yet none of these critics have examined parallels between Native American writers' preoccupation with translation and other ethnic writers' concern with this subject, and none of these critics have argued for the idea of a trope that involves transmigrating tongues and transcoding ethnicity so that the language of hegemony is refashioned. Moreover, while Arnold Krupat has contended that "it seems virtually impossible to speak of Native American literatures, both oral and written, without speaking of translation in the very many senses that word has taken on today" and that Native American literary texts contain a translated, "re-colonized" English marked by traces of Native American language ("Postcoloniality" 164, 177), Krupat here pays little attention to the language of the texts themselves. My book focalizes this question: *What* is the language of the text? On both a lexical and a thematic level, how does the text transmigrate another language into English? And what questions of language and identity underlie these transformations, these transmigrations of English itself? Krupat's postulation that Native American writers participate in "anti-imperial translation" is valuable, but it is not enough. We must look closely at the language of the texts and at what is (and is not) translated in them to understand how this anti-imperial impulse functions.

One of the indispensable ideas operational in translation theory is that we are all, always, on some level caught in the process of translation. Language is not a perfect medium, and it is not transparent. At some point in our lives everyone has to learn to translate.

I say something to you. You do not understand. I must reword it, rework it—translate it, in a sense. Students in freshmen composition classes must routinely learn how to translate their thoughts into standardized, academic discourse. Many postmodern theorists argue that we are all, to some degree, exiles in language—that we can constitute ourselves as subjects only by separating ourselves from the mother and the mother tongue. As translator Claude Lévesque phrases this in a comment to deconstructive critic Jacques Derrida, "I know that, for you, in order for any language to be a language, it can only be—structurally—a place of exile, a medium where absence, death, and repetition rule without exception" (143). There is a telling moment in Toni Morrison's novel *Beloved* (1987) when Paul D. tells Sethe, "You got two feet, Sethe, not four" (165). Paul D. can only understand Sethe's killing of one of her own children as the behavior of a brutal animal with four legs rather than the act of a human being, much less a loving mother. "Right then a forest sprang up between them; trackless and quiet" (165) is Morrison's next concise comment. Paul D. and Sethe no longer speak the same language, which is a failure of translation in its broadest sense—they manifest an inability to find the words that might cross the forest, bridge the opposite sides of their experiences as man and woman, as enslaved and freed selves.

Morrison's *Beloved* is very attentive to processes of storytelling and of locating the language to bring unspoken experiences into the realm of the spoken, or at least the speakable. It is also concerned with whether characters who speak African American Vernacular English are empowered or disempowered in relationship to the dominant discourse (Standardized English) and in society. When Sixo, for example, logically and eloquently argues in dialect that he had a right to steal, cook, and eat Schoolteacher's shoat in order to make himself a better worker and thereby "improve" Schoolteacher's property, he is still beaten because "definitions belong to the definer—not the defined" (190). Sixo cannot manipulate or renovate the language of hegemony, and eventually he gives up speaking English altogether except for his final naming of his progeny as Seven-O. In certain key moments, then, *Beloved* engages with questions of translation, but the novel as a whole does not focalize the trope of translation as it is used here: it does not assess how translation might transcode ethnicity and hybridize tongues so that a new mode of discourse is created out of the fission and fusion between African American Vernacular English and Standardized English. Translation is a major trope undergirding ethnic literature as a whole, but some texts stress this trope more than others; this book therefore focuses on texts in which translation is an explicitly discussed subject and translation struggles are integral to the plot's final movement. Most of these texts, in fact, use the term "translation" to describe this struggle. For example, the theme of translation surfaces more insistently in Kingston's *The Woman Warrior* than in *China Men*, and it comes up more often and more explicitly in *Tar Baby* than in any other work by Morrison. For each chapter I selected texts that specifically emphasize the trope of translation, the transcoding of ethnicity, and the attempted movement toward a syncretic voice or text. This does not mean that in these texts other terms or tropes are not employed at times, such as storytelling, bilingualism, multilingualism, or codeswitching; I will also consider these practices extensively. However, in the specific texts I discuss, the trope of translation is emphasized above these other linguistic practices, and other linguistic methodologies are most often deployed in the service of a larger translative enterprise or struggle.

As mentioned above, from a postmodern viewpoint we are all always-already caught in the process of translation. And as Eric Cheyfitz points out, it is not only ethnic American individuals who struggle over questions of language and cultural identity. Anglo-Americans tend to figure themselves as monolingual and monocultural, but this is not exactly the case; many Anglo-Americans have forgotten an ethnic language that their parents or grandparents or great-grandparents spoke (Yiddish, Irish, Polish, Italian). So perhaps it is not surprising that the topic of translation is broached by some Anglo-American writers, such as Cormac McCarthy in *Blood Meridian* (1985), T. C. Boyle in *The Tortilla Curtain* (1995), and Barbara Kingsolver in *The Poisonwood Bible* (1998). However, I do not discuss such texts because the trope of translation functions in a radically different manner in them. More specifically, often the translator is portrayed as evil, and translation transgresses or destroys ethnic cultural values. The mission of the translator frequently entails colonization and decimation of indigenous peoples and their languages as well. In such works, then, translation as trope often concerns a portrayal and critique of the attempted dominance of hegemony and hegemonic discourses over disenfranchised peoples and marginalized dialects, and as such it does not involve a transcoding of ethnicity. For example, in McCarthy's *Blood Meridian* the character known as "the Judge" uses his knowledge of many languages (Native American, Spanish, Latin, German, and English) and his ability to translate to destroy almost every individual he comes into contact with and to steal any texts that contain indigenous languages. In *The Tortilla Curtain* the translator figure uses his language skills to rape and abuse a Mexican woman named, ironically, América and to swindle her husband out of his last possessions. And in *The Poisonwood Bible* Kingsolver's missionary father-figure produces ludicrous translations of the English Bible into African language—translations that never cross the boundaries between Africa and America, between the Congolese discourse and the English spoken by the missionary family. In these texts there is little hope that translation can create a syncretic reconciliation between competing languages and cultures, although Kingsolver does suggest that the younger generation may eventually move beyond the cultural and linguistic binarisms her novel so painstakingly explicates and reproaches.

Obviously, these novels are only three from the vast corpus of contemporary fiction written by Anglo-Americans, but I use them to suggest that the trope of translation, when it is represented by Anglo-American writers (which is infrequent), is deployed in a manner dissimilar from the way this trope is deployed in ethnic American literature. Certainly the topic of how these three novels, to which I might add works such as John Griffin's *Black Like Me* (1962), William Styron's *The Confessions of Nat Turner* (1966), and Don DeLillo's *White Noise* (1985), deploy the representation of ethnic discourse and the trope of translation would be an excellent subject for another book, but I am confident that such a book would reach conclusions that diverge from those I reach here. These differences, of course, should not be tied to biological aspects of race or ethnicity but to sociohistorical and political ones. Anglo-American writers for various reasons may be more invested in a critique of the (white) translator figure and of translation, whereas ethnic writers are more invested in showing an (ethnic) translator who can mediate binarisms, transmigrate tongues, and reformulate cultural and linguistic practices.

Certainly, some authors of ethnic American literature represent translators who endeavor to use translation for colonialistic purposes and who do not see language barriers as permeable. In general, however, their texts depict the failure of this impulse and the dismantlement of numerous binarisms—hegemonic discourse versus marginal dialect, empowered subjectivity versus the disempowered "other," and American versus ethnic. In doing so, many of these writers create a new mode of language and a new construction of ethnicity for their characters that exceeds the sum of the parts. The commonalities I will discuss in this book between the writers—the commonalities that are "transethnic" in that they cross ethnic boundaries—are fourfold. First, these authors value writerly, active, resistant translation more than readerly, passive, or literal translation. Translation as trope, then, works to remodel and remake the "source text"—the parent's ethnic language and world—but also the "target text"—the language and culture of the United States. But, second, this remodeling is not exclusively deconstructive, and indeed, an effective translation can occur only when there is respect for both the "source text" and the "target text" —a sense that both possess something that is worthy of translation and preservation. A third point of parallelism in these texts is an additive rather than subtractive attitude toward language itself —a politics, in other words, of language diversity. Many of these writers imply that the more languages, codes, or dialects one has in one's linguistic reservoir, the more effective an individual will be as a translator and storyteller and the more agency he or she will wield as a subject. Codes, dialects, and tongues are amassed, blended, and transformed; the aural or oral is mingled with the written; new kinds of words are formed through fusion between different languages; and new dialects are created through commingling of tongues within English, such as African American Vernacular English (AAVE) and Standardized English (SE). Furthermore, multiple discursive identities are not sutured over in favor of "one" voice, of a homogenous tongue. Finally, and logically, it follows that these writers indicate that both the dominant discourse and the "minority" tongue may undergo significant revision and remodeling within the spaces of translation. Both disenfranchised and hegemonic discourses may be remade through this conga-ing, this fusion, this fission. In certain texts something new is created by this process of encroachment, revision, and reappropriation— a mode of language that can no longer be viewed as a "source" or a "target" but must be viewed as both, simultaneously.

Of course, not all writers from all ethnic groups formalize this trope in precisely the same way. As Ang articulates, it is crucial to pay attention "to the particular historical conditions and the specific trajectories through which actual social subjects become incommensurably different *and* similar" (545), something I take into account in this book. It is also crucial to comprehend that social categories of race and ethnicity *continue* to play a constitutive role in the formulation of identity. Therefore within and across particular groups there will be differences in how ethnic identity and language are interlinked, but some significant commonalties as well, as outlined above.

I also want to emphasize that although this trope of translation often moves toward resolution of ethnic conflicts, many of these texts frequently stress the limitations of this process and what translation as trope fails to achieve. Perhaps this seems paradoxical, but it is not, for this simultaneous loss and gain is at the heart of translation. As I explain in the next section, some theorists view translation as an exclusively positive process (a form of cultural enrichment of the target culture), whereas others view it as an exclusively negative process (a form of colonization of the source culture). But the most prescient translation theorists emphasize the multiple cultural and linguistic roles of loss *and* gain that translation can actually perform concurrently. In discussing translation in the past, Susan Bassnett argues that since Roman readers knew both Greek and Roman, the translated text was considered as a kind of metatext in relation to the original. Therefore, "the translated text was read *through* the source text" (45). In the current context, the majority of U.S. readers are predominantly monolingual, but metaphorically one way of figuring translation is as a kind of palimpsest. Certain practices of translation within the texts discussed can allow us to hear/read two cultures and to hear/read (at least) two voices at once. As Simon argues, "translation is not only the appropriation of previously existing texts in a mode of vertical succession; it is the materialization of our relationship to otherness, to the experience—through language—of what is different" (160). Translation as trope can be a representation of both differences and similarities within and between languages—and within and between cultures. It can allow us to hear a double voice: the voice of the source text/culture as it speaks through the target text/culture, and the voice of the target text/culture as it is modified by interaction with the source text/culture. Ethnic American writers use the trope of translation, then, to speak in a double voice that finally attempts to dismantle the line between a process of translation that colonizes and a process of translation that enriches, and to undermine the demarcation between the "majority" discourse and the "marginal" dialect.

AS INDICATED ABOVE, numerous translation theorists have examined similar questions: whether translation can move beyond a model of appropriation/domination, whether writers can produce "resistant" translations that are strange and estranging, and whether translation must of necessity replicate binarisms present in the power relations and language politics of the "real" world or can somehow move beyond them. In this section I therefore discuss recent developments in the field of translation theory relevant to the overall project. The first two ideas from this field concern what translation is *not*. Translation is not a *literal* transfer of meaning from one text to another, and translation is not *only about language*. To take the first point, in the translation of literary texts it has become a given that the translator must strive to do more than render literal meaning, for to render the literal meaning of something like a poem is to lose its spirit. Translation is often figured as an interpretation of a literary text rather than an actual rendering of it. As André Lefevere phrases this idea, translations "are only one type of text that makes an 'image' of another text" (15). Recognizing the impossibility of literal translation, theorists argue that translation is about finding metaphors or analogies, about choice and freedom of interpretation, and about the creation of a coauthored literary text.[10] The translator is portrayed as being both a reader and a writer of the source text (Díaz-Diocaretz 9), or as creating a new text that takes on a life of its own (Weinberger and Paz 1). In the current moment, translation is seen as a creative and interpretive act.

In the past some individuals saw translation as a secondary, derivative, and often feminized art. And in the twentieth century, authors such as Vladimir Nabokov have tried to hold to a literal standard of translation (127). But most contemporary translators endorse ideas of "free translation." Still, they have not abandoned all notions of "faithfulness" to the source text. According to Philip Lewis, translators need to shift their attention from the signified to the "chain of signifiers" (43). In other words, translators need to shift from specific meanings of words to the larger linguistic and social world these words convey. In a discussion of translating a Tamil poem, for example, A. K. Ramanujan speaks of translating "not only Tamil, its phonology, grammar, and semantics, but this entire intertextual web, this intricate yet lucid second language of landscapes which holds together natural forms with cultural ones in a code, a grammar, a rhetoric, a poetics" (57). Translators try to capture a text's connotative meanings, its intertextual and extra-textual worlds. But translators also need to understand the target culture's values—the audience for whom they are translating the text. Translation must therefore be seen as a negotiation between cultures—a back-and-forth movement between source culture and target culture. As Ramanujan later argues, "To translate is to 'metaphor,' to 'carry across.' . . . Yet 'anything goes' will not do. The translation must not only re-present, but represent, the original. One walks a tightrope between the To-language and the From-language, in a double loyalty" (61–62).

Later in this introduction I discuss paradigms of translation that move beyond a binary model of this process, but it should be noted here that the use of such terms as "fidelity" versus "infidelity" or "literal" versus "free" translation is problematic. In a discussion of the issue of fidelity, Robert Wechsler hypothesizes that the best translators need to be creatively unfaithful to the source text—that is, faithfully unfaithful (107). Barbara Johnson explicates this differently when she speaks of the translator's loyalties being split between "a native language and a foreign tongue." The translator must therefore be estimated not as "a duteous spouse but as a faithful bigamist" ("Taking Fidelity" 142–43). Perhaps this begs the issue of *to* what, exactly, the translator is supposed to be a faithful bigamist. Certainly, this varies with each translator and the employment to which each translation will be put. The paramount matter for many translators is cognizance of their double loyalties, their tendencies toward both infidelity and fidelity—in short, that translation becomes the subject of creative and conscientious deliberation. According to Wechsler, "balancing, rather than fidelity, is the central ethical act of translation, the act that allows for the redemption of losses, for respecting a work's integrity, for the recreation of another, freestanding work of art" (140). But this balancing can occur only when the translator has thought carefully and creatively about his or her obligations to both the words and the worlds of the source text, as well as the words and the worlds of the target text.

For translation is often about the clash and conflict between worldviews—about cultural power and disempowerment. The second point, then, concerns how translation embodies struggles not only over language but also politics and ideology. Numerous theorists have argued that translation must be understood as occurring within a political context and a structure of power relations (Chamberlain 66; Lefevere 27; Mehrez, "Translation" 121; Simon 160; Venuti 10). What is chosen for translation is often a matter of what the translating culture decides to value, and how it gets translated often has much to do with the translator's own political or cultural horizons. To give an example, when networks wanted to bring the Japanese cartoon *Pokémon* (or "Pocket-Monsters") to U.S. television, they removed many traces of Japanese culture from the cartoon. When the characters eat food that is considered to be too specific to Japan, such as sushi, more generic American food may be painted into each frame of the cartoon. Or the food remains the same, while a reference to American food is introduced. When the characters are eating rice balls, for example, they comment on how delicious their donuts taste. Dubbing is also used so that the characters appear to be speaking American English. Television producers clearly felt that to make this cartoon popular in the United States they had to "Americanize" it—which says much about their perception of U.S. culture and their perception of Japan. As Lawrence Venuti cautions, it is "essential to recognize that translation in its many aspects—from the selection of foreign texts to the implementation of discursive strategies to the reviewing and teaching of translations—wields enormous power in the construction of national identities and hence can play an important geopolitical role" (13). Perhaps this is why so many ethnic writers have fastened on translation as a trope: it is an example of the powerful ideological and cultural forces at work within what appear to be "neutral" language practices. Yet as Simon argues, translation also "participates in many different ways in the generation of new forms of knowledge, new textual forms, new relationships to language" (160). Translation is not exclusively about words—it is also a telling example of the way words *and* worlds can intersect, clash, and be remade.

Having established what translation is not, now I will consider three different formulations of what translation can be. Some theorists see translation as a positive process of cultural exchange and interchange. Wilhelm Von Humboldt, a well-known theorist, argues in 1816 that translation is a form of linguistic enrichment:

> Translation, especially poetic translation, is one of the most necessary tasks of any literature, partly because it directs those who do not know another language to forms of art and human experience that would otherwise have remained totally unknown, but above all because it increases the expressivity and depth of meaning of one's own language. For it is the wonderful characteristic of languages that, first and foremost, each one accommodates the general needs of everyday life; yet, through the spirit of the nation that shapes and forms it, a language can be infinitely enriched. (56)

Translation, then, can encourage the growth and expansion of the target culture's own language. Translation also preserves works that might otherwise be lost. Walter Benjamin contends that since "a translation comes later than the original, and since the important works of world literature never find their chosen translators at the time of their origin, their translation marks their stage of continued life" (73). For Benjamin, then, translation generates a kind of literary afterlife. More recently, Yves Bonnefoy has argued that the best translators understand that translation is not about conquering but about sympathy (191): "What we gain through translation . . . is the very thing we cannot grasp or hold: that is to say, the poetry of other languages" (188). These writers focus on translation as a positive paradigm for cultural and linguistic interaction—an interaction that enriches both the source and the target culture's language and literature.

Throughout this book I will consider other theorists who view translation as a positive process. Certainly, translation can perform a beneficial cultural and linguistic function, but seeing translation as either purely positive or purely negative is somewhat problematic. Like language itself, translation can take on a multiplicity of roles, and it can perform many different functions, often simultaneously. Translation theorists who work with paradigms that are exclusively positive or negative sometimes ignore this multiplicity. For example, Eliot Weinberger and Octavio Paz argue that "the relationship between original and translation is parent-child" (9). But is it possible that sometimes the translation becomes the "parent" and the original text the "child"? Such might be the case for some writers whose art was recognized only through translation. Edgar Allan Poe, for example, became more popular in the United States after his works had been translated into French. And Abraham Cahan's original draft of *Yekl*—written in English—was not published in English until after he had translated it into Yiddish and printed it serially in a Yiddish newspaper.[11] In these situations it is difficult to tell what is the "parent" and what the "child." Furthermore, an exclusively positive view of the translated text as the smiling child or grandchild of the parent text does not help us see the multiple cultural and linguistic roles translation actually performs.

On the other hand, many recent theorists view translation as being essentially about colonization and cultural disempowerment, and these views are also problematic. Translation has certainly been used in the past to expand particular ideologies or to force various "foreign" cultures to conform to "civilizing" influences.[12] Lori Chamberlain cites a particularly graphic example of this colonialist impulse from Thomas Drant, a sixteenth-century translator. Speaking of his translation of Horace, Drant says:

> First I have now done [with Horace] as the people of God were commanded to do with their captive women that were handsome and beautiful: I have shaved off his hair and pared off his nails, that is, I have wiped away all his vanity and superfluity of matter. . . . I have Englished things not according to the vein of the Latin propriety, but of his own vulgar tongue. . . . I have pieced his reason, eked and mended his similitudes, mollified his hardness, prolonged his cortall kind of speeches, changed and much altered his words, but not his sentence, or at least (I dare say) not his purpose. (Chamberlain 61–62)

Translation functions as a kind of violent penetration of the source text—and yet somehow Drant still feels he has captured Horace's "purpose." Translation also has a long history of being about conquest, as Wechsler explains: "Throughout most of classical and modern history, the translator did whatever he wanted with the works he translated. This was true of the Romans, who took what they felt like taking from Greek culture and made it theirs. As Friedrich Nietzsche wrote, 'In those days, to translate meant to conquer'" (67). One way of envisioning translation, then, is as a mechanism of cultural dominance and appropriation.

Even translation theorists who do not explicitly perceive translation as colonization have a kind of colonialist bent; many paradigms that appear to be "neutral" still figure translation as a power struggle. The translator may choose to have the source text overpower the target text or vice versa, but one culture or the other will always dominate. In a well-known essay published in 1938, Friedrich Schleiermacher argues the following:

> Either the translator leaves the writer alone as much as possible and moves the reader toward the writer, or he leaves the reader alone as much as possible and moves the writer toward the reader. . . . In the first case, the translator takes pains, by means of his work, to compensate for the reader's lack of understanding of the original language. He seeks to communicate

to his readers the same image, the same impression that he himself has gained—through his knowledge of the original language—of the work as it stands, and therefore move the readers to his viewpoint, which is actually foreign to them. If, however, the translation seeks to let its Roman author, for example, speak as he would have spoken and written as a German to Germans, it does not move the author to where the translator stands; . . . on the contrary, it moves the author immediately into the world of the German readers and transforms him into one of them. (42)

A translator can either turn German into English or force English readers to "become" German. Schleiermacher's point is well taken, but he may replicate another set of binaries. In Schleiermacher's model a reader is either German or English, and the translator either moves the reader toward the source text or the source text toward the reader. Is there a more dynamic way of conceptualizing translation? Can a translated text become German/English—or can the reader be, if but for a moment while reading a text, a "Germenglish" person?

One final group of theorists attempt to formulate models of translation that are more dialogic and syncretic as well as more aware of the way translation can play positive and negative roles, even simultaneously. From a postmodern standpoint, translation is able to deconstruct binarisms such as source text versus target text. I have already referred (by way of Claude Lévesque) to Jacques Derrida's idea that we are all, to some degree, exiles within language. For Derrida, there is no original, uncontaminated, pure language that we can speak with ease; there is only a language that makes us aware of what we lack, of what we have lost. Therefore, there would be no pure, original text to be translated—only versions of other texts that are themselves impure, inauthentic. Perhaps this is why, in *The Ear of the Other*, Derrida argues that "translation is writing; that is, it is not translation only in the sense of transcription. It is a productive writing called forth by the original text" (153). Glossing this statement, Chamberlain argues that "in attempting to overthrow the binary oppositions we have seen in other discussions of this problem, Derrida implies that translation is both original and secondary, uncontaminated and transgressed or transgressive" (70). In another text, Derrida contends that something is always left over when one translates—something that blurs the distinction between the original text and its translation. Derrida thus exposes the impossibility of "the dream of translation without remnants" ("Living On" 119). Such notions of a translated text as both original and secondary, composed both of speech and of remnants of speech, and as "speaking" the source culture as well as the translated culture, attempt to move beyond a binary model of translation toward a model that foregrounds translation as difference. As another postmodern theorist, Maurice Blanchot, comments, "Translation is the sheer play of difference: it constantly makes allusion to difference, dissimulates difference, but by occasionally revealing and often accentuating it, translation becomes the very life of difference" (83). For Blanchot, translation should not establish hierarchies and binarisms; rather, it should foreground the ambiguity at the heart of language itself. I am not arguing, of course, that these theorists are entirely successful in trying to move translation beyond binarism but simply pointing out that they make this attempt.

How, then, might a translator preserve the remnant that persists and foreground translation as difference, as a process of being both lost and found? Translation theorists Lawrence Venuti and Samia Mehrez have two approaches to this question. Venuti focuses on a concept of resistant translation—translation that emphasizes the actual process of translation and refuses to efface cultural differences. A resistant translation of *Pokémon*, for example, might have preserved the sushi of the original and also have left traces of Japanese speech or language in the English speech so that viewers were aware they were watching a translated text.[13] In Venuti's terms the "fluent" translation that emerged could only efface cultural differences and make translation invisible. For Venuti, a resistant translation makes the translator's work (more) visible, but it also helps to "preserve the linguistic and cultural difference of the foreign text by producing translations which are strange and estranging, which mark the limits of dominant values in the target-language culture and hinder those values from enacting an imperialistic domestication of a cultural other" (13). A resistant translation, we might say, moves toward syncretism: differences in culture and language are brought together, but they are not resolved or harmonized. Difference is not covered over or synthesized but allowed to remain.

Samia Mehrez's critical essays on works of literature written by postcolonial bilingual writers illustrate a particular translation practice that can be termed "resistant."[14] Mehrez argues that such works create a language in between dominant and marginalized discourses. This newly forged language challenges both indigenous, conventional models of literature and the dominant models of the colonizer. The ultimate goal of this literature is to "subvert hierarchies by bringing together the 'dominant' and the 'underdeveloped,' by exploding and confounding different symbolic worlds and separate systems of signification in order to create a mutual interdependence and intersignification" ("Translation" 122). By drawing on more than one culture, more than one language, and more than one world experience within the same text, these writers defy a notion of "original" text or "original" language.

Mehrez borrows a term from the Moroccan writer/theorist Abdelkebit Khatibi and calls this practice "radical bilingualism." Whereas a bilingual text would use only one language at a time, a radically bilingual text maintains a constant movement between different languages or even between different layers of the same language. Mehrez discusses Khatibi's novel *Amour bilingue* as an illustration of conscious radical bilingualism. To take just one example, on Khatibi's title page the French title (*Amour bilingue*) appears in bold red letters at the top of the page; at the bottom of the page is its translation, written in Arabic calligraphy (*Fata Morgana*). Both titles are "readable" to the non-Arabic (French) speaker, but only the French title makes sense. The monolingual reader must move back and forth between these titles, trying to understand them. Furthermore, the title page contains an Arabic symbol that a non-Arabic reader could not decipher. The title page thus undermines expected hierarchies between dominant and minority discourses, between the translator and the translated. Mehrez postulates that such texts force the readers to become bilingual, as well as showing the presence of one language within another ("Translation" 134). This is a capacious metaphor for translation: translation can be a form of radical bilingualism and can encourage the reader to think/speak/read in more than one voice. Most important, translation as radical bilingualism refuses to privilege one language over another or one culture over another but focuses instead on translation as a constant migration of language from one system of signs to another system—from systems of signs that are also, paradoxically, shown to be contained within each other.

As I illustrate in the next section, the ethnic writers discussed sometimes become trapped in a binary conceptualization of translation. But some of these writers—such as Cherríe Moraga and Susan Power—call on notions of translation that show characters speaking two (or more) languages at once or that force the reader to become a translator. This form of radical bilingualism dismantles the line between the translator and the reader, between the dominant language and the "disempowered" one(s).

Before we begin the next section, two other concerns relevant to this study must be assessed. The first has to do with the role of gender in translation. Both linguistically and culturally, women frequently are portrayed as the connecting link, the mediator, between the ethnic and the American, and in the texts I discuss, it is most often female characters who are the translators. What occurs when a woman (such as Maxine Hong Kingston) attempts to translate from a parent culture or tongue that appears to devalue women? Numerous translation theorists have discussed this issue, arguing that women translators must learn to speak through and against the translated text and to use their translations to make alterations in constructs of gender.[15] Writers such as Kingston and Moraga use translation to contest and revise the dominant cultural scripts they encounter both as "minorities" and as women. In the next chapter I discuss in greater detail the concept of a resistant feminist translation practice that works to deterritorialize and decontextualize a source text perceived as containing negative messages about gender and race. In the works discussed in this book, women are placed under a strong imperative to translate and mediate, an imperative that they sometimes resist and sometimes reconfigure. African American women writers, in particular (as demonstrated in Chapter 4), use the trope of translation to claim an empowered speech, and they thereby counter a long tradition in many African American works written by men (from Frederick Douglass onward) in which the assertion of voice is associated with an identity as a "free man." For many women characters, translation offers a way of revising social scripts of both race and gender that have made it difficult for them to claim an authorized cultural voice.

At times in Kingston's *The Woman Warrior*, however, the narrator states that she cannot translate Chinese culture, not only because of her gendered relationship to it but also because it is fundamentally untranslatable—it is too alien and strange in content to make a successful transition to the "American" world. As I explain in the next chapter, the notion of "untranslatability" is not viable; anything can be translated, if the translator wants to find a way to translate it. Of course, something *is* lost in translation, but as Rushdie suggests, something is also gained. So, as Bonnefoy states, it is only when "a work does not compel us [that] it is untranslatable" (192). Characters who refuse to translate are often avoiding the intercultural and interlingual demands that translation entails. And they are implying that the parent culture does not compel them or that it lacks usable "cultural capital"—material value in the new world they inhabit. Translation is always possible, even when the translated item/text does not exist in the target culture. As Roman Jakobson argues, "We never consumed ambrosia or nectar and have only a linguistic acquaintance with the words 'ambrosia,' 'nectar,' and 'gods'—the name of their mythical users; nonetheless, we understand these words and know in what contexts each of them may be used" (144). Any experience or object is conveyable in *some form* in any existing language—provided the translator wants to strive to convey it.

From this summary, it should be apparent that translation theorization vivifies many crucial debates about ethnic heritage, linguistic identity, and cultural struggle. So it should not surprise us that the trope of translation has also preoccupied ethnic writers from a wide range of backgrounds. The book begins with David Wong Louie's *Pangs of Love* (1992), Fae Myenne Ng's *Bone* (1993), and Maxine Hong Kingston's *The Woman Warrior* (1976), because these writers have a very clearly formulated stance in relationship to the question of how one transmigrates tongues and transcodes ethnicity. These three Chinese American texts demonstrate that translation can occur only when the translator respects and values the source text—the parents' world and language—and interacts with it in a positive and "writerly" way. In Chapter 2 I examine two post–World War II Japanese American novels that also portray translation's connection to formulations of ethnic identity—John Okada's *No-No Boy* (1957) and Cynthia Kadohata's *The Floating World* (1989). After the forced internment of thousands of American citizens of Japanese descent in camps euphemistically called "relocation centers," writers struggled to re-create a productive relationship between the ethnic and the American. In these texts it is only by living *in* translation—in the spaces and gaps between racial and linguistic identities—that characters are able to transcode their ethnicity and find the ancestral voice they need to survive.

Chapter 3 takes up these concepts in Native American literature, beginning with N. Scott Momaday's *House Made of Dawn* (1968), a novel in which the main character, Able, suffers because he has lost a viable relationship to his native language and the ability to translate it. I then discuss Leslie Marmon Silko's *Ceremony* (1977), a work in which the protagonist, Tayo, does learn to translate and tell his story. Most important, Tayo learns how to speak English in such a way that he conveys Native American values and meanings; he becomes, in short, a radical bilingual who transmigrates his native tongue *and* English. Susan Power's *The Grass Dancer* (1994) portrays another character who becomes a radical bilingual—Red Dress —an individual from the past who speaks both Dakota Sioux and English simultaneously, transforming both languages. In Sherman Alexie's novels *Reservation Blues* (1995) and *Indian Killer* (1996), the relationship to the indigenous tongue has become even more tenuous. In these books few individuals from the Spokane tribe speak the language or are even interested in learning it. *Reservation Blues* implies that one can maintain a connection to the Native American culture and transcode ethnicity without the language, but *Indian Killer* shows the dire consequences of removal from the land and the language: alienation, violence, and death.

Chapter 4 is concerned with the subject of intralingual translation (translation within a language or between dialects) in several works by African American women writers. Toni Morrison's *Tar Baby* (1981) and Danzy Senna's *Caucasia* (1998) both feature light-skinned heroines who can "pass" in various ways (linguistically or socially) as white; in both novels heroines lose their connection to their families and ethnic communities when they no longer translate between African American Vernacular English and Standardized English. Sherley Anne Williams's *Dessa Rose* (1986) and A. J. Verdelle's *The Good Negress* (1995) also detail struggles between an enfranchised, written language and a vernacular, oral tongue. In fact, *Dessa Rose* is fundamentally about a translation struggle. Who will tell Dessa's story: the white man Nehemiah, who wants to write it in Standardized English that effaces Dessa's subjectivity and agency, or Dessa herself, who insists on speaking, singing, and signfyin' her story? Similarly, *The Good Negress* stages a conflict between African American Vernacular English and Standardized English when the young heroine is encouraged to give up her southern dialect in favor of "the king's English"—standardized, "proper" English. Yet both texts finally move toward hybridized dialects that entail a continual process of exchange and translation between African American oral discourse and Standardized English. Through this exchange ethnicity is transcoded, and both tongues are transmigrated.

In Chapter 5 I discuss four Chicano/a writers: Richard Rodriguez, Nash Candelaria, Cherríe Moraga, and Abelardo Delgado.[16] Many critics have argued that Richard Rodriguez is an assimilationist who turns his back on the Mexican Spanish tongue, but in his autobiographical trilogy—*Hunger of Memory* (1982), *Days of Obligation* (1992), and *Brown* (2002)—Rodriguez uses English oppositionally, thus exposing its faults, as well as its fault lines. Once again English is transmigrated, but Spanish also undergoes change in this process. In Nash Candelaria's novel *Memories of the Alhambra* (1977), the question of translation is negotiated through a father and son; while the father struggles to be "purely" Spanish (rather than Chicano or Mexican American), the son struggles to recover a Mexican Spanish language he has never been taught. The son does finally learn to translate, and in so doing he transcodes his ethnicity and accepts his status as a Chicano. These texts are written primarily in English, with a small amount of Mexican Spanish included. Cherríe Moraga's *Loving in the War Years* (1983) and Abelardo Delgado's *Letters to Louise* (1982), on the other hand, use both Spanish and English. Moraga and Delgado codeswitch in their texts—that is, they move from Spanish to English—but they also create a third dialect that creatively fuses Mexican Spanish and English and includes terms such as "mexicatessen" and "los slow ones." Through these fusions they move toward a new form of language that exceeds both Spanish and English, and they create a more dialogic concept of ethnic identity.

In Chapter 6 I examine debates over language policy in order to comprehend the current situation of multilingualism and cultural translation in the United States. "Official" language policy (as reflected by the curtailment of bilingual education and the passage of "English Only" legislation) is contrasted with the ongoing bilingualism of some contemporary ethnic communities and the work of performance artists such as Guillermo Gómez-Peña, who constantly stages scenes of cultural translation. I contend that in the United States today there is an unofficial realm of multilingualism and translation that undercuts official language policy. This unofficial realm of multilingualism and translation constructs a sociolinguistic space where languages divide to conga and the concept of the "native speaker" is renovated. In this unofficial realm, ethnicity is still being transcoded and tongues are still being transmigrated.

The conclusion of the book returns to a topic discussed in this chapter—the idea of a transethnic trope specific to ethnic American literature. Undergirding this trope is a fascination with moving beyond certain kinds of impasses, certain kinds of gaps that haunt cultural translation and ethnic discourse itself. What finally is lost in translation? And what is found? What happens to the "untranslatable" remnant about which Derrida has theorized? I develop the metaphor of the "lost-and-found space" of translation; a lost-and-found space allows for loss, recuperation and recovery, and finally the continual *exchange and reformulation* of diverse and often divergent cultural and linguistic entities. At one point in Ng's novel *Bone*, the main character, Leila, becomes frustrated with her mother's Chinese speech. "She had a world of words that were beyond me" (22), Leila comments. But Leila does learn to translate. By realizing that the "gap" is a productive opportunity for transcoding ethnicity and transmigrating tongues, Leila succeeds in translating her mother's world and her mother's words. The remnant may be preserved, then, within the notion of the "gap," or lacuna, in the text, within the lost-and-found space in discourse and in language itself. Translation sometimes replicates divisions between languages and cultures, and translation can reinforce numerous binarisms that have kept individuals disempowered: high culture over "low" culture, civilized nations over "savage," Anglo-Americans over all "minorities." Yet translation foregrounds the hope of a creative fusion and fission between languages and cultures that does not destroy differences but rather creates something new *precisely* out of these differences and out of an acknowledgment of the "gap" or "loss" that haunts translation and all discourse. Postmodern theorists have argued that we are all alienated from language, that we are all "lost in translation." Yet the works discussed in this book offer productive ways of acknowledging this loss but also of finding ourselves in and through translation—ways of locating a mode of cultural voice that renovates the racial and linguistic politics of the textual and actual worlds we inhabit.

I

An Impossible Necessity

Translation and the Re-creation of Linguistic and Cultural Identities in the Works of David Wong Louie, Fae Myenne Ng, and Maxine Hong Kingston

The transformations that take shape in print, that take the formal name of "translation," become their own beings, set out on their own wanderings. Some live long, and some don't. What kind of creatures are they?—Eliot Weinberger and Octavio Paz, *Nineteen Ways of Looking at Wang Wei*

IN THE TITLE story of David Wong Louie's collection *Pangs of Love*, the English-speaking narrator tries to communicate with his mother, who speaks mostly Chinese and has learned only a few English phrases from the television she watches constantly. But the protagonist fails: "I know what I want to say in English. My mind's stuffed full with the words. I pull one sentence at a time from the elegant little speech . . . and try to piece together a word-for-word translation into Chinese. Yielding nonsense" (95). "Poetry," Robert Frost has said in a famous formulation, "is what gets lost in translation,"[1] and some authors have argued that the poetry of *any* literary form is decimated by translation. The narrator of "Pangs of Love" seems to share the view that translation of his "elegant little speech" is impossible. And so mother and son remain locked in separate linguistic and cultural worlds.

Yet, eventually, some of the characters in Louie's collection learn to translate. To some, translation may seem "impossible" in a pure sense—but it is also absolutely necessary. Susan Bassnett observes that while some theorists perennially lament translation's impossibility, still, "in spite of such a dogma, translators continue to translate" (135). This formulation of translation as "an impossible necessity" enables an understanding of the linguistic and cultural reconciliation enacted by certain works of contemporary Chinese American literature. In these works, the words of the foreign language or "source text" (the various dialects of Chinese) literally must be translated into the new tongue or "target text" (American English) so that parents and children, first and second generation, can communicate with each other. As a symbolic trope in these texts, however, translation evokes the concept of a crossing of borders, a permeation of barriers erected between what seem to be separate and contradictory cultural and linguistic entities.

Louie's *Pangs of Love*, Fae Myenne Ng's *Bone*, and Maxine Hong Kingston's *The Woman Warrior* portray the difficulties of translation, of reaching across borders that appear to be impenetrable by language, by cadences, by culture.[2] Second-generation characters in these texts all confront what appear to be irresolvable translation dilemmas, and they articulate the sense that Chinese culture and language (which are initially configured as "foreign" and "other" for the second generation) are untranslatable. To succeed as translators these characters must move from a literal to a metaphorical understanding of the process of translation. Following Roland Barthes's theory that some texts are more writerly than readerly, translation theorist Willis Barnstone speaks of writerly translations that involve an active participation with the source text. A writerly translation would be creative and imaginative, rather than passive, literal, and constrained; it might also evoke the notion of coauthorship (230). In these Chinese American texts, then, the characters must become writerly translators who understand how their dual and at times conflicting cultural heritages as Chinese Americans can be mediated and transcoded. Through acts of writerly translation the protagonists learn to transcode the source text—the parents' linguistic and ethnic heritage—and disarticulate Chinese ethnicity from a discourse that labels it alien and useless in the "modern" world of the United States. They also learn to transcode the "target text," their own cultural and linguistic horizons as "Americans"; they must understand themselves as Chinese Americans possessed of multiple ethnic heritages. These characters finally realize that it is precisely their divergent cultural/linguistic heritages that engender the ability to produce new meanings, new stories, writerly translations that break down the binary opposition between the ethnic and the American, enriching and finally re-creating both cultural terrains.[3]

ALTHOUGH MANY ETHNIC WRITERS employ the trope of translation in their works, this trope is extremely pronounced in Asian American literature. Perhaps this is because, as Shih-Hsiang Chen observes in a discussion of Chinese-to-English translation, the extreme differences between these languages focalize the question of "the translator as creator" (254). Chinese, in particular, is a language with a high degree of syntactic ambiguity (Aaronson and Ferres 152). The various dialects of the Chinese language differ from those of English in numerous ways. Bernhard Karlgren reports an average of ten different word meanings corresponding to each Chinese syllable in a small dictionary; therefore, Chinese words (depending on how a word is defined) may have three to sixteen times as many meanings as English words (20). Also, as Doris Aaronson and Steven Ferres explain, word meanings in Chinese are radically polysemous; homographs for a word such as "wen," for example, can mean such diverse things as "hear," "smell," or "news" (146). In Chinese, function words, prepositions, and articles are often omitted, and pronoun forms are few and optional. This leads Aaronson and Ferres to conclude that "the extent to which context determines the exact meaning will be far greater in Chinese than in English" (147). Therefore, an ability to understand context is required to disambiguate, to create a meaningful translation of a particular word, sentence, or phrase.

Chinese American writers such as Louie, Ng, and Kingston often configure the difficulties inherent in Chinese-to-English translation as both linguistic and cultural problems of context sharing between generations. "Pangs of Love" and "Inheritance," two short stories from Louie's collection, demonstrate that given the extreme differences between the linguistic systems of China and America, language can easily function as a barrier between what is Chinese and what is American. Yet these stories also point toward the healthy context sharing and interpermeation of cultures that the trope of "translation," in its broadest sense, evokes.

The title story, "Pangs of Love," depicts a literal breakdown in communication that symbolizes a more problematic loss of generational and cultural connection. The narrator cannot tell his mother that his American girlfriend, Amanda (or Mandy), has left him for a Japanese man, and his brother (called Bagel) cannot tell his mother that he has no intention of marrying a Chinese woman because he is homosexual. Gaps between the language of the mother (Cantonese Chinese) and the children (American English) seem at first glance to be the source of these characters' inability to communicate. The protagonist informs the reader, "My mother has lived in this country for forty years and, through what must be a monumental act of will, has managed not to learn English" (75). For his part, the narrator speaks little Chinese: "Once I went to school, my Chinese vocabulary stopped growing; in conversation with my mother I'm a linguistic dwarf" (78). The mother and son inhabit the same physical space (they share an apartment), yet they are trapped in separate linguistic terrains, and little genuine conversation occurs.

Although these examples seem to illustrate a literal problem in translation (the sons speak mostly English, the mother only Chinese), they actually represent a metaphorical problem, symbolic of these characters' refusal to cross the borders that separate the seemingly contradictory cultural terrains of America and China and to transcode the corresponding ethnic identities these terrains represent. Willis Barnstone suggests that translation includes the notion of transportation (15), so when the narrator calls his mother a "linguistic dead-end street" (84) he implies that her refusal to learn English signifies an unwillingness to transport herself to an American context; she views Americanness as a negative ethnicity and refuses to transcode it. Her insulation from American culture is so complete that she "seems out of place in a car, near machines, a woman from another culture, of another time, at ease with needle and thread, around pigs and horses" (86). Mrs. Pang embodies the traditions of the Chinese past, dreaming her son will marry "a Chinese girl who will remember [her] grave and come with food and spirit money" (88). These values have become transmuted in the United States, yet she fails to comprehend this. Therefore, there is little communication, as her final words in the story demonstrate: "How can I be your mother if nobody listens to what I say?" (98). First- and second-generation individuals remain in their separate and mutually inaccessible cultural universes, and the binary divisions between languages and cultures, between what is "Chinese" and what is "American," remain intact.

As Octavio Paz has argued in a famous formulation: "Each civilization, as each soul, is different, unique. Translation is our way to face this otherness of the universe and history" (159). Yet neither Mrs. Pang nor her sons can face "this otherness of the universe and history," this otherness of the world they do not inhabit, or refuse to inhabit. Clearly, Mrs. Pang sees "otherness" in her sons' world. For example, with tears in her eyes she asks the narrator about Bagel's lifestyle: "Ah-Vee-ah, all the men in this house have good jobs, they have money, why don't they have women? Why is your brother that way?" (97). Here Mrs. Pang does try to translate her sons' world into terms she can understand. But as Paz also argues, a successful translation must be an act of love and participation, reflecting both a respect for the source text and a desire to share the source text with the world (153). Mrs. Pang has no respect for her sons' world, calling the narrator a "crazy boy" when he tells her Mandy no longer loves him (96) and calling Bagel a "hammerhead" when he tries to explain that he does not want a girlfriend (97). Mrs. Pang desires comprehension of her sons' lives, but her lack of respect for their choices and perspectives impedes a successful transmission of information, a successful translation.

Yet if Mrs. Pang fails as a translator because she cannot participate in her sons' world, her sons also fail because they devalue her world. The narrator describes his interactions with his mother as "putting in time" (76), as if he is on a chain gang. He also calls conversation with her "a task equal to digging a grave without a shovel" (78), an entombment for which he lacks both the language and the patience. Albrecht Neubert and Gregory Shreve explain that "if a translation is to succeed, there must be a situation which requires it. There must be a *translation need*. Many academic examples of so-called 'untranslatability' are actually examples of texts for which a receptive situation does not exist" (85). Similarly, to illustrate the idea that there is no such thing as "untranslatability," Willis Barnstone uses the examples of the translation of *Moby-Dick* in Poland (where there is no whaling industry) and of the biblical translation of the phrase "lamb of God" for Eskimos who had never seen a lamb. In each case, the translator invented words or found analogies within the culture that made these "untranslatable" words coherent for his or her respective audiences (41). "Untranslatability," then, is a product not of words but of an unmotivated situation. Because the narrator of "Pangs of Love" does not see any need to translate his mother's world, he fails as a translator. Although "love" appears in the story's title, the love and receptive motivation that might enable translation are figured as conspicuously absent from the text.

Louie also demonstrates that translation is a matter of motivated situations, rather than linguistics per se, through the narrator's former girlfriend. Although she is an English-speaking Anglo-American, she manages to communicate with Mrs. Pang: "[Mandy] spoke Chinese, a stunning Mandarin that she learned at Vassar, and while that wasn't my mother's dialect Mandy picked up enough Cantonese to hold an adult conversation, and what she couldn't bridge verbally she wrote in notes" (80). Beyond "bridg[ing] verbally" the barriers that appear to separate her language from Mrs. Pang's, Mandy also manages to cross the borders between their two cultures: Mandy and Mrs. Pang "conspired together to celebrate Chinese festivals and holidays, making coconut-filled sweet-potato dumplings, lotus-seed cookies, daikon and green onion soup, tiny bowls of monk's food for New Year's Day" (80). Unlike the narrator, then, Mandy is receptive to Mrs. Pang's worldview and diligently translates their cultural and linguistic differences into positive signs of intercultural connection. Louie's text therefore demonstrates that language can be either a bridge between cultures or a barrier; translation can either maintain or destroy cultural divisions. Louie does not hold to a monolithic view of translation; he sees the multiple social, cultural, and linguistic functions it can serve.

Through the character of Mandy, the story also illustrates that translation should be a writerly process of actively and imaginatively bridging gaps between languages and cultures. Yet this lesson is not transmitted to the narrator, who cannot succeed as a translator both because he refuses to transcode his mother's Chinese culture and because he remains trapped by a readerly conceptualization of translation. The narrator's translations are literal and constrained, as the "transcription" of his translation process quoted at the beginning of the chapter shows. In trying to "piece together a word-for-word translation into Chinese" (95), the narrator takes a literal approach to the process of translation. Rather than thinking metaphorically about how he might convey his sentiments, he becomes formulaic and simplistic: "I abandon this approach and opt for the shorter path, the one of reduction, simplicity, lowest common denominator" (95). The narrator sees translation as a reduction, rather than an expression, of his experience, and ultimately he conveys nothing. The narrator also constantly devalues his mother and his mother's Chinese traditions, seeing them as "alien" and "other." Consequently, he never transcodes them or disarticulates them from the negative cultural baggage with which they are associated in the United States. The narrator seems to long to become "American," and so translation as trope functions in this text to show how tongues are *not* transmigrated, how ethnic identity is *not* transcoded, when the ethnic remains separated from and devalued by the American.

Louie's story "Inheritance," on the other hand, depicts Chinese American characters who engage in a more positive, active, and metaphorical process of translation, for the central character, Edna, moves from a readerly attempt to translate her mother's life to a writerly one. She also moves beyond seeing her metaphorical "inheritance" as a Chinese American in a purely negative light;

finally, she finds a way to transcode this ethnicity. Edna's deceased mother (who initially is the strongest representative of Chinese traditions) seems to have been lost in translation. Indeed, Edna wonders if her bitter and reclusive mother has transmitted anything positive: "Had I inherited my mother's hand, which was warm only after she hit her little girl, which for comfort reached for angry fistfuls of her child's hair?" (224). As in "Pangs of Love," language at first seems to be the source of the problem. Edna explains: "Once my sister started school and infected our home with English, I stopped learning Chinese, and after that my mother . . . who masterfully avoided linguistic accommodation of any form—spoke to me as to a little child" (207). Yet the mother's refusal to learn English— her avoidance of "linguistic accommodation"—also reflects her cultural identity: she lets her husband, Edsel, "negotiate this American life for her" (207), staying at home to perform traditional Chinese ceremonies she does not explain to Edna (202). She sees Americanness itself as negative and refuses to transcode it, opting instead for a "pure" Chinese identity. Once again, parent and child inhabit the same physical space but remain in separate linguistic and cultural terrains.

What cannot be translated may be lost in a kind of cultural and linguistic silence, an isolation or physical death that betokens a more symbolic loss. Edna's mother does not explain the Chinese traditions or her own life to her daughter, and so Edna has no access to them as an adult. However, Louie depicts the necessity for adaptation and some degree of linguistic and cultural accommodation through Edna's father, who does begin transcoding his ethnic identity in ways that his daughter eventually comprehends. Edsel is described as being "very old-world Chinese" (202), but after the death of his wife and his other children, he begins to communicate with his only surviving child. His conversations reflect an adaptation to the American world in which he and Edna live: "He started to talk to me a lot—something Chinese fathers aren't predisposed to do. . . . He pronounced us friends and demanded that I call him Edsel, straying again from Chinese-father orthodoxy" (202). Edsel does not abandon "traditional" Chinese values, for he pressures Edna to have a large Chinese wedding and give birth to many children. Yet, to find a translation between his daughter's universe and his own, he adapts his language and behavior to the new world she inhabits. Edsel is willing to engage in a metaphorical translation of his own system of values into his daughter's world, and he is willing to transcode his own ethnic identity as "Chinese" so that it is not separate from the Americanized context his daughter inhabits. Language therefore becomes a symbolic bridge that allows a syncretic fusion and permeation of cultures.

Edna's mother, on the other hand, refuses translation of the seemingly binary opposite cultures of China and America to the very day of her death. Louie demonstrates this symbolically through the character of Mrs. Woo, an elderly woman who reminds Edna of her deceased mother. Like Edna's mother, Mrs. Woo speaks no English and is purely Chinese, castigating Edna for being "not quite the real thing, neither Chinese nor American" (208). The protagonist can find no response to Mrs. Woo's vision of "cultural purity"; Edna believes that if she "said what was on my mind in the language I thought it in, that would simply confirm what [Mrs. Woo] thought" (208). Standing in for Edna's dead mother, Mrs. Woo illustrates symbolically that Edna has found no way of communicating with her mother, of translating her maternal inheritance. Edna's incomprehension of her mother causes her to see her inheritance negatively: "How could I be sure that I'd tamed my hand, that I'd taught it to be patient and soothing? For years I feared my mother in myself, for things do run in the family. We died young; who could guarantee the safety of my children?" (224). Who can guarantee that Edna will not be lost in translation to her children, just as her own mother was lost?

Louie portrays Edna as having stark options: she must either learn to translate her mother's life or face the possibility of her own death. After Mrs. Woo's children send her to a nursing home, Edna wanders into Mrs. Woo's apartment. She turns on all the stove's gas burners and thinks, "All I wanted was warmth. One match now and I could solve every problem" (224). Faced with her inability to understand her maternal legacy, Edna considers suicide—she considers being lost in translation. Yet Edna does not kill herself. Instead, she finds a more writerly notion of translation that allows her to transcode her ethnicity and transmigrate her mother's tongue. Edna has been thinking rather literally of what she inherited—her mother's hands, her mother's cruelty, her mother's linguistic and cultural rigidity—but she must think more metaphorically. Looking out the window of this American apartment, Edna imagines seeing "limestone mountains in mist, birds in wooden cages, women in rice paddies whose legs were spread wide. Scenes of South China I knew from calendars Edsel hung in our home," and she realizes that "this was the mystery wound in my DNA, this the very color of my genes, this my inheritance" (224–25). Edna's heritage is not just her mother's bitterness, lack of cultural accommodation, and violence but the entire history of China as well. Edna inherits a vision broader than the limited perspective her mother's life has given her: "I looked out at the yard again, but now, instead of the smallest things, I saw over impossible distances" (224). Despite her mother's recalcitrance, Edna finally translates her heritage into something vast and powerful, rather than something constricting and painful.

Edna also apprehends that her inheritance encompasses not just her mother's rigidity and lack of accommodation but also her father's flexibility and willingness to change, to be a "friend" to his child. In so doing, she transcodes the meaning of Chinese ethnicity itself. After looking out Mrs. Woo's window, Edna goes upstairs and watches her sleeping father. In the story's final words—"My father" (225)—Edna recognizes that her inheritance is not a readerly, literal translation of her mother's life but a writerly, metaphorical inheritance from both parents, and indeed from all of China. Edna's translation of her own life and of her parents' also renders the binary oppositions of parent/child and China/America inoperative, for the story's final image figures Edsel as a child, "smacking his lips, tasting his mouth, making funny noises, as he rubbed his eyes with the backs of two small fists" (225). Edsel is both Edna's father, pressuring her to have a "traditional" Chinese marriage, and her child, sucking his thumb in her American apartment. Moreover, Edna's writerly translation of her inheritance breaks down oppositions in another sense, affirming an identity that is neither purely Chinese nor purely American. Finally, both Edna and Edsel are Chinese Americans who have learned to synthesize their dual heritages and create new cultural and ethnic identities for themselves. As cultural translators, they move beyond binarism, beyond either/

or dualisms into a more capacious understanding of how translation can syncretize worlds and words. They transcode the meaning
of their ethnicity so that it can function positively in the new world
of America, and in so doing they become Chinese American.

In both of Louie's stories, translators must attempt to cross barriers not only of culture and language but also of gender. The male
protagonist of "Pangs of Love" attempts (and fails) to translate
his mother's worldview. In "Inheritance" Edna finally succeeds in
translating between her paternal and maternal inheritances, and
Edsel can only translate between his daughter's world and his own
when he strays from "Chinese-father orthodoxy" (202) and has real
conversations with her. Yet the burden of translation is not shared
equally by the male and the female characters. In both stories women
(Edna and Mandy) make stronger attempts than any of the male
characters to mediate between cultures, to move beyond a binary understanding of languages and worldviews. Perhaps this should come
as no surprise since, as numerous translation theorists have pointed
out, translation is often viewed as a "feminized" or subservient profession. In the works I discuss in this book, women often suffer real
physical or psychological impairment, sometimes resulting in death,
when their translations fail. "Inheritance" suggests that Edna's inability to translate is life threatening, and as Kingston's and Ng's
texts also demonstrate, for female characters translation is often
about their very survival. Kingston and Ng investigate more extensively than Louie how gendered familial relations—and a parent/
ethnic culture that is itself seen as devaluing women—inflect translation difficulties, but in Louie's texts gender plays a role, and
women characters most often bear the heaviest burdens as translators, as the links between divergent worldviews. And the need for
syncretic and writerly, resistant translations that transcode ethnicity is all the more pressing when the "source" text (or parent/ethnic
culture) is one that appears to devalue women.

Neubert and Shreve describe translation as an attempt to cross
both linguistic and extralinguistic (social and cultural) frontiers
(41). This concept is operative in "Inheritance"; for example, Edsel
must learn to bridge both linguistic and cultural gaps separating
his world from his daughter's. Ng's central character in *Bone*, Leila
Fu, shares this concept of translation as a crossing of both linguis-

tic and cultural frontiers. As an actual translator for a school in San Francisco's Chinatown, Leila's job is about "being the bridge between the classroom teacher and the parents," about "getting the parents involved, opening up a line of communication" (16). Leila can converse in both English and Chinese, yet she also recognizes situations in which the Chinese attitudes conveyed by the use of Chinese prohibit translation: "I use my This Isn't China defense. I remind them 'We're in America.' But some parents take this to heart and raise their voices. 'We're Chinese first, always'" (16). Leila stops the argument there, for, like Mrs. Pang and Edna's mother, these parents employ language to refuse a compromise between Chinese and American cultures rather than to create a bridge between them. And Leila sees and understands this refusal for what it is: not a literal inability to translate but a metaphorical one, a symbolic refusal to begin crossing cultural divisions, transcoding ethnicity, and transmigrating tongues.

In her own life, Leila claims to be unable, literally, to translate some of her feelings: "I have a whole different vocabulary of feeling in English than in Chinese, and not everything can be translated" (18). She also suggests that her parents have this problem; about her mother she says, "She had a world of words that were beyond me" (22). But Leila can, in fact, translate her mother's "world of words": "Mah grunted, a huumph sound that came out like a curse. My translation was: Disgust, anger. There's power behind her sounds. Over the years I've listened and rendered her Chinese grunts into English words" (22). Leila has discovered how to decode the metaphorical meanings behind her mother's Chinese grunts, to translate them into a language that crosses the barriers between Chinese and English. Leila has also learned to find linguistic transmigrations between her mother's world and her own, as the following exchange about Leila's husband, Mason, demonstrates:

> "What?" I was too upset to stop. "What?" I demanded again. "You don't like Mason, is that it?"
> "Mason," Mah spoke his name soft, "I love."
> For love, she used a Chinese word: to embrace, to hug.
> I stepped around the boxes, opened my arms and hugged

Mah. I held her and took a deep breath and smelled the dried honeysuckle stems, the bitter ginseng root. (23)

Leila translates her mother's Chinese term for "love" into an English word that is meaningful to herself and her readers, and the translation is both literal (from the Chinese word to the English meaning) and metaphorical (from the world of China, ginseng, and the mother to the world of the daughter). The Chinese word for "love" that Leila's mother uses is thus transmigrated into the English language. Leila's mother feels angered that her daughter has married without the traditional Chinese wedding banquet, and Leila feels defensive about her choice of an American marriage in a city hall with only her sister as witness. Yet the word Leila's mother uses for "love" acts as a bridge between the two women, a translation that encourages, rather than inhibits, communication. This translation allows a crossing between the daughter's modern world of America and the mother's traditional world of China and shows that mother and daughter are compromising rather than remaining on opposed sides of a cultural divide.

Ng's main character speaks more Chinese than do Louie's characters, yet this is only part of her success as a translator. As Neubert and Shreve explain, translation is a constructed (or learned) competence (43), an active process of problem solving that must be acquired (86). Since "Chinese appears to be a more context-sensitive language than English," a context of shared experiences and knowledge is necessary (Aaronson and Ferres 148). Leila is a successful Chinese-to-English translator, then, both because she actively problem-solves in order to translate difficult words and sounds and because she is willing to understand and transcode her mother's cultural context. As a child, Leila hated the responsibility of translation: "What I hated most was the talking for Mah and Leon, the whole translation number. Every English word counted and I was responsible. I went through a real resentment stage" (17). Yet Leila grows away from her resentment, although her statement on this subject is still somewhat tentative: "I'm over that now, I think" (17). As an adult, Leila does not resent translating, and she shares her parents' context in order to bridge her world and theirs. Leila also has a respect for her parents and for the Chinese culture that is completely absent in any of the second-generation characters in "Pangs of Love." For example, after the suicide of Leila's sister Ona, Leila's mother can only be consoled by the Chinese "sewing ladies" who "knew all the necessary rituals to get through this hard time" and who succeed in "plucking the pain out" (105). Leila recognizes that these women have an art valuable to her own life: "Bringing the right foods was as delicate as saying the right words. The sewing ladies knew, in ways I was still *watching and learning from*, how to draw out Mah's sadness and then take it away" (105, emphasis added). According to John Felstiner, "translation acts not merely to convey or extend but to regenerate tradition" (116), and one can observe this regeneration occurring in *Bone*. Translation grants tradition new life: the ways of the Chinese sewing ladies will continue to be meaningful in new contexts and new historical frameworks. Furthermore, in this passage ethnicity itself is transcoded. It does not represent something alien, foreign, other, and separate from the American (as it does in "Pangs of Love") but something positive, useful, and part of the American context and world. The Chinese sewing ladies, after all, exist *in* America (in an American Chinatown), not in the "alien" or "foreign" ethnic world of China.

Yet translation is a two-way street, as Neubert and Shreve explain: "Translation is motivated by a common desire to cross that frontier. The source language . . . user and the target language . . . user want to communicate with one another" (41). In "Pangs of Love," Mrs. Pang sees no value in her sons' world, and at times in *Bone*, Leila's mother also seems unwilling to share in her children's world and selfish in her insistence that they adapt to hers. Nina (Leila's youngest sister) complains that her parents "have no idea what our lives are about. They don't want to come into our worlds" (33). Nina believes her parents, like Mrs. Pang, are stuck in their traditional ways: "We keep on having to live in their world. They won't move one bit" (33). Nina's statements have a certain degree of truth, but they are somewhat hyperbolic; change on the part of the parents is occurring slowly. Leila's stepfather, Leon, for example, rejects the "traditional" Chinese view that sons are of more value than daughters, saying that "five sons don't make one good daughter" (3). Like Edsel in "Inheritance," Leon strays from "Chinese-father orthodoxy," and Leila's ability to translate the parent culture may be enabled by change in its gender structure and change in gendered family relations. Similarly, despite its nontraditional, non-Chinese ceremony, Leila's mother accepts her daughter's marriage to Mason. Earlier, Leila's mother had also accepted Leila's decision to live with Mason before marriage, reacting with tolerance and understanding: "'Give it a test.' She nodded, and then muttered, almost to herself, 'Remember to have a way out'" (191). Both Leila's mother and father demonstrate a certain flexibility in their cultural beliefs, a willingness to transcode and adapt Chinese traditions of gender and marriage so that they can function in new ways in the child's "American" context.

Communication and translation are enabled, then, by willingness to transcode ethnic identity. The novel also suggests that those who cannot find a compromise between their two cultures may not survive; like Edna's mother or Mrs. Pang, they may be lost in translation. Ona, the middle daughter, commits suicide, and one of the catalysts of her death is an inability to translate between disjunctive worldviews. Shortly before her death, Ona falls in love with Osvaldo Ong, the son of her parents' business partner. When Osvaldo's father embezzles the business's money, however, Ona's father, Leon, forbids her to see Osvaldo. According to Leila, Leon reverts to a Chinese "old-world" view that sees women—or, more specifically, daughters—as property controlled by the father: "When things went sour, Leon got dangerously old-world about his control over Ona" (112). But Ona has grown up in the "new world" of America, and she believes that she has the right to choose her own romantic partner and to be self-defined. She continues to see Osvaldo until her father forcibly ejects her from the family's home in Chinatown. Ona is not comfortable, however, in a world that is completely American, as Leila explains: "Ona told me about how she felt outside Chinatown. She never felt comfortable . . . she never felt like she fit in" (173). Ona is thus part American and part Chinese in her belief system, but she is unable to transcode either culture; they remain as separate and inassimilable linguistic and cultural terrains in her psyche.

As the middle child, Ona should be in a perfect position to syncretize the world of her Chinese parents and the world of America.

Nina, the rebellious younger child, looks down on her parents' customs and flees three thousand miles to New York. Leila, the dutiful oldest daughter, has trouble leaving her parents to live her own life. Ona can find comfort in neither of these extremes: oscillating between them, she is ultimately destroyed by the tug-of-war between America and China. Ona cannot find a translation between new-world and old-world values, between her desire to have a life of her own and her need for paternal acceptance, between Leon's definition of her as a dutiful daughter and her own need to be self-defined. Ona also cannot discover a language to bridge these conflicts, and so she falls into a silence and invisibility that foreshadow her eventual suicide: "Ona got used to keeping everything inside, to holding the seeds of herself secret from us, and we got used to her shadowy presence" (112). And because Ona's family cannot translate her life back into words, she seems to be lost in translation, as Leila explains: "Ona has become a kind of silence in our lives. We don't talk about her" (15). Literally, the family does not speak of Ona, but more metaphorically they refuse to translate her life out of the void of death and silence and back into the living world of language.

Yet Leila eventually tells Ona's story. Therefore, the novel should be construed as a breaking of the silence surrounding Ona's life, and Leila's narration of the novel must be read as an attempt to ensure that Ona is not lost in translation. Leila tells us that "Ona was a counter" who "counted off the days till Leon was coming home" and then counted "out ninety-nine kisses to keep him safe" (88). Ona counts, and Leila's narrative *recounts* her life in language that lives and breathes with Ona's very personality: "Ona had always been the forward-looking one. She was always excited about the next day, the tomorrow. . . . Ona wanted to be a smart old goddess. She wanted to be a seawoman and sail the world, to see everything Leon saw" (88); "If Ona were here, she would count the living; Ona would tell us that there are more living than dead" (89). Although her parents insist on keeping secrets, a deeper cultural wisdom stresses the need for articulation; Leila remembers the advice of the sewing ladies: "Talk. Talk good things and urge the sadness away" (132). If Ona is to be a living presence, rather than a dead relic, her life must be translated back into active language, into a living story.

In the end, it is the power of storytelling that the novel endorses: "Family exists only because somebody has a story, and knowing the story connects us to a history" (36). Leila's recounting of Ona's life breaks down the barrier between the past and the present, between her parents' Chinese silence about the shameful suicide and Leila's own need for expression, between an Ona who is lost in translation and an Ona who is living, breathing, and counting. It also breaks down the barriers between an "old-world" patriarchal view of Ona as a silent and passive possession and a "new-world" view of Ona as a self-defined American individual. In Leila's translation of Ona's life, Ona is both a sweet daughter, counting out kisses for her father, and a salty sailor, sailing the world. Leila creates a writerly translation of Ona's life that mediates not only between the Chinese and American but also between a silent, passive "text" that is forgotten in the past and an active, spoken one that is re-created in the present.

In each of the works discussed so far, storytelling plays a central role in intergenerational communication and in translation itself. For what is elided, specifically, when no translation occurs, are the stories: the stories of the parents' culture, the stories of the children's world, and the stories of the syncretic reconciliation that translation might enact between them. The parent culture (figured here as the ethnic) is often silenced or forgotten when the children (figured here as the American) cannot translate it into comprehensibility. However, in its most active and writerly sense translation has the capacity to push the ethnic back into language, into cultural circulation, into stories, when it is in danger of being lost in a void of silence, of unintelligibility. In these works, storytelling and translation are therefore closely and crucially interlinked: both function as potential conduits between not only China and America but also the silenced and the spoken, between what is lost in the void of the past and what lingers in present cultural memory and circulation. Storytelling becomes crucially embedded, then, within the larger discursive enterprise of translation.

This concept of storytelling as a translation between not only China and America, but also the silenced and the spoken, underlies Maxine Hong Kingston's *The Woman Warrior*. Like *Bone*, the book begins with the breaking of silences about a suicide: Kingston's protagonist is told to be silent about her aunt's death, but she insists on writing about it (3, 16). By imagining and writing a more positive story for this woman, Kingston creates a translation of her aunt's life that crosses the borders between the Chinese injunction to be silent about this shameful suicide and her American need for a myth of ancestral strength.[4] Throughout the novel, however, the protagonist is preoccupied with a series of seemingly irresolvable translation paradoxes: How can she translate the patriarchal Chinese stories she hears about her ancestors into a positive cultural legacy that she can use in the difficult world of America ("Unless I see [my aunt's] life branching into mine, she gives me no ancestral help" [8])? How can she incorporate a sexist Chinese language into her own writing in a way that does not debilitate her ("There is a Chinese word for the female *I*—which is 'slave.' Break the women with their own tongues!" [47])? How can she transcode false cultural myths about a China she has never seen into a meaningful and useful cultural legacy in America ("What is Chinese tradition and what is the movies?" [6])? Facing such paradoxical problems, Kingston is sometimes tempted to conclude that her Chinese heritage is untransportable and even disabling—that it is not worth transcoding or disarticulating from the discourse of the alien, the foreign, the other. Yet the movement toward a resolution of these translation dilemmas is the plot of *The Woman Warrior*, for as the protagonist shifts from a readerly to a writerly translation process, she apprehends that her conflicting cultural heritage actually enables the ability to produce unique translations that break down the divisions between cultures, translations that finally transcode and reanimate both cultural and linguistic terrains.

An analysis of the text's movement toward a more positive and writerly process of translation must begin with the question of Kingston's own silences and of how these silences coincide with problems in the translation of her cultural and linguistic identity. Gender plays a clearer role in Kingston's translation problems than in Louie's or Ng's texts, and as I argue later, Kingston's protagonist does eventually develop a feminized and resistant practice of translation. Initially, however, she seems stymied by the difficulties that race and gender impose. To use Louie's term, "Chinese-father orthodoxy" defines Kingston's identity as silent and passive; however, she cannot completely accept the individualism of an American identity, an American "I." Both King-Kok Cheung and David Leiwei Li have noted Kingston's problematic conceptualization of the word "I" (Cheung, *Articulate Silences*; Li, "Naming"). Yet this difficulty is one of translation, for the Chinese feminine "I" is sexist and demeaning, while the American "I" is too slippery for her to grasp: "How could the American 'I,' assuredly wearing a hat like the Chinese, have only three strokes, the middle so straight?" (166). Literally, Kingston cannot transcode the English "I" into terms she can understand as a Chinese living in America. But she adamantly rejects the female Chinese character for "I," claiming that it offers her no positive linguistic or cultural identity but only an identity as a "slave" (47).[5] Thus Kingston's silence and lack of "I"dentity are not a product of either her Chinese or her American heritage. Instead they are produced by the interplay of both heritages and by her inability to find a meaningful transcoding of these two linguistic and cultural terrains and the divergent conceptions of femininity they seem to promote. This point is also made in terms of Kingston's own problems with language: at times her silences are figured as the product of being a "Chinese girl" (166), while at other times they are linked to a desire to be "American-feminine" (11, 172). In fact, Kingston's muteness is created by gaps between the linguistic and cultural systems she has access to and by her lack of facility in bridging these gaps through a meaningful translation that takes account of both linguistic and cultural universes. Therefore, the struggle in the book is to open up these silences, translate them, break them into language and into stories. Kingston's own body is sometimes figured as a text; in the mythological episode "White Tigers," for example, her parents carve words on her back that report the crimes against her family (34–35). Yet Kingston struggles in the book not to be a text, an icon of the divided, marked, scarred ethnic American body/self, but rather to speak a text that transcodes this body/self into a new entity.[6]

Kingston must learn to engage in a writerly process of translation that re-creates the scripts of cultural and gendered identity and voice that have silenced and disempowered her, and she must use her translations to speak through and against derogatory constructs of race and gender. Yet like Leila in *Bone*, as a young girl

Kingston resents the process of translation, and she refuses the problem solving that translation of necessity entails. For example, when a druggist erroneously sends medicine to her family's home (an omen of bad luck) and Kingston must ask for candy (or "sweetness") to amend this evil omen, she does not even try to translate this custom, to make it comprehensible to the druggist. Instead, she demands some "sample candy," which the druggist initially refuses to give to her:

> "We don't give sample candy, young lady," he said.
> "My mother said you have to give us candy. She said that is the way the Chinese do it."
> "What?"
> "That is the way the Chinese do it."
> "Do what?"
> "Do things." I felt the weight and immensity of things impossible to explain to the druggist. (170)

Instead of translating or transcoding the custom, she resorts to repeating the same words, words that explain little: "That is the way the Chinese do it." Her failure underscores the underlying ethnic conflict: the second generation is alienated from the first generation's traditions, lacking both the language to explain these customs and the respectful motivation necessary to create a successful translation of them. Kingston is afraid that her mother will make her "swing stinky censers across the counter, at the druggist" or "throw dog blood on the druggist" (170). Chinese ethnicity is here portrayed as baggage that cannot—and should not—be transcoded or disarticulated from a discourse that would label it foreign, other, or savage. Kingston's mother, for her part, refuses to participate in her daughter's world or even to acknowledge the difficulties of her daughter's position, saying callously, "You just translate" (170). Although one critic has argued that in Kingston's writing the process of translation is "transparent" because Kingston tends "to smooth away the linguistic ruptures resultant from intertextual/intercultural transposition" (Huang 153–54), it should be clear that here and elsewhere Kingston foregrounds the very arduous and *visible* process of intercultural translation in which her protagonist is expected to engage.

These problems of/in translation are compounded by the fact that the heritages of the first and the second generation are configured as disjunctive and inaccessible. The parents speak Chinese and hide their real names from authorities and from their children. They also conceal the meaning of their Chinese heritage; repeatedly, Kingston makes the point that parents will not explain many of the Chinese customs to their ghostlike, "barbarian" children (121, 183–85). The immigrants also denigrate American culture and, by extension, the world their children inhabit: "They called us a kind of ghost. Ghosts are noisy and full of air; they talk during meals. They talk about anything" (183–84). The parents, then, see little of value in "the American" and refuse to transcode it, maintaining instead a "pure" Chinese ethnic identity. For their part, the children mostly ignore their parents' customs, speaking in English (128) and refusing to translate. When Kingston's maternal aunt, Moon Orchid, asks a child what he is reading about, he responds: "I don't know the Chinese words for it" (134). This could be read as a literal statement of an inability to disambiguate, but the fact that the "child's" vocabulary includes sophisticated Chinese words such as those for "thermometer" and "library" belies this literal interpretation of the incident. If translation is a learned competence (Neubert and Shreve 43), it seems clear from these examples that the process of learning has stopped.

Yet, as do Ng and Louie in their books, in *The Woman Warrior* Kingston suggests that those who do not learn this process of translation run the risk of ending up insane, dead, or isolated. Like Louie and Ng, Kingston also implies that women, in particular, bear the heaviest burden as translators and stand to suffer the greatest losses when their translations fail. The stories of Moon Orchid and of Crazy Mary demonstrate this point. At the urging of Kingston's mother, Moon Orchid comes to the United States prepared to reclaim the husband who moved there thirty years ago. But Moon Orchid's husband has remarried and become extremely Americanized. He considers Moon Orchid untransferable, saying, "She'd never fit into an American household. . . . [She] can barely talk to me" (153). Indeed, Moon Orchid's cultural alienation is so great that she cannot fit herself into the American world at all, and she eventually goes insane and dies in a mental institution.

Moon Orchid's insanity takes a peculiar form from the point of view of language and translation theory. As her insanity progresses, she claims that she understands other immigrants—the Mexicans: "This time, miraculously, I understood. I decoded their speech. I penetrated the words and understood what was happening inside" (156). Moon Orchid's claim demonstrates a point translation theorists and the texts discussed so far have detailed: shared experience, rather than language facility itself, enables translation. But does Moon Orchid actually understand the Mexican immigrants? Has she penetrated through their dialect to a pure language bound together by commonalties, a pure language hidden beneath the babble of impure tongues? This episode raises a question central to translation theory: are all languages tied together by a universal, underlying language, as translation theorists such as Paz (157) have wondered? If so, then the translator might seek to recover this common, underlying language. As a translator, Moon Orchid seems to find a pure language that undergirds all language, and in the mental institution she repeats this idea when she discusses the other inmates: "We understand one another here. We speak the same language, the very same" (160). Of course, Moon Orchid is insane, and she dies shortly after making this statement. Through the example of Moon Orchid, then, Kingston rejects the notion of a locatable *reine sprache*—a pure language that underlies all languages. If such a language exists, Kingston seems to say, it is a language of insanity, one that cannot survive in a real-world social context. The novel also indicates that what control Moon Orchid does achieve over her language through her "translations" exists only in a fantasy; she retreats into an imaginary, pure language that cannot survive in the real world of disjunctive and imperfect translations and tongues.

The connection between insanity, untranslatability, and the retreat into a "pure" language no one can understand is also alluded to in the story of Crazy Mary, another recent Chinese immigrant, a story Kingston herself fears replicating. Mary's family leaves her in China when she is a toddler, and by the time they have enough money to send for her she is twenty years old and completely insane. Like Moon Orchid, Mary speaks a "pure" language all her own, composed mainly of "growls" and "laughs" (187), a language no one can translate. And like Moon Orchid, Mary's insanity and her "pure" language seem to have been produced by cultural and linguistic alienation; as Kingston notes, "Their other children, who were born in the U.S., *were normal and could translate*" (187, emphasis added). But insanity and lack of translation are not just a problem for recent Chinese immigrants; Kingston fears insanity herself. Kingston talks to people in her head, drops dishes, picks her nose while cooking, wears wrinkled clothes, limps, and has a mysterious illness. Although some of this behavior is affected, she wonders if this could be the onset of insanity: "Indeed I was getting stranger every day"; "I did not want to be our crazy one" (190). Through her adoption of these odd mannerisms, she resists being married off in what she sees as "traditional" Chinese fashion. Yet her refusal to transcode her parents' heritage into something useful in her own life exposes her to the risk of becoming like Crazy Mary and Moon Orchid: untranslatable, insane—caught in a fantasy world of one's imagination, trapped in a linguistic universe of one's own, using a pure (yet insane) language.

Kingston comments early in the book that she "could not figure out what was [her] village" (45); does she belong in a Chinese world, or does she belong in an American one? Ultimately, Kingston uses language to break down this division, stating, "My job is my own only land" (49). On a literal level, this statement refers to the fact that in an agricultural society, a peasant without land had no food and work. Literally, Kingston's job (writing) is the equivalent of land: it gives her food and work. But Kingston is not in the agrarian, rural world of China; she is in the urbanized, industrial world of the United States. This statement must therefore be translated as a symbolization of the way that Kingston's writing helps her mediate her disjunctive cultural heritage, transcode her ethnicity, and find place: when Kingston writes, she finds her "own only land" by breaking down the binary oppositions that have disabled her. In the same passage, Kingston comments that nobody has "united both North American and Asia" but that as "a descendant of eighty pole fighters, I ought to be able to set out confidently, march straight down our street, get going right now" (49). Through her writing, Kingston breaks down the oppositions that separate North America and Asia, syncretizing and transcoding her dual and at times conflicting cultural heritage as a Chinese and an American in order to create something new.[7]

Translation has been characterized as a search for correspondences between a source text and a target text, but such correspondences can be found only when the translator believes the source text has something useful and relevant to communicate. To transfer this analogy to Kingston's own struggle, she must value her parents' culture before she can translate it into her own life, before she can find correspondences. In an episode in her later volume *China Men*, Kingston finds herself conversing fluently and easily in Chinese with her paternal aunt, and she comments, "I was speaking well because I was talking to her; *there are people who dry up language*" (206, emphasis added). Kingston senses a love, respect, and tolerance on the part of her aunt, which enables her ability to translate. Similarly, when Kingston compliments her aunt on her English, the aunt responds that her children refuse to talk to her: "They shout at me and tell me I'm too stupid to understand. They hardly come home, and when I ask them what they're doing, they say I'm dumb" (*China Men* 206–7). Both women possess a translating consciousness—the ability to intertwine words and worlds. And in *China Men*, Kingston's and her aunt's mutual respect regenerates and interanimates their ability to find points of connection and of correspondence.

Despite some negative feelings between mother and daughter, this mutual respect is also present in *The Woman Warrior*, and it enables Kingston's finding of correspondences between her own world and her mother's. Kingston realizes that she and her mother share the gift of storytelling and that all her life she has been in the presence of a great power, her mother "talking-story" (19–20). And her mother finally realizes that she needs her daughter, saying: "I want you here, not wandering like a ghost from Romany" (107). But Brave Orchid (Kingston's mother) does also accept, finally, her daughter's choice of a distant domicile, saying: "The weather in California must not agree with you. . . . Of course, you must go, Little Dog" (108). Brave Orchid's use of the nickname "Little Dog" is highly significant, demonstrating a protective and loving care for her daughter. As Kingston explains, "Little Dog" is an "endearment," "a name to fool the gods" (109) since both Kingston and her mother were actually born in the Chinese year of the dragon. At other times in the book Kingston misconstrues her mother's use of Chinese customs and traditions, but here she understands this endearment, this translation of her status. In Chinese tradition, people born in the year of the dragon are said to be powerful, energetic, and strong, and Kingston here takes pride in the Chinese heritage she shares with her mother: "I am really a Dragon, as she is a Dragon. . . . I am practically a first daughter of a first daughter" (109). The term "Little Dog" also functions as a blessing from her mother, as a linguistic entity through which the mother and daughter achieve peace. When Kingston's mother uses this term, Kingston feels "a weight lifted from me. The quilts must be filling with air. The world is somehow lighter" (108–9). As in *Bone*, a Chinese term and its English translation ("Mason I love," "Little Dog") suggest cultural compromise, intergenerational reconciliation, and transmigration of the Chinese tongue into English, rather than the "drying up" of language.

The translation of "Little Dog" is also a writerly translation that makes both Kingston and her mother active participants in the creation of meaning. Like Edna and Leila, Kingston must learn to be a writerly translator or she will be unable to create such successful translations. In one chapter, for example, Kingston literally translates her mother's statement that she is ugly, but her readerly translation fails to take account of the Chinese cultural context in which, as Kingston's mother explains, "that's what Chinese say. We like to say the opposite" (203). Some of Kingston's translations of Chinese ideographs also rely on a literal translation. About the word for mountain, for example, she comments that it "look[s] like the ideograph 'mountain'" (20). Kingston cannot translate certain words, such as *Sit Dom Kuei* (a kind of ghost) because she seeks a literal, uncontextualized dictionary definition of them: "I keep looking in dictionaries under those syllables. 'Kuei' means 'ghost,' but I don't find any other words that make sense" (88).[8]

Yet Kingston sometimes finds more writerly and contextualized translations. She finds multiple meanings for the phrase used to refer to immigrant children, "Ho Chi Kuei." Kingston translates "kuei" as "ghost," but *ho* and/or *chi* are more confusing and could mean: "'centipede,' 'grub,' 'bastard carp,' 'chirping insect,' 'jujube tree,' 'pied wagtail,' 'grain sieve,' or 'casket sacrifice'" (204). However, Kingston rejects these translations because she finds them irrelevant to the way "Ho Chi Kuei" is used, to the term's social context. Instead, she begins a more writerly process of translation: "Perhaps I've romanized the spelling wrong and it is *Hao* Chi Kuei, which could mean they are calling us 'Good Foundation Ghosts.' The immigrants could be saying that we were born on Gold Mountain and have advantages. Sometimes they scorn us for having had it so easy, and sometimes they're delighted" (204–5). Kingston has moved from a literal examination of the word's meaning to a more metaphorical way of translating and transmigrating it; she is now striving to apply it to her own life and to her interactions with her relatives. In so doing, she asserts control over the process of translation, actively participating in it and transcoding her parents' ethnic heritage. More important, this writerly process of translation allows Kingston to create a positive cultural legacy for herself, one in which the prior generation does not disparage the children's experience. According to Lorraine Dong and Marlon Hom, phrases such as "hu-ji," "hu-ji hauh," "hu-ji doi," and "hu-ji nui" are all new terms created out of the Chinese experience in the United States that refer to Chinese Americans (13, 22). Dong and Hom translate "hu-ji," for example, as "product/son of the earth," a term "usually but not always derogatorily used by the older generation for the younger" (22). Similarly, "hu-ji hauh" means literally "a native head" (22), again perhaps a pejorative term for the younger generation. By disregarding such negative translations of the phrase "Ho Chi Kuei" and creating a more positive reading of it, Kingston deconstructs the pejorative way her generation has been construed, creates a more positive relationship to her parental culture and language, and promotes the permeation of cultures that translation in its most metaphorical sense engenders. In the end, then, through translation she transcodes the meaning of the parent culture's ethnicity so that it signifies something positive that can grant her ancestral strength.

Kingston also suggests that such a writerly process of translation enables this ability to break down the disjunctions between her Chinese and American heritage: "I like to look up a trouble-some, shameful thing and then say, 'Oh is that all?' . . . It drives the fear away and makes it possible someday to visit China, where I know now they don't sell girls or kill each other for no reason" (205). It may seem odd that the act of looking up words such as "Sit Dom Kuei" generates confusion about China, while the act of looking up other words drives away fear and creates an acceptance of this world. But in this latter instance of using the dictionary, Kingston searches in a less literal way and finds a more writerly and metaphorical process of translation that allows her to allay her fears and be more accepting of her Chinese heritage. After all, "*Hao Chi Kuei*" (204) (which Kingston translates as "Good Foundation Ghost") may be Kingston's invention, her transcoding of the nega-tive term Ho Chi Kuei into something positive and meaningful in her own world. Like all good translations, "Good Foundation Ghost" gives voice to the source text while also allowing for the translator's creative, inventive, and artistic point of view. Hao Chi Kuei, in opposition to Ho Chi Kuei, reflects a compromise and even a peace between the world of the Chinese immigrants and that of their American offspring.

A writerly process of translation also helps Kingston mediate the conflicting gender roles she has inherited as a Chinese Ameri-can. Looking up words and translating them makes it possible for Kingston, as previously noted, to understand that China is not a land where they "sell girls [and] kill each other for no reason" (205). And yet Kingston still finds herself confronting an antagonistic source culture—a culture that appears to devalue women and in-cludes maxims such as "'girls are maggots in the rice'" and "'it is more profitable to raise geese than daughters'" (43). Discussing the role of gender in translation, Carol Maier argues that "the transla-tor's quest is not to silence but to give voice, to make available texts that raise difficult questions and open perspectives. It is essential that as translators women get under the skin of both antagonistic and sympathetic works. They must become independent, 'resisting' interpreters who do not only let antagonistic works speak . . . but also speak with them and place them in a larger context by discuss-ing them and the process of translation" (4). In the chapters "No Name Woman," "White Tigers," and "Song for a Barbarian Reed

Pipe," Kingston portrays antagonistic myths from Chinese culture, but she also slowly learns how to transcode these myths—to speak through them and against them so that they give her "ancestral help" as a woman and as a Chinese American.

In "No Name Woman" Kingston first imagines the antagonistic story—the story of a woman who is forced into marriage, raped while her husband is away, and then silenced "as if she had never been born" (3). But this is not a story that Kingston finds helpful: "Unless I see her life branching into mine, she gives me no ancestral help" (8). To find "ancestral help" in this story, then, Kingston begins to retranslate it. She sees her aunt as a woman who perhaps was in love, who perhaps stood at the mirror and "combed individuality into her bob" (9). Most important, Kingston gives voice to her aunt's silenced life. Her mother explicitly tells her that "you must never tell anyone . . . what I am about to tell you" (3) and "don't tell anyone you had an aunt" (15). Yet Kingston does tell the story, translating it out of silence into language: "I alone devote pages of paper to her" (16). In this text, however, Kingston is unable to formulate a resistant translation. She does tell the story, and she does attempt to revise it, but in the end she remains faithful to the outlines, at least, of the source text. Perhaps this is why Kingston describes her aunt as "forever hungry" and waiting "silently by the water" to pull Kingston down into the well (16). The ghost is still hungry because Kingston has not written a text that nourishes it, that gives it life and substance.

In "White Tigers," on the other hand, Kingston becomes more of a feminist and resistant translator. As an author, Kingston has been accused of being unfaithful to the original version of the myth of Fa Mu Lan, but her response is insightful in terms of how she views her translation of it: "Sinologists have criticized me for not knowing myths and for distorting them: pirates correct my myths, revising them to make them conform to some traditional Chinese version. They don't understand that myths have to change, be useful or be forgotten. Like the people who carry them across the oceans, the myths become American. The myths I write are new, American" ("Personal Statement" 24). Kingston takes the story of Fa Mu Lan out of its original context and rewrites it. Such deterritorialization, decontextualization, and contamination of a source text may be emblematic of a feminist practice of translation (see Flotow-Evans 44). Kingston also seems to have explicitly feminist goals in her adaptation of this myth, as her statements indicate: "I take the power I need from whatever myth. Thus Fa Mu Lan has the words cut into her back; in traditional story, it is the man, Ngak Fei the Patriot, whose parents cut vows on his back. I mean to take his power for women" ("Personal Statement" 24).[9] In Barbara Godard's performative theory of feminist translation, "Translation . . . is production, not reproduction" (91). Such a goal seems to be at work in "White Tigers." Kingston does not so much mistranslate the myth as retranslate it—not reproduce the myth but actually attempt to produce it in a new way.

In Kingston's new translation of the myth of Fa Mu Lan, the heroine can lead her people in successful battles (42), give birth (40), and slay the baron who makes demeaning comments about women (43). She can then return home and become an example of "perfect filiality" (45). Kingston's story, then, portrays a woman who can "have it all": who can be both man and woman, heroic warrior and dutiful daughter, a legend and a mother/wife. But there is something hyperbolic about this translation, as Kingston well knows. And, most problematic, it does not fit with her own life; like the story of No Name Woman, it does not give her "ancestral help." Back in the United States, Kingston still feels that "my American life has been such a disappointment" and that "I could not figure out what was my village" (45). Although she recognizes that "the swordswoman and I are not so dissimilar" (53), Kingston ends this piece with the words of the crimes flowing off her skin: "The reporting is the vengeance—not the beheading, not the gutting, but the words. And I have so many words—'chink' words and 'gook' words too—that they do not fit on my skin" (53). Kingston has tried to become a resistant translator who can perform the source text so that it is given a feminist emphasis, but from this ending it appears that she herself cannot avoid "becoming" the source text—an icon of the divided and scarred ethnic, feminine self. The source text has not, in short, been transcoded.

In the text's concluding chapter, "Song for a Barbarian Reed Pipe," however, translation finally enables a transcoding of Kingston's understanding of Chinese cultural and gender structures that is effective in the American world Kingston inhabits. In this chapter, writerly, resistant translation produces a positive fusion between two seemingly dissociated and contradictory cultures, as well as a productive reconsideration of gender roles. On the cultural level, the last chapter reflects a syncretic reconciliation between the Chinese and the American, the mother's world and the daughter's. Because a translation gives voice to both the source text and the translator's unique perspective, some translation theorists argue that it should be viewed as coauthored. According to Barnstone, then, translation is "the work of two artists, or a double art" (13).[10] Literally, Kingston's final chapter is the product of at least two artists (Kingston and her mother), as Kingston states: "Here is a story my mother told me. . . . The beginning is hers, the ending, mine" (206). In a more metaphorical sense, however, this chapter is also collaborative, a double art, for Kingston translates her mother's story while also revising and rewriting it so that it can be her own. Calling herself "an outlaw knot-maker" (163), she twists this traditional story of Chinese culture into a new and unique Chinese American design.

The original Chinese story is based on the life of Ts'ai Yen, the first great woman poet of China. Ts'ai Yen was captured by an invading army in A.D. 195 and then spent twelve years in "barbarian" lands. Finally, she was rescued and returned to her own land, leaving her two children behind. As Cheung explains, then, "The Chinese version highlights the poet's eventual return to her own people, a return that reinforces certain traditional and ethnocentric Chinese notions" ("'Don't Tell'" 171). The original version also emphasizes separation between not only the "barbarian" and the "Chinese," but also the mother who returns to China and the children who remain in the foreign land. Kingston's retelling of this story does not avoid the idea of cultural and linguistic dislocation, for she tells us that Ts'ai Yen's "barbarian" children do not speak her language and even make fun of their mother's speech (208). However, Kingston's version suggests that translation overcomes this separation. When Ts'ai Yen hears the "barbarian music," she begins singing Chinese songs that cross the barriers between cultures: "Ts'ai Yen sang about China and her family there. Her words seemed to be Chinese, but the barbarians understood their sadness and anger. Sometimes they thought they could catch barbarian phrases about forever wandering" (209). The songs also function as a bridge between the mother's language and the children's: "Her children did not laugh, but eventually sang along when she left her tent to sit by the winter campfires" (209). In Kingston's version of the story, Ts'ai Yen finds a way of bridging the barriers between the new "barbarian" world and the old world of China, the world of the children and the world of the mother.

Read on a metaphorical level, "A Song for a Barbarian Reed Pipe" suggests that Kingston has found a way of deconstructing the binary oppositions that separate mother and daughter, China and America—a way of transcoding Chinese ethnicity and transmigrating the Chinese tongue into English. Kingston says that Ts'ai Yen "brought her songs back from the savage lands, and one of the three that has been passed down to us is 'Eighteen Stanzas for a Barbarian Reed Pipe,' a song that Chinese sing to their own instruments. It translated well" (209). In choosing to conclude her work with "It translated well," Kingston suggests the symbolic meaning of translation as a trope for cultural syncretism and intergenerational conjunction. Although the process is fraught with conflict, in this story and in the book as a whole Kingston creates a translation that allows her to break down some of the barriers between East and West, as well as to take strength from the interplay and interpenetration between her disjunctive cultural and linguistic terrains. She does not, then, as Yunte Huang claims, eradicate differences between texts or cultures "in order to create a unitary text" (162) but, rather, allows differences between the mother and the daughter, China and America, and the East and the West to remain and even to power and animate her text and her translations.

This story also breaks down the distinctions between male and female and between active and passive that Kingston finds in Chinese legends, thereby facilitating her ability to locate "ancestral strength" in her Chinese culture. Successful translators sometimes pillage, and it should be noted that, in a sense, Kingston pillages the story of Ts'ai Yen, reconstructing its gender biases so that the female poet can serve as a more active and resistant model for Kingston's own process of translation. The original version of this story emphasizes the sadness of the mother's leave-taking:

> The seventeenth stanza. My heart aches, my tears fall.
> . . . .
> Now I think again and again, over and over,
> Of the sons I have lost.
> . . . .
> I will never know them again
> Once I have entered Chang An.
> I try to strangle my sobs
> But my tears stream down my face. (Ts'ai Yen 7)

The poem is a mournful catalogue of what the author has lost: her homeland, her children, her identity. Moreover, in the original version, Ts'ai Yen is passive, carried from one place to another, co-erced into marriage, raped, and then forcibly separated from her children. Kingston's text recognizes that on a literal level Ts'ai Yen remains passive: "After twelve years . . . Ts'ai Yen was ransomed and married to Tung Ssu so that her father would have Han descendants" (209). But on the level of language and translation, Kingston's Ts'ai Yen is active, pursuing communication with the "barbarian" culture and with her own children, bringing "her songs back from the savage lands" and translating them into Chinese (209). In Kingston's version, the pillaged (Ts'ai Yen) becomes not precisely a pillager but certainly someone willing to integrate herself actively into another culture and then "borrow" its cultural artifacts when she leaves. This is a form of translation that Kingston respects, one which begins to break away from a strictly gendered notion of activity and passivity in Chinese women. Indeed, Ts'ai Yen is both active and passive. As Barbara Johnson might say, Kingston has been able to translate a difference between men and women (male = active versus female = passive) into a difference within (Johnson, *Critical Difference* 102). And while not denying the poet's passive traits, Kingston highlights the activity of Ts'ai Yen's character and writing as the grounds on which translation is enabled. The more active understanding of Ts'ai Yen that Kingston achieves through her translation, then, enables a breaking down of binarisms not only between East and West, parent and child, and the Chinese and the American but also between the feminine and masculine. Kingston portrays the antagonistic source text, but she also transcodes it through a resistant process of translation.

Kingston's *The Woman Warrior* also adds a new idea to the trope of translation, one that can be read backward into the other two texts. The songs of Kingston's Ts'ai Yen do not merely translate "barbarian" music into Chinese or make Chinese words understandable to "barbarians." In fact, Ts'ai Yen's syncretic product combines the two languages, the two worlds, even the two genders, producing a *new* entity—a dynamic, regenerative, resistant song. As I have argued, however, Kingston's text seems to demonstrate that there is no such thing as a pure and universal language, and we could extend this to say that there is no such thing as a pure and universal story, an original Ur-text that precedes all other texts. There are only stories that are versions of other stories, words that are translations of other translations. Therefore, as Paz says, "originality in a given translation is untrue in that no text is entirely original because language itself, in its essence, is already a translation." Yet, even so, "all texts are original because every translation is distinctive. Every translation, up to a certain point, is an invention and as such constitutes a text" (translated in Barnstone 5). Each act of translation, then, is old and new, repetitive of past texts/traditions and a new text/tradition in its own right.

In the end it is this capacity for being both old and new, of the past and of the present, that gives translation its power as a trope. In Chinese American texts such as *Pangs of Love*, *Bone*, and *The Woman Warrior*, translation breaks down the binary oppositions between past and present, first-generation and second-generation experiences, between the Chinese and the American, between a silenced story and a spoken reality, and, sometimes, between the feminine and the masculine. Translation finally produces an evolving, fluid, intergenerational, intercultural text. As Neubert and Shreve note, translation can play a significant role in cultural change; translation can liberate by creating "new paradigms and new ways of living" (3). It is this dynamic, intercultural growth between and across nations and time frames that translation, in all its metaphorical senses, ultimately engenders. The works of Louie, Ng, and Kingston express both the difficulties of translation as well as the necessity of constructing a new interlinguistic and intercultural heritage to constitute Chinese American identity—a heritage in which the Chinese and the American interanimate and finally re-create each other.

2

Finding a "Home" in Translation

John Okada's *No-No Boy* and

Cynthia Kadohata's *The Floating World*

tas-key-tehhh
wrong language
the line of white heels
in half
moons over my head
fade away . . .

hellllllllllp

still
wrong language

I will come up for air
in another language
all my own.

—Mitsuye Yamada,
"Drowning in My
Own Language,"
in *Camp Notes
and Other Writings*

MITSUYE YAMADA'S POEM "Drowning in My Own Language" (1988) movingly articulates the struggle of Japanese Americans living in the wake of World War II—after the forced internment of Japanese American citizens in U.S. prisoner of war camps—to find a language of their own. Somewhere between Japanese and English (both figured as "wrong language[s]") there must be "another language / all my own." In this new language, Japanese American individuals will come up for air, finding a mode of translation that creates a home in the interstices between languages and cultures.

I argued in the previous chapter that contemporary Chinese American writers such as Louie, Ng, and Kingston sometimes depict the failure of translation, yet as a whole their works formulate a practice of writerly translation that creates transcoded ethnic identities and transmigrated tongues. This process is much more conflicted for Japanese American writers in the wake of World War II. During World War II approximately 110,000 Japanese Americans were rounded up and shipped to "relocation" centers. Two-thirds of these individuals were American citizens. This action was taken even though the U.S. government had commissioned studies showing that these individuals posed no threat and were loyal to the U.S. government.[1] Several years later this loyalty would be tested when Japanese American men were asked to fight for the United States and put in jail as "No-No boys" if they refused.

Historian Roger Daniels argues that these events marked a profound rupture: "The relocation was and is the central event in Japanese American history, the event from which all other events are dated and compared. 'Before the war' and 'after camp' are the phrases that provide the essential periodization of Japanese American life" (4). For Japanese Americans the relocation also represented a sharp break between a sense of self as belonging to the new culture and a sense of self as irrevocably alien. As one Nisei (second-generation Japanese American) writes, "Suddenly, I became an explicit Jap, a beast, a lecherous threat to white womanhood, a person without ethics, totally devious and sneaky, ugly, and hated. . . . It was Jap, Jap, Jap, and it permeated popular radio shows, newspapers, government pronouncements" (Mass 160).[2] Or as John Okada phrases this in his preface to *No-No Boy*, "As of that moment, the

Japanese in the United States became . . . animals of a different breed. . . . Everything Japanese and everyone Japanese became despicable" (vii). The break is so profound that for many years individuals were unable to confront their feelings about it. Repression, denial, and blaming the self for the government's behavior are all characteristic psychological aftereffects (Mass 160–61). And many Japanese American writers do not write directly about the internment. Authors such as Toshio Mori, Valerie Matsumoto, and Lonny Kaneko tend to depict this displacement through metaphors and elisions, through gaps and silences.[3]

In this chapter I examine two novels that probe this gap, this rupture, this silence—John Okada's *No-No Boy* (1957) and Cynthia Kadohata's *The Floating World* (1989). I have chosen these novels because in them translation struggles between the ethnic and the American are structured in a similar manner but also because the thirty-two-year gap that separates them illustrates how historical and cultural ethos contribute to processes of transcoding ethnicity and transmigrating tongues.[4] Both novels examine a similar set of translation questions ubiquitous for Japanese Americans in the 1950s and 1960s: How can one inhabit a transcoded, syncretic identity when part of this identity (the "American" side) has been denied, while the other part (the "Japanese" side) has been denigrated? Where is the space/place where one can be both Japanese *and* American in a culture that forces one to choose, a culture within which one is either Japanese *or* "American" but not both? Okada's work, written shortly after World War II, probes the idea that translation might be of use in reconciling the dilemma faced by Ichiro, the protagonist, but ultimately, this idea is not brought to textual fruition. As André Lefevere has observed, translation can be allied with cultural capital, and what gets translated has much to do with what is considered to be socially valuable and credentializing speech.[5] In the novel's time period (1950s) Japanese ethnicity was still devalued. Okada portrays a character who never quite learns how to transcode his Japanese ethnicity or disarticulate it from the racist discourse of the "Jap," and one who mostly abandons (rather than transmigrates) his ethnic tongue. The novel does present certain characters who undermine cultural binarisms through their practices of translation, but they remain peripheral figures who only hint at a future hope for the transcoding of ethnicity and the transmigration of tongues—a hope that goes unrealized within the text.

In *The Floating World*, Cynthia Kadohata retrieves this hint of hope, using translation to suggest that the conflict between being Japanese and American can be refigured and transcoded in productive ways. Both *The Floating World* and Kadohata's second novel, *In the Heart of the Valley of Love*, make few direct references to the internment.[6] Yet especially in *The Floating World* the internment is, as literary critic Yuko Matsukawa has suggested, "the unwritten center" of the text.[7] Like Okada, then, Kadohata is concerned with whether translation allows Japanese Americans to repair the schisms in subjectivity caused by the war and to transcode their ethnicity. Kadohata is also concerned with whether translation can create a home: a bricolaged space of placement in displacement. And like Okada's novel, Kadohata's begins in the 1950s. Of course, Kadohata's novel is published in the 1980s when Japanese Americans (for better or worse) have assumed the mantle as America's "model minority," so the transcoding of ethnicity has become less arduous; Japanese ethnicity now has "cultural capital." Yet this is only part of the reason that Kadohata's text deploys the trope of translation to renovate ethnic identity. Another part of the novel's positivity in utilizing this trope is that Kadohata learns from a text such as *No-No Boy* about how binarisms are structured in this time period and about how ethnicity is devalued, and also because she retrieves the hint of hope embodied by his text—a hint of hope that finally does reside in translation. Indeed, in *The Floating World* it is only by living *in* translation that individuals can find the "ancestral strength" they need to survive and to make a space for themselves in the world. I would suggest, then, that by returning to this time period Kadohata both pays homage to and rewrites the textual and linguistic translation dilemmas of the earlier novel and the earlier time period. What is important for Kadohata is that individuals maintain a "translating consciousness"—the ability to see the world as composed of multiple and intersecting identities, languages, and cultural frames of reference. Such a consciousness can ultimately transmigrate the Japanese tongue to a space within the English language—a space where the discourse of the "Jap" no

longer functions to derail the processes of translation, as it does in
No-No Boy.

IN TOSHIO MORI'S "The Travelers," one character comments: "We
Nisei are . . . like the seeds in the wind" (130).[8] During World War
II, Japanese American communities in the United States were forcibly destroyed, and this dislocation continued after the war's end.
Some communities rebuilt, but literature from this time period
portrays a continual pattern of movement. Is this because, as one
of my students argued recently, "a moving target can't be hit"? In
the wake of World War II, did Japanese Americans feel that the
only safe space was a no-home, a not-place, a floating world? Or,
to interpret this theme of movement more positively, did these individuals actually find place *through* movement? And how do questions of translation play into this search for "home," a search which
is surely allied with the attempt to find an ethnic identity and a
voice that move beyond the binary choice of being *either* Japanese
or American?

In the novels I discuss, there are often contradictory formulations of home. Some individuals seek an originary home—a place
where the self was not always-already displaced. And some individuals try to find home in an assimilative sense of being "American."
Both these strategies fail. To find home, individuals must realize
that there is no place where they are not already displaced. But
language—and more specifically translation itself—is one way to
formulate a renovated sense of home. Language can create what
Salman Rushdie has called an "imaginary homeland." "My job is
my own only land" (49), Kingston's protagonist comments in *The
Woman Warrior.* For Kingston's protagonist her job—writing—
creates and even re-creates her land, an imaginary homeland that
transcodes past and present, where she has been and where she is,
the ethnic and the American. It is this re-creative, imaginary power
of translation that both Okada's and Kadohata's novels reach toward in their formulations of home.

No-No Boy is filled with a nervous energy that often takes the
form of both a geographic migration and a linguistic displacement
that bespeaks the characters' sense of homelessness. Literally, no

one in this book can sit still. "Pa," Ichiro notes, is incessantly moving as if "his trousers were crawling with ants" (9). Ichiro himself is constantly on the move. He returns (by bus) to Seattle after two years in a relocation center and two years in prison; he walks to his house, walks to a friend's house with his mother, rides the bus past the university he once attended, is driven around in his friend Kenji's car, drives Kenji to Portland, drives Kenji's car back, walks around some more, and delivers Kenji's car to Kenji's family. The novel finally ends with Ichiro still roaming the streets, chasing after the meaning of America: "He walked along, thinking, searching, thinking and probing, and, in the darkness of the alley of the community that was a tiny bit of America, he chased that faint and illusive insinuation of promise as it continued to take shape in mind and heart" (251). Perhaps we can see in this constant migration a strategy of placement—of finding home in and through movement. But the novel seems to belie this notion through the character of Kenji. Kenji urges Ichiro to face his problems: "The kind of trouble you've got, you can't run from it. Stick it through. Let them call you names. . . . They just need a little time to get cut down to their own size. Then they'll be the same as you, a bunch of Japs" (163). Go home and face your problems, Kenji counsels—but what exactly is home in this context?

Interestingly, certain characters also employ a refusal to translate to maintain illusionary conceptualizations of home. For example, Ichiro's mother sees Japan as her home. She plans to return with her family to Japan someday (13, 20, 25), and she and her husband "still feel like transients even after thirty or forty years in America" (25). So, of course, she does not learn to translate between Japanese and English. This is a way of preserving her dream of home, as the narrative voice notes about the Issei (first-generation immigrants from Japan) in general: "They rushed to America with the single purpose of making a fortune which would enable them to return to their own country. . . . *They continued to maintain their dreams by refusing to learn how to speak or write the language of America*" (25–26, emphasis added). Both Ichiro and the narrative voice criticize this attitude. For example, Ichiro recalls how his mother once destroyed a phonograph he had borrowed because she did not like his American records, and the narrative voice comments: "He *justly* felt after all these years that she had been very unfair" (205, emphasis added). From the narrative point of view, Ichiro's anger and hostility toward his mother—even after her death—is "just." Mrs. Yamada is trying to prevent American culture and the sounds of the English language (the records) from infecting her Japanese home. Apparently this goal is one that the narrative voice considers unreasonable.

Nor is Mrs. Yamada successful in this goal. Both her sons adopt American English and refuse to speak Japanese. Linguistically, then, they attempt to be "American" and to locate their homes in this new geographic and linguistic terrain. Moreover, throughout the novel Ichiro longs to find home by becoming "American." In a long meditation, Ichiro wonders: "Where is that place they talk of and paint nice pictures of and describe in all the homey magazines? Where is that place with the clean, white cottages surrounding the new, red-brick church with the clean, white steeple, where the families all have two children, one boy and one girl, and a shiny new car in the garage and a dog and a cat and life is like living in the land of the happily-ever-after? Surely it must be around here someplace, someplace in America. Or is it just that it's not for me?" (159). Rushdie comments that America can deprive you of your own dreams and replace them with a commodified version of the dominant society's mass-produced fantasies (124). Although Ichiro does see the flaws in this American discourse of the home, he also spends much of the novel longing for it and longing to be "American." But because he did not fight in the war, he feels he is not "American": "I made a mistake and I know it with all the anguish in my soul. . . . Am I really never to know again what it is to be American?" (81–82). Throughout the novel Ichiro regrets his decision not to fight in the war (34, 81, 220) and longs to be a true "American" who fought for America (16, 34, 51, 232).

In reading these passages, I find it difficult to decide where Okada himself stands. Is he critical of individuals who translate themselves into "Americans" and adopt an American discourse of the home in which everyone (so the story goes) lives "happily ever after"? Or does he feel that this is a normal process: immigrants sink their roots into the soil and adopt the languages and identities of the new homeland, forgetting their native tongue and its values?

I read Okada as being most interested in depicting the contradictory ideologies running rampant in America during the postwar time period, rather than in judging them. Ichiro himself is caught up in these contradictory ideologies: understanding why he did not fight but also wishing he had; wanting to find a home in America as an American while also realizing the limitations of America for one who is not white (104); longing to speak and think like an "American" even as he subconsciously laments the loss of the mother tongue. Furthermore, in this particular historical context, dilution, hybridity, or the inhabiting of a nonbinary identity are seen as weaknesses, rather than strengths. "I wish with all my heart that I were Japanese or that I were American. I am neither" (16), Ichiro tells Kenji. Ichiro also feels he has let the two warring sides of his identity destroy him. As he tells Kenji: "Me, I'm not even a son of a bitch. I'm nobody, nothing. Just plain nothing" (76).

Looking, then, more closely at the novel's translation problem, we can see that (like the works discussed in Chapter 1) the language gap between the generations, as well as between the ethnic and the American, is abundantly clear: "[Ichiro's] parents, like most of the old Japanese, spoke virtually no English. On the other hand, the children, like Ichiro, spoke almost no Japanese. Thus they communicated, the old speaking Japanese with an occasionally badly mispronounced word or two of English; and the young, with the exception of a simple word or phrase of Japanese . . . resorting almost constantly to the tongue the parents avoided" (7). Studies have shown that in situations where an individual has access to two languages, the code or language one speaks has more to do with social network than with generational status (Milroy and Wei 146). And children who speak English rather than an ethnic tongue may do so not because they are second- or third-generation individuals but because the ethnic tongue represents a "dispreferred" or disfavored language (Milroy and Wei 150). In *No-No Boy* the younger generation's social network is composed of other individuals who speak English, and the dispreferred language is Japanese. This indicates that the children are attempting to formulate an identity as "pure" Americans. The parents, for their part, maintain a linguistic and cultural identity as Japanese by refusing to learn English. Neither parent nor child, then, has begun the process of transcoding ethnicity.

Translation is portrayed as being crucially necessary to bridge these linguistic and cultural gaps, but the burden is placed on the older generation. Kenji's father remembers hearing a lecture in the camps by a young Japanese American sociologist. The sociologist argues that the parents do not know their children: "How many of you are able to sit down with your own sons and daughters and enjoy the companionship of conversation? How many, I ask? If I were to say none of you, I would not be far from the truth. . . . Change, now, if you can, even if it may be too late, and become companions to your children" (125). To understand their children the older generation must learn to converse in English, but no mention is made of the children learning more Japanese to understand their parents. In the novel as a whole, many of the characters see assimilation into American English as a strength and indeed a necessity. Japanese ethnicity is to be discarded rather than transcoded or renovated.

Furthermore, codeswitching is often presented as a weakness. Three types of language are represented in this book: a pure Japanese, a kind of discordant Japanese inflected by English words or discursive patterns, and a standardized American English. These languages are written in English, but they each have their own distinctive syntactic patterns. Ichiro's mother appears to speak a kind of pure and formal Japanese, constructing sentences such as: "If you have come to doubt your mother—and I'm sure you do not mean it even if you speak in weakness—it is to be regretted. Rest a few days. Think more deeply and your doubts will disappear. You are my son, Ichiro" (15). Ichiro's father also speaks Japanese (7), but his language contains American English words and is often portrayed as being grammatically incorrect: "Ya, Ichiro, you have come home" (6); "Mama is gone to the bakery" (7); "Ya, four is best; a whole case, better. Sonagabitch, I'm thirsty. Sonagabitch, cold too. Plenty cold" (173; see also 177, 188, 189). Pa appears to be able to codeswitch, but when he does so he sounds foolish. After falling down in the street while hurrying home to drink his liquor, he says, "Okay. . . . Everything okay. Just fall" in "halting English" to the inquiring faces clustered around him (174). Some bilinguals speak of infecting English with the values and discursive patterns of other languages. For instance, according to Coco Fusco, a performance artist and writer such as Guillermo Gómez-Peña (discussed in more detail in Chapter 6) is "very interested in subverting English structures, infecting English with Spanish, and in finding new possibilities of expression within the English language that English-speaking people don't have" (157). But of course, this can work in the opposite direction: the ethnic language can also become infected—or even taken over—by English. Words such as "ya" (yes) and "sonagabitch" (son of a bitch) are evidence that Pa's Japanese has been "infected" by English. The result, from Okada's point of view, is not a hybrid or transmigrated language of strength but a dialect that sounds broken, foolish, and diluted.

Has the younger generation been more successful at infecting English with other languages? For the most part, the Nisei speak an Americanized English that does not appear to contain any traces of the ethnic tongue. For example, in refusing a job from Mr. Carrick, Ichiro says: "You've no apology to make, sir. You've been very good. I want the job. The pay is tops. I might say I need the job, but it's not for me" (152). This polite speech includes American colloquialisms ("the pay is tops") and complex grammatical constructions characteristic of someone who is perfectly comfortable speaking English. English is clearly Ichiro's "home" tongue. The Japanese language, on the other hand, is alien, as the following quotation shows: "His father had described the place to him in a letter, composed in simple Japanese characters because otherwise Ichiro could not have read it. The letter had been purposely repetitive and painstakingly detailed so that Ichiro should not have any difficulty finding the place. . . . The Japanese characters, written simply so that he could read them, covered pages of directions as *if he were a foreigner* coming to the city for the first time" (6, emphasis added). Metaphorically, Ichiro is a "foreigner" in the Japanese language, lost in the simple Japanese characters. This image graphically depicts his linguistic and cultural estrangement from the ethnic world.

Even more problematic, because he allies Japanese language and the ethnic identity it represents with his mother, he has little desire to transcode this ethnicity or transmigrate this tongue. Ichiro feels that his mother is a "stranger" (11) and that her "sharp, lifeless" language (10) is not his. In fact, the Japanese tongue may function as a kind of "bad mother" for Ichiro. Claude Lévesque discusses the Quebecois writer who writes in English yet continues to cherish a dream of fusion with a maternal tongue "that will refashion an identity for him and reappropriate him to himself" (143). But the dream of fusion with the maternal tongue is, of course, illusionary, for no language is capable of undoing the lack that exiles us from the mother, the lack that actually produces subjectivity and speech proper. Lévesque goes on to argue that "the maternal tongue could therefore only be the language of the bad mother . . . that is, of the mother who has always already weaned her child, who keeps her distance" (144). Ichiro thinks he recalls a time when he spoke a language that fashioned an identity for him and fused him with his mother: "There was a time when I was your son. There was a time . . . when you used to smile a mother's smile and tell me stories. . . . I was the boy in the peach and you were the old woman and we were Japanese with Japanese feelings and Japanese pride and Japanese thoughts" (15). Ichiro blames his mother for his cultural confusion and sees her as a bad mother; the tongue she speaks is therefore a bad mother tongue. Yet he fails to realize that his sense of exile is not only due to her influence but also inherent in the nature of language itself. There would always come a time when he would be exiled from the mother and the mother tongue. Ichiro cannot learn to translate, then, because he does not understand the problematic nature of language, of speech, and of the dream of fusion with a perfect and nourishing tongue.

Ichiro often refuses to engage in a dialogue with this tongue, with this culture, and with its values. As discussed in Chapter 1, translation is possible only when the translator respects and values the parent's culture and wishes to transcode it rather than discard it. Ichiro can speak some Japanese (158) but still feels that he will never be able to communicate meaningfully with his parents. Kenji speaks of a time when Ichiro will "want to talk to [his parents]" and they will talk "all through the night," to which Ichiro responds: "It won't ever happen to me" (139). In many places in the novel, it is clear that Ichiro feels he has little to learn from his parents. A linguistic or cultural identity as a Japanese American appears to provide little, if any, usable cultural capital. On another level, the translation problem of this novel has to do with Ichiro's failure to find a home in *any* language. Ichiro is estranged from the bad mother tongue and its identity. Yet because he did not fight in the war he also feels cut off from the "American" world of English. So Ichiro lacks an empowered voice within both discursive terrains and within both ethnic identities.

Translation might resolve this dilemma, but as indicated above it is the parents who bear the burden of translating themselves into English-speaking Americans to communicate with their children. For example, Kenji and his father communicate well with each other (118, 131), and this has much to do with the fact that Mr. Kanno has finally allowed himself to become, to some degree, an assimilated, English-speaking "American." Ichiro also believes that if his father was more like Mr. Kumasaka (the father of the dead soldier Bob), Ichiro might be able "to pour out the turbulence of his soul" to Mr. Kumasaka (27). Recalling that Ichiro envied Mr. Kumasaka's comfortably furnished home, we must conclude that what would enable Ichiro to communicate with Mr. Kumasaka is not his language facility but his ability to adapt to America. Mr. Kumasaka, in other words, has mostly abandoned his Japanese ethnicity and tongue and translated himself into an English-speaking American, and for Ichiro this not only enables but even creates the grounds for communication. In this context translation becomes assimilation: the language and identity of English takes over you and remakes you as an "American." And translation seems to affirm, rather than deconstruct, the binary divisions between languages and cultures. One is either Japanese or American; one speaks either Japanese or English. Those who speak both languages and attempt to reside in both categories of identity—such as Pa—are seen as weak, diluted, or foolish.

Does the novel present an alternative to this assimilative and colonizing view of translation? Given the time period, it seems logical that the novel is pessimistic on this subject. Yet there are (to use Okada's own phrase) "insinuation[s] of promise" (250) about what the future might hold. One such glimmer of hope lies in the final scene of the novel in which Bull, a rabidly pro–United States Japanese American man who has fought in the war, cries over the death of Freddie, a no-no boy: "Then he started to cry, not like a man in grief or a soldier in pain, but like a baby in loud, gasping, beseeching howls" (250). Bull's ability to see that he and Freddie are not so different may be a sign that the binary divisions between being Japanese and being American are breaking down and that the process of transcoding Japanese ethnicity has begun. And perhaps the binary divisions between languages are breaking down. Bull's cry is not so much language as something before language—something that may return to the presymbolic babble of the child. Bull becomes "an infant crying in the darkness" (250), and Okada perhaps signifies that language itself may be rejuvenated out of such moments of crisis. Language returns to its origin in sounds, in baby talk, in babble, and out of this return a new language can be born.

Another glimmer of promise lies in the idea that some people (including Ichiro) do see the need to cross barriers of language and culture through translation. Mr. Carrick, for example, speaks a little Japanese, which he learned from some Japanese friends (149). And it is no coincidence that Mr. Carrick offers Ichiro a way back into "the real nature" of the United States (153)—which in this specific context refers to a country where cultural and linguistic diversity is appreciated rather than assimilated. Another man—Mr. Morrison (the director of the Christian Rehabilitation Center where Ichiro seeks work)—also recognizes the importance of being multilingual and multicultural. After speaking a few phrases of Japanese, Mr. Morrison comments: "Only way to get to know the people is to learn the language, I say. I learned it and I got to know them" (219). Like Carrick, Morrison realizes the value of attempting to translate between languages and cultures; he realizes that without doing so, true understanding cannot occur. These two characters move beyond the assimilative notion of translation—translation as acculturation.

Some characters in this book do, of course, endorse the idea that translation and multilingualism is unnecessary—that becoming "American" and speaking American English is the only cultural capital, the one path to success. Yet Ichiro knows this is not the "solution" to his problems. "Tell me, Mother, who are you? What is it to be Japanese?" (104), Ichiro thinks at one point. And he continues this meditation about his mother's life, which is also his plea for communication and translation:

> Tell me about the house in which you lived and of your father and mother, who were my grandparents, whom I have never seen or known because I do not remember your ever speaking of them except to say that they died a long time ago. Tell me everything and just a little bit and a little bit more until their lives and yours and mine are fitted together, for they surely must be. . . . Begin from the beginning when your hair was straight and black and everyone was Japanese because that was where you were born and America was not yet a country beyond the ocean where fortunes were to be made or an enemy to hate. Quick, now, quick, Mother, what was the name of your favorite school teacher? (105)

Earlier, Ichiro seemed to long for an illusionary *fusion* with a mother tongue, but here he works more productively to engage in a *dialogue* with this tongue. Numerous individuals have criticized the novel's assimilationist stance and its rejection of all things Japanese. Gayle Sato argues, for example, that "recovery of 'American' identity is enacted through a rejection of 'Japanese'" and that "the plot of *No-No Boy* boils down to a single rhetorical gesture— Ichiro's reaffirmation that he is 'American'" (242, 241).[9] In this passage from the novel, however, a different perspective emerges, if but for a moment, as Ichiro attempts to gain ancestral strength by *understanding and transcoding* his mother's world so that it signifies something positive rather than representing only negative cultural baggage he must discard. And in the face of her silence he is even willing to be a writerly translator who can engage actively and creatively with the source text. This active type of translation could allow Ichiro to fit his life into his parents' life, to see how he might be interconnected with his parents' Japanese heritage through processes of transcoding. Okada postulates that it is individuals like Ichiro (individuals who reside in a kind of middle ground between identities and languages) who have the potential to become translators. Ichiro does not realize this potential, but the novel gestures to a future in which translation and multilingualism—rather than monolingualism and assimilation—might be possible.

In teaching *No-No Boy*, I have found that students often react hostilely to it, which has always puzzled me. But perhaps this has something to do with the novel's uncompromising nature. It provides only brief hints about how one might create a transcoded identity or transmigrate the ethnic tongue into English. It reflects —rather than resolves—the contradictory ideologies of "America" and being "American" in the postwar time period. As Jinqi Ling argues, while the novel appears to tell the story of the "prodigal" son who recognizes his errors and embraces the promise of "America," within this conventional form Okada creates "a protagonist who fails to piece together his fragmented past" (360).[10] The novel also illustrates how we are caught up in binary thinking—thinking that may finally destroy us—yet it offers little to undermine this binary way of thinking. So many of the characters die: Ma kills herself, Freddie is literally cut in half in a car accident, and Kenji dies from a wound that eats him up from inside.

Ichiro survives, but in the end what has he learned? Perhaps only that the middle ground is the place from which translation and a transcoded ethnic identity might emerge. Those who chose to inhabit only one identity—like Kenji, the patriotic American, or Freddie, the rebel no-no boy, or Mrs. Yamada, the "pure" Japanese —are killed off by the narrative. Ichiro is caught in the middle ground between languages and cultures, between being "American" and being Japanese, in the no-man's-land of being "nobody." Yet he survives. Perhaps in this middle ground, this borderland between languages and cultures, Ichiro will at last find a home in and through translation. And this, finally, is John Okada's insinuation of hope.

PUBLISHED FORTY-FIVE YEARS after the end of World War II, Cynthia Kadohata's *The Floating World* returns to an earlier time period (the 1950s and 1960s) to refind or reinvent the glimmer of hope present in a novel such as *No-No Boy*. Hybridity and the inhabiting of multiple positions of ethnic identity simultaneously become a kind of power in this text, rather than a source of weakness. Of course, because Kadohata writes out of a postmodern sense of the world and identity as irrevocably fractured, it is much easier for her to depict an individual finding home in hybridity and in a fragmented subjectivity. Yet both Okada and Kadohata believe that hope lies in the in-between space, in the middle ground, represented by translation. And for both writers hope lies in individuals who possess, or who might come to possess, a translating consciousness.

In "Translation and Literary History," G. N. Devy discusses individuals who possess this consciousness. Devy argues that "if we accept the structuralist principle that communication becomes possible because of the nature of signs and their entire system, it follows that translation is a merger of sign systems. Such a merger is possible because systems of signs are open and vulnerable" (185). Translation exploits the instability and openness at the heart of language. And the translating consciousness sees the potential openness of language systems; in so doing it brings closer together sign systems that are seen as materially different. Devy points out that in India and many other nations, "several languages are simultaneously used by language communities as if these languages formed a continuous spectrum of signs and significance" (185). The translating consciousness sees the source language and the target language not as separate linguistic registers but "as parts of a larger and continuous spectrum of various intersecting systems of verbal signs" (185). Olivia, the narrator of *The Floating World*, possesses this translating consciousness. She is interested in the differences and similarities between languages, but she is also interested in creating a voice that can move comfortably between languages as if they were part of a continuous spectrum of verbal signs. She transmigrates the Japanese tongue into English, but she also sutures these two languages together to create new interpretations of her world and of the languages themselves.

This transmigration of languages is the only way to create "home." Home is not found in a physical space, as the novel makes abundantly clear, or in physical migrations. Olivia's family constantly moves from place to place, and when Olivia finds an apartment it sits next to a freeway so that "from the kitchen window you could see cars flickering between the hedges" (125). Throughout the novel Olivia is in love with the road, with travel, and with dislocation and relocation, and she lyrically describes them: "Once we started traveling, a part of me loved that life. . . . I remember how fine it was to drive through the passage from morning to noon to night" (4). In *The Floating World* characters sometimes speak of a time long ago, before a home had been lost: "With all the older people I knew, even my parents, I occasionally saw the fierce expression as they exclaimed over something that had happened years ago, losses in a time and place as far removed from my twelve-year-old mind as the dates in a schoolbook" (24–25). What exactly are these losses? Are they the losses of a home, a business, and a safe space, because of internment? This remains unclear, but what is apparent is that the older generation remembers and longs for a time when they were not displaced—when they had not lost that something that made them placed and stable.

Nevertheless, the novel intuits that there is no such stable place —there is only placement in displacement, home in the spaces between languages and cultures. Olivia first learns this lesson from her maternal grandmother, Hisae Fujiitano. When the family is on the road, Hisae tells them they are traveling in "ukiyo," or the floating world. The floating world is "the gas station attendants, restaurants, and jobs we depended on, the motel towns floating in the middle of fields and mountains. In old Japan, ukiyo meant the districts full of brothels, teahouses, and public baths, but it also referred to change and the pleasures and loneliness change brings" (2–3). This passage is crucial for several reasons. First, Hisae is able to take a term for the districts of Japan and transmigrate it so that it signifies something meaningful and useful in the new American world she and the family move through. Second, that she names it in Japanese ("ukiyo") while still applying it to the American context indicates that Hisae is interested in moving between languages and cultures, as well as in finding points at which cultural differences break down and can be remade. Hisae, in fact, injects Japanese words into the English language—words such as "ukiyo" (2), "hakujin" (8), and "shimeru" (2)—and then translates them for her granddaughter: "floating world," "white people," "to close." And Olivia inherits this translative, injective, or even infective power from her grandmother. For example, Olivia redefines "ukiyo" for herself: "For a long time, I never exactly thought of us as part of any of that [ukiyo]. *We* were stable, traveling through an unstable world while my father looked for jobs" (3). For Olivia, ukiyo becomes a symbol of stability in instability, of placement in displacement. Ukiyo also becomes a symbol of how one can move between languages in such a way that their differences are undermined.[11]

As in Louie's story "Inheritance," a central question this book probes is what children learn from their ancestors. Hisae is a cruel, vindictive woman, and her grandchildren often hate her. But she possesses a unique ability to transmigrate herself and her world and to make a home in between languages and cultures. And this is precisely what Olivia inherits. Hisae owns "a valise in which she carried all her possessions, but the stories she told were also possessions" (3). Olivia believes these fantastic stories, and after the death of her grandmother she inherits the responsibility of telling them: "When she was gone my brothers begged me to tell them the stories again" (28). As we have seen, storytelling and translation are often allied. Of course, to retell her grandmother's stories Olivia must retranslate them. What seems most crucial, however, is that the grandmother functions as a key figure for how Olivia learns to intermesh her Japanese heritage with her present reality as an American. The Japanese heritage is not discarded, then, but rather transcoded through processes of translation.

For without translation, this ethnic heritage will be lost. And some of it has already been lost. In discussing names, for instance, Olivia relates that at the start of World War II, the public schools made Hisae's children anglicize their names: "Satoru, Yukiko, Mariko, Haruko, and Sadamu became Roger, Lily, Laura, Ann, and Roy." Now "their original names are just shadows following them" (2). The original names are no longer a lived reality—but they persist, enunciated in language first by Hisae and then by Olivia. Some parts of the heritage are lost, but some parts are strengthened when Olivia takes over the role of storyteller, of translator. And unlike Ichiro, Olivia sees and values her connection to the older generation. For example, she says that her grandmother's name is "a name sort of partway between mine and those of my ancestors" (1). Symbolically, the grandmother stands in a middle space between Japan and the United States, and Olivia learns to value this middle space and take up the role of cultural mediation, translation, and transcoding.

Like Hisae, Olivia possesses the ability to move between languages and to translate in order to remake her world and her identity. Hisae is an Issei—she moved to the United States when she was a girl (2). For Olivia, she represents a connection to Japan and the world of the "past." Yet it is crucial that Hisae is also fluent in two languages. Not only does she translate words such as "ukiyo" into English for her grandchildren, but she also keeps a diary in two languages: "I got her opinion through her diaries, small parts of which were in Japanese" (91). While it might be postulated that she writes parts of her diaries in Japanese so that her grandchildren will not be able to read them, I would argue exactly the opposite. By writing parts of the diary in Japanese, Hisae encourages her granddaughter to understand them—to become a translator. Codeswitching, as I contend in Chapter 5, can be mystifying but also beckoning, especially to a curious, nosy, multilinguistic character such as Olivia.

And Olivia is intrigued by this codeswitched discourse, as she relates: "Translating [the diaries] was difficult—my mother did all the hard parts. . . . But the project was well worth my time. It was good for me to have someone to consult with" (91). The diaries, then, link the three generations of women—the grandmother, the mother, and the daughter—in an interlingual and intergenerational act of communication and translation. Olivia is clearly a writerly translator who understands, as Derrida has phrased it, that translation is not transcription but a productive writing called forth by the original text (*Ear* 153). Like Kingston's protagonist, Olivia also sees translation as collaboration and coauthorship. In this context, translation is a linguistic act that undermines binarisms such as self versus "other," past versus present, and the ethnic versus the American.

The translation of Hisae's diaries is mentioned at numerous points in the novel (91, 92, 95, 96, 98, 125, 148). Thus it is important to consider what Olivia learns from these diaries. First, she learns the value of adaptation and even of instability. The grandmother, Olivia finds, grows less certain of herself with age (148); the diaries, then, are about growth, change, and the value of uncertainty. She also learns about her grandmother's life in Japan (98) and about the beauty and power of this world. And she learns about sex, for her grandmother is a woman who had three different husbands and seven lovers (96). For Olivia, the diaries convey important knowledge about her ethnic heritage as well as information she can use in her present life. Through their translation, Olivia therefore attempts to find a link to her past ethnic heritage but also to create a future for herself in which she can be both ethnic and American. The diaries are also described as changing over time: "Some of the diary pages started to change and warp, as if they were alive, growing" (95). This image suggests that the diary is not a stable artifact of Japanese language and culture but something that can transmute and transform itself to adapt to a changing reality. The diaries become an important symbol for the creative and generative nature of translation, much like Leslie Marmon Silko's almanac in *Almanac of the Dead*, which I discuss in the next chapter.

Finally, and most important, from these diaries Olivia learns to mediate and transcode differences between racial, linguistic, and cultural identities. The following statement about their translation illustrates how this transcoding impulse works: "And I liked the two languages, Japanese and English, how each contained thoughts you couldn't express exactly in the other. For instance, because you didn't use spaces between words in the same way in English and Japanese, certain phrases—such as 'pure white' or 'eight slender objects' or 'how many people'—seemed to me like only one word in Japanese. Seeming to use only one word changed slightly the meaning of what I was saying. It made me think about what exactly was pure white and not merely white" (91–92). Initially, Olivia is interested in thinking about the differences between languages, "how each contained thoughts you couldn't express exactly in the other." Two words (such as "pure white") become one in Japanese, causing Olivia to reflect on what the English words "pure white" might really mean. Finally, Olivia's concept of "pure white" is no longer purely Japanese or American; it is both. Or rather, the process of translating *between* the languages has caused Olivia to situate her understanding of particular terms *within* two intersecting language systems. Olivia has developed, in short, a translating consciousness that treats the source language text and the target language text "as parts of a larger and continuous spectrum of various intersecting systems of verbal signs" (Devy, "Translation and Literary History" 185). This translating consciousness lets her see not only how languages intersect but also how racial identities intersect and may be remade and transcoded. It is no coincidence that in the above passage Olivia is thinking about "what exactly was pure white and not merely white" (92). In the United States, a land of immigrants, is anyone "pure white"? And as a Japanese American, is she "pure white," "merely white," or not "white" at all? This passage about the translation of the grandmother's diaries breaks down not only linguistic identities but also cultural and racial ones.

Olivia's ongoing struggle to translate these diaries therefore speaks to her need to understand and deconstruct the categories of race and identity that inscribe her. Without translation, these categories rigidify or become assimilative, as in *No-No Boy*. Hisae appears to speak both Japanese and English, and her daughter Laura speaks English with a Japanese accent. But Olivia's parents are glad that their daughter's English is uninflected. "If you couldn't see her, you wouldn't even know she was Japanese" (8), they say proudly. When Olivia speaks to strangers, she feels she is taunting them with her perfect English: "See, I can talk like you, I was trying to say, it's not so hard" (8). Language is used here for domination and also homogenization—Olivia's perfect English allows her to efface her ethnic identity. The translation of the grandmother's diaries stands in opposition to this type of communication, for it is clearly about transcoding racial and ethnic heritage and also about investigating and undermining divisions between languages and cultures.

Furthermore, from her grandmother Olivia learns to create a home in translation—a floating linguistic and cultural world. Given the historical background of this novel, such a revised concept of home is logical. The novel is set in the 1950s and 1960s when, as Olivia notes, "it could be . . . hard for Japanese to get good jobs" (4). The narrative implies that well after the end of World War II, Japanese Americans still face discrimination (a fact that historical research has corroborated). The family lost their houses during the war and they do not seem to have recovered a firm sense of home, a firm sense of who they are and where they fit in this American world. Olivia's maternal grandparents abandon their boarding-house in San Francisco and move to Hawaii at the start of the war (2, 28). Perhaps they move to avoid internment; in Hawaii the Japanese American population was too large a segment of the workforce to be conveniently evacuated.[12] Olivia's own father appears to have been interned during the war and then drafted, although the novel is not definitive on this subject. We do learn, however, that the father, who is known as Charlie-O, worked in the fields of California as a child and then lived in Los Angeles "before the area became a ghost town during the war" (118). We are also told that Charlie-O was in the army during the war, where he learns how to let his hands, and not his heart, "feel for [him]" (120). It seems likely, then, that Charlie-O and his family were in the camps during the war and that Hisae's family moved to Hawaii to avoid internment.

The war therefore represents a rupture in the family's psyche and in their concept of home, a break that has been difficult to overcome. The older generation exclaims fiercely over "something that had happened years ago," "losses in a time and place" long past (24–25). It is logical to assume that these losses have to do with the internment. And the legacy that the older generation passes on to the children is one of fear: "My parents had taught me many things they hadn't meant to teach me and I hadn't meant to learn. One of those things was fear, their first big fear, during the war" (121). The internment is only mentioned once explicitly: "Some of my parents' friends used to live on the east side of 99, but when the war started, there was a law that Japanese had to move west of the highway, so they packed up all their things and moved across the street. The next year they were interned" (140–41). The "they" here is not very specific, but the point Kadohata makes has to do with the effect of the internment—the way it bred fear in all Japanese Americans, a fear that was passed down to the next generation. And this is a fear of ethnicity itself—a fear of actually being Japanese, rather than a "pure American."

Yet the grandmother is never described as possessing this fear. After all, it is Hisae who describes ukiyo to Olivia and who applies this Japanese term to the American landscape, using her translation to find placement in her displacement and to transcode her identity. And as an adult, Olivia finds home in such displaced, transplanted, translated spaces. For example, her apartment next to the freeway gives Olivia "that old feeling [that I liked] of being displaced and safe at the same time" (126). Eventually Olivia resides in the postmodern and surreal landscape of Los Angeles, where she is amazed at "how all those varied worlds out there coexisted, including the world I lived in, and the world that in the future would touch me" (138). From Hisae, Olivia learns to allow for the existence of multiple homes, multiple time frames, and multiple languages. The novel also considers—and rejects—several more traditional ideas of home, as well as several more traditional definitions of "American" identity. For example, in one scene in the novel the family visits model homes. Like Ichiro's concept of the perfect white house, these homes seem beautiful but unattainable: "Each house was more beguiling than the one before. The last one had splendid white carpets, and chairs I thought were so old they were made before Obāsan was born" (148). The parents are impressed by all this luxury, but Hisae does not even bother to take off her shoes before entering the houses (148). Hisae knows that such Americanized homes are not for her family. Eventually the family creates a home where "intricate lace curtains hung in all the windows, but none of the curtains matched, and baskets, statues, and pottery sat in every corner. Nothing matched yet it all matched" (69). This image suggests that home is found in hybridity, in bricolage, in placement amid displacement—not in a stable, model, perfect "American" home. Clearly, home is an analogy for an American identity that involves acceptance of hybridity, difference, multiculturalism, and multilingualism. Everything does not have to "match."

Kadohata's novel participates in a discourse of postmodernism in which we are all displaced linguistically (alienated from language) and geopolitically (our homes have been lost, or perhaps they never existed). But it adds to this discourse by providing the perspective of an individual who is forced out of an old home and an old language because of race but who still manages to transcode her ethnic identity and transmigrate the words of the ethnic tongue into English. Rushdie has argued that displaced individuals must, "of necessity, make a new imaginative relationship with the world, because of the loss of familiar habitats" (125). For Kadohata, racial and linguistic identities play into this search for a floating world and offer productive occasions for the retheorization of home and voice. And this is finally the lesson that the grandmother teaches: how to find a home in change and the pleasures of change and instability; how to find speech in the gaps between being "pure white" and something else; and how to use translation practices to create a hybrid, bricolaged, multilingual Japanese American subjectivity and voice.

In *No-No Boy* Ichiro never translates his mother's story, her history, or her legacy, and he cannot transcode the lives of the Issei and the Nisei in a way that provides ancestral strength. So it is not surprising that even at the end of *No-No Boy*, Ichiro remains displaced and homeless. He has not learned to live in translation, and he has not found an identity/voice that enables his survival, although the novel does gesture to a moment in the future when this might occur. Conversely, Olivia learns to value translation and her ethnic heritage. Her grandmother's diaries and the stories of the ethnic "past" teach lessons about how to survive in the present moment and provide important emotional and psychological capital. Through translation Olivia finds a shifting but viable ethnic identity and voice—a voice that speaks to the fact that she can make her home in the floating world, in the gaps and spaces between languages and cultures. Like Mitsuye Yamada, Olivia will not drown but will come up for air in another language all her own—a transmigrated voice that can renovate the language of hegemony.

3

Translation as Revelation

The Task of the Translator in the Fiction

of N. Scott Momaday, Leslie Marmon Silko,

Susan Power, and Sherman Alexie

Translation keeps putting the hallowed growth of languages to the test: How far removed is their hidden meaning from revelation?—Walter Benjamin, "The Task of the Translator"

"ABEL WALKED INTO the canyon. His return to the town had been a failure, for all his looking forward. He had tried in the days that followed to speak to his grandfather, but he could not say the things he wanted; he had tried to pray, to sing, to enter into the old rhythm of the tongue, but he was no longer attuned to it. And yet it was there still, like memory" (58). In this early passage from N. Scott Momaday's *House Made of Dawn* (1968), Abel, a young Jemez Pueblo man, struggles to connect to his culture and identity through recovery of his native tongue. This language would allow him to pray and would show "him whole to himself" (58). Yet for the majority of the novel Abel fails to translate his English thoughts back into his native tongue. The language *is* there, but he cannot reach it.

When the novel ends, a wounded, battered Abel is running in the snow. Under his breath he begins to sing, but this is an equivocal moment: "There was no sound, and he had no voice; he had only the words of a song. And he went running on the rise of the song. *House made of pollen, house made of dawn. Qtsedaba*" (212). Does Abel learn to translate? "House made of pollen, house made of dawn" are in italics, which might lead us to believe that they are spoken in a Native American tongue, and the final addition of the word "*Qtsedaba*" supports such a reading. But what of Momaday's telling us that "there was no sound, and he had no voice"? Is Abel translating, or is he dying of exhaustion, alone and unheard, in the frigid landscape? Has Abel learned to pray? Has he reached revelation? And what does it mean to pray in an oral language that is, quite literally, disappearing from the face of the earth with each succeeding generation?

I begin with these questions about *House Made of Dawn* because they illustrate the dilemma present in all the novels I will discuss in this chapter—the dilemma of how one can translate and find revelation in a language that is rapidly being extinguished by social and cultural forces. Momaday's *House Made of Dawn* and *The Way to Rainy Mountain* (1969) debate a series of ideas about translation that another early writer—Leslie Marmon Silko—will revise and reformulate in her novel *Ceremony* (1977) and return to in *Almanac of the Dead* (1991). More recently, writers such as Susan Power, in *The Grass Dancer* (1994), and Sherman Alexie, in *Reservation Blues* (1995) and *Indian Killer* (1996), have continued to wrestle with these issues. It is not my intention to discuss all these works in detail, but I will argue that in them, translation struggles signify conflicts not only of Native American identity but also of cultural survival. I will focus on two interrelated aspects of this struggle: the innovative methods these writers formulate to enable the survival of a native tongue through transmigration of it into English, and the connection between translation and revelation. In "The Task of the Translator," Walter Benjamin argues that "translation keeps putting the hallowed growth of languages to the test: How far removed is their hidden meaning from revelation, how close can it be brought by the knowledge of their remoteness?" (76). For many of these Native American writers, translation is about a leap of faith that enables the character to speak a sacred language, a language he or she may not previously have known. Through translation a kind of cultural voice is recovered that transcodes ethnicity, but at its most pure this voice does put "the hallowed growth of languages to the test." This sacred voice reveals the hidden structure of the world, the hidden intermeshing of humanity, nature, and the sacred forces that vivify the world and all things in it.

I do not mean to suggest, however, that a Judeo-Christian understanding of revelation can encompass these writers' ideas. Indeed, these texts criticize Christianity and even the most sacred revelatory text, *The Revelation of Saint John the Divine*. In Momaday's *House Made of Dawn*, for example, John Big Bluff Tosamah argues that after preaching "In the beginning was the Word," Saint John should "have stopped" since "there was nothing more to say" (93). Native American writers, then, reclaim the sacred power of the word without explicitly allying the word with the Word, with Christianity or a specific divinity. Benjamin, too, focuses in his essay on the sacred power of the word rather than the Word, arguing that "it is the task of the translator to release in his own language that pure language which is under the spell of another, to liberate the language imprisoned in a work in his re-creation of that work" (81). For Benjamin, capturing the "eternal life of works" (80–81) has more to do with understanding the resonances and interconnections between linguistic systems and less to do with finding a divine Truth, a divine Word.[1] For Momaday, Silko, Power, and Alexie the word is an emblem of the interconnections between humanity and the world's spirit rather than a sign of the Christian "God's" power.

Of course, in many Native American cultures the word is also sacred in and of itself; language is extremely powerful and does create reality.[2] However, the works I discuss span a thirty-year time period in which recovery of "the word" shifts away from a concern with retrieval of a homogeneous language system or dialect toward something more metaphorical. While an earlier writer such as Momaday is interested in literal recovery of the oral native language, later writers are more concerned with transmigrating values and ideals of the native language into spoken and written English so that English itself is changed. In discussing why he writes in English, Salman Rushdie states: "Those of us who do use English do so in spite of our ambiguity toward it, or perhaps because of that, perhaps because we can find in that linguistic struggle a reflection of other struggles taking place in the real world, struggles between the cultures within ourselves and the influences at work upon our societies. To conquer English may be to complete the process of making ourselves free" (17). Later writers do attempt to "conquer English" and also (in Gustavo Pérez Firmat's terms) to "conga" English (*Life* 22) through various translation strategies. In Silko's *Ceremony* English becomes a kind of palimpsestic, hybrid discourse; Susan Power employs a radical bilingualism in which two distinct voices are spoken at once; and Sherman Alexie turns to a kind of violent revelatory discourse as a way his characters "translate" a Native American language they may never have learned. Over time, then, there is less interest in translation's literal ability to recover "the word" and more interest in how, on a metaphorical level, it might allow two or more discourses to coexist in a sometimes uneasy alliance, a sometimes violent syncretism.

Linguistic Recovery in N. Scott Momaday's *House Made of Dawn* and *The Way to Rainy Mountain*

Many critics have argued that *House Made of Dawn* primarily depicts Abel's successful struggle for voice.[3] Yet the novel also concerns the larger question of how a variety of Native American individuals within Euro-American culture learn to translate between their native language and the dominant one and transmigrate values and terms from indigenous cultures into the English language and context. When Abel is compared with these individuals, he must be seen as only partially successful in finding voice. I will argue in this section that Abel's conception of translation is limited by a focus on the recovery of a pure and untainted tongue. When Momaday returns to these questions in *The Way to Rainy Mountain*, he illustrates a more flexible methodology for translating Native American cultures and languages and for transcoding ethnicity.[4]

In *House Made of Dawn* Abel returns to his home among the Jemez Pueblo after fighting in World War II only to find that he has lost his connection to his culture and language. Abel is an orphan; his mother has died, and he never knew his father, who was from another tribe (perhaps Navajo). The figure of the "mixed-raced" orphan who does not know his or her place within the culture will reappear in several of these texts as an embodiment of a particular translation problem. It is difficult enough to translate when one can speak to one's relatives, as Kingston illustrates in *The Woman Warrior*. But what if the parents are gone, dead, or of unknown racial heritage? How can ethnicity be transcoded when it was never really known? Abel's grandfather Francisco tries to teach his grandson about the language and culture, but Abel cannot avail himself of this ancestral help.

One problem lies in the specific way Abel structures his translation dilemma. Abel seeks to recover a pure language that bears no traces of other languages. In a flashback from his childhood, Abel describes this language: "He remembered the prayer, and he knew what it meant—not the words, which he had never really heard, but the low sound itself, rising and falling far away in his mind, unmistakable and *unbroken*" (13, emphasis added; see also 20–21, 170–71). Interestingly, this pure language transcends the words themselves: "He knew what it meant—not the words . . . but the low sound itself." Abel struggles, then, to gather the threads of his "fallen" language into a unified, unbroken tongue: "He was alone, and he wanted to make a song out of the colored canyon, the way the women of Torreón made songs upon their looms out of colored yarn, but he had not got the right words together. It would have been a creation song; he would have sung lowly of the first world, of fire and flood, and of the emergence of dawn from the hills" (59). Colored yarn on a loom is gathered together, woven into a picture, a unified song, by the weaver. As an image of language this passage seems to suggest an illusionary unity which might have existed when language was first "created" (hence Abel's reference to "a creation song") but which is not possible in the contemporary context. Nonetheless, Abel wants to rebuild himself through this language's unbroken harmony: "Had he been able to say it, anything of his own language—even the commonplace formula of greeting 'where are you going'—which had no being beyond sound, no visible substance, would once again have shown him whole to himself" (58). Abel attempts to recover a pure language of authentic and whole selfhood.

Momaday's novel implies, though, that such a strategy of linguistic recovery is not viable. As Bernard Selinger argues, the novel reflects "ambivalence about the likelihood of acquiring wholeness and authority" (46). The attitudes toward language expressed in the text also reflect this ambivalence—there is no pure language that will restore unbroken selfhood. And so like Ona in Ng's *Bone*, Abel becomes stranded between languages and cultures. He cannot recover the native language he has lost, but he also has difficulties expressing himself in English. With his friends Ben Benally and Milly, for example, he is always described as silent or as lacking the English words to express his painful experiences (120, 143, 145, 153, 175, 182). Ben describes this scenario of being caught between languages: "And they [white social workers] can't help you because you don't know how to talk to them. They have a lot of *words*, and you know they mean something, but you don't know what, and your own words are no good because they're not the same; they're different, and they're the only words you've got" (158). Although Ben says his words are "no good," by speaking them Ben does at least attempt to translate Abel's situation into language.

Unlike Ben, Abel has little interest in expressing his thoughts in English. For example, when he is put on trial for murdering an albino man named Juan Reyes, Abel observes that "word by word by word these men were disposing of him in language, *their* language, and they were making a bad job of it" (102). Abel sees English as a foreign and fallen tongue: *their* language. At first he tries to defend himself in this tongue, but then he gives up: "He sat like a rock in his chair, and after a while no one expected or even wanted him to speak" (102). Killing Juan Reyes may be an attempt to find "voice" through violence and to remove something Abel perceives as "impure" from the culture (the albino man, who is of Jemez Pueblo descent but white skinned). But the search for voice through violence is often unsuccessful, as my discussion of *Indian Killer* will show. Furthermore, Abel constructs a binary opposition between the "foreign" tongue (English) and the "pure" native tongue—a binary that he cannot transcode. Seeking a pure and authentic native tongue, he is unable to undertake the intercultural, interlinguistic burdens of translation.

What Abel fails to realize—and what Momaday makes abundantly clear—is that in the contemporary world, languages are never pure but rather fallen and broken, "tainted" with traces of other languages. Yet there can be strength in this brokenness. For example, the people of Abel's town have absorbed aspects of Euro-American culture and language without losing their own identities. The narrative voice tells us that "the invaders were a long time in conquering [the people of the town]; and now, after four centuries of Christianity, they still pray in Tanoan to the old deities of the earth and sky. . . . They have assumed the names and gestures of their enemies, but have held on to their own, secret souls; and in this there is a resistance and an overcoming, a long outwaiting" (58).[5] The people of the town assume "the names and gestures of their enemies"—a linguistic and social transformation—yet they hold on to their own "secret souls." As Momaday tells us in *The Way to Rainy Mountain*, in many Native American cultures the name is sacred, so it is highly significant to take on the enemy's names. This is accommodation of a sort, but it may function as a form of resistance. In a discussion of linguistic hybridity, Homi Bhabha argues that "resistance is not . . . the simple negation or exclusion of the 'content' of an other culture. . . . It is the effect of an ambivalence produced within the rules of recognition of dominating discourses as they articulate the signs of cultural difference and reimplicate them within the differential relations of colonial power" ("Signs" 172). The signs of Euro-American culture—its names and customs—are reimplicated, rearticulated in the context of the traditional Tanoan language. This produces ambivalence, but also a kind of power that emerges from linguistic hybridity, from broken and scattered languages.[6]

Indeed, the townspeople's language is not pure but a mixture of dialects. Abel's grandfather Francisco describes hearing this language: "Out of the doorways he passed came the queer, halting talk of old fellowship, Tanoan and Athapascan, broken English and Spanish" (75). In this mixture of tongues there is power; after all, it is the Euro-American languages (English and Spanish) that are described as "broken." I discuss Francisco's role as a translator later, but here I want to note that unlike Abel, he sees language as scattered and fallen rather than whole. The translator does not gather or unify language but speaks and embodies its brokenness. Athapascan, one of the languages Francisco mentions, is itself a family of Native American languages including Chippewa, Hopi, and Navajo. In Cree, the word "ahthapskaaw" means "there are reeds here and there." This sentence illustrates that any spoken language is composed of multiple other languages. Language is a scattering, not a gathering, of reeds, of discourses.

Benjamin postulates that "pure language" is not an original, unbroken tongue but the totality of all linguistic systems: "Rather, all suprahistorical kinship of language rests in the intention underlying each language as a whole—an intention, however, which no single language can attain by itself but which is realized only by the totality of their intentions supplementing each other: pure language" (75). Translation, then, can push us closer to pure language, but it cannot actually create it. Translation "thus ultimately serves the purpose of expressing the central reciprocal relationship between languages" (73). There can be a kind of strength and a resistance in looking for reciprocity between languages, between different discursive systems; for Benjamin, this is how we move toward (but yet do not attain) "pure language." But Abel refuses to look for reciprocity between languages—to find points of convergence and divergence, points where transmigrations might occur. Instead, he sits outside language, locked into his silence.

Yet as I have indicated, other individuals in *House Made of Dawn* do find ways of transcoding their ethnicity and transmigrating their tongues. I want to look more closely at these individuals and at the discursive landscape of the book before returning to the novel's ending. First, it is crucial to note that *House Made of Dawn* is a multilingual text—and a text that refuses to separate languages and cultures into neat compartments. Consider, for example, Francisco's meditations on food: "He smelled the odor of boiled coffee, and was good. He cared less for the sweet smell of piki and the moist, broken loaves of sotobalau, the hot spicy odors of paste and posole" (75–6). None of the "foreign" words in this list are italicized; we might say, then, that none of the words are "othered" typographically and that languages are therefore allowed to mingle without separation. The number of culturally inflected words in this passage also is significant: "piki," "paste," "posole," and "so-tobalau" would all be somewhat foreign terms to many Anglo-American readers. Yet these words do not come from *one* culture but from (at least) three: Spanish, Native American, and English. Momaday does not translate these terms for his reader, leaving the reader who knows only English to struggle with these unfamiliar dialects. Finally, in this passage, it is (again) English that is broken: "He smelled the odor of boiled coffee, and was good."

I dwell on this passage because it emblematizes the way languages mix and mingle in the book as a whole. The text is written in English, of course, but speckled with words from several other languages (Tanoan, Navajo, Spanish, French, Latin): *dypalon* (1); *piñones* (6); *yahah* (10); *teah-whau* (12); cacique (10, 81); arroyo (12); Bahkyush (19); Angelus (25); *hombre* (27); soutane (46); OMO FATU-OUS (47); kiva (51, 78, 85, 188, 199, 207); Padre (73); *Díné* (76), *In principio erat Verbum* (91); Tai-me (96, 131); peyote (109–11); Ä'poto Etódǎ-de K'ádó (132); *culebra* (141, 183); *Tségihi* (146); ketoh (167, 168, 171); *concho* (171); *najahe* (172); *Ei yei* (182); Ei yei (187); *Esdzá shash nadle* (187, 188); *Dzil quigi* (187); mesas (188, 197, 211); Yeí bichai (188); vigas (193, 207); *diablo blanco* (195); *ayempha* (195); *mucho frió* (195); *muchacho* (206); and *Qtsedaba* (212). Some of these words are italicized and some are not, but very few are translated. This is not an exhaustive list, but I am exhausted after typing it, finding um-laut and other accent marks, looking up words, searching through several different dictionaries—but surely not as exhausted as Abel is from negotiating this thicket of language, this multilingual world of words. Yet Momaday demonstrates how crucial this negotiation is. The world is not unilingual, and only by negotiating its multi-lingualism can we find our relationship to language and become effective translators.

Momaday also shows that "separate" languages are actually imbri-cated in each other. A word such as "peyote," for example, has roots in Spanish, Mexican, and Native American cultures and has now passed into the "English" language so that most English speakers would not need to look it up. And the word "cacique" has meanings in both Spanish and Native American cultures. Languages mix and mingle, creating and re-creating each other. This is particularly apparent in the speech of Abel's grandfather Francisco.[7] Francisco often speaks in a blend of Tanoan and Spanish (7, 195); he also speaks enough English to communicate with Abel after the war, when Abel can no longer speak his native tongue. Francisco is an effective translator who finds the language to tell his grandsons the oral stories of the culture: "These things he told to his grandsons, carefully, slowly and at length, because they were old and true, and they could be lost forever as easily as one generation is lost to the next, as easily as one old man might lose his voice, having spoken not enough or not at all" (198). On his deathbed, Francisco tries desperately to communicate with Abel: "Still [Abel] could hear the faintest edge of his grandfather's voice . . . going on and on toward the dawn. . . . The voice had failed each day, only to rise up again in the dawn" (197). But Abel cannot hear his grandfather's words: "He listened to the feeble voice. . . . His mind was borne upon the dying words, but they carried him nowhere. . . . The words ran together and were no longer words" (195–96). Does Abel eventually learn to translate his grandfather's memory into some language, whatever that language might be?

The answer to this question—and to the question of what language Abel might eventually speak—can only be understood by looking at two other translator figures in the book: Tosamah and Ben Benally. Tosamah, a Kiowan preacher who may (or may not) be a stand-in for Momaday, criticizes the *Revelation of St. John*, but he also preaches about the power of words and about the fundamental link between translation and revelation. Discussing his grandmother, for example, Tosamah says: "You see, for her, words were medicine; they were magic and invisible. They came from nothing into sound and meaning. They were beyond price" (96). Language is an instrument of "creation" and "magic." By telling the oral stories of her culture, by translating them so that Tosamah can understand them, Tosamah's grandmother brings him closer to something "sacred and eternal" (95), something "timeless" (95). Through the link to his grandmother and her stories, Tosamah finds revelation.

Yet this revelation is not achieved through a pure language. Like Francisco, Tosamah's grandmother speaks a language that syncretizes cultures. The grandmother is described as a "Christian," yet she never forgets "her birthright" (132)—the spirit of her culture. She is also described as sometimes praying in a language Tosamah does not know: "I believe [her prayers] were made of an older language than that of ordinary speech" (133). Still, she does make herself understood to her grandson, and he passes on her stories (in English) to his followers (the group of Native Americans from various tribes who attend his religious services). Like his grandmother, then, Tosamah demonstrates a linguistic hybridity and an ability to transmigrate stories into a new tongue so that they are not lost. Furthermore, the two sermons Tosamah preaches—"The Gospel According to John" (89) and "The Way to Rainy Mountain" (90)—indicate his interest in moving across and between languages and in finding points of convergence and divergence between the Bible and his grandmother's stories, between English and Kiowan, between Native American and Anglo-American cultures and religions.

Tosamah is not, of course, a perfect character. He berates Abel, calling him a "longhair" (149) and contributing to his downfall. Tosamah may preach about the sacred power of the word and about the need for syncretism and transmigration of tongues, but it is unclear if Abel absorbs—or is even present to hear—these lessons. It is Abel's friend Ben who offers Abel a more positive way to transmigrate his culture and find a mode of voice. Ben also has something Abel is not given in the novel—a first-person voice with which to tell his stories (139–90). He also has some knowledge of his own Navajo language and culture, as the following passage reveals: "I used to tell him about those old ways, the stories and the sings, Beautyway and Night Chant, I sang some of those things, and I told him what they meant, what I thought they were about" (146). Ben here attempts the intercultural and interlinguistic tasks that translation entails, transmigrating his culture to a new context (English) so that Abel can understand it. He also relates the songs and prayers in a language composed of both his original tongue (Navajo) and English:

Tségihi.
House made of dawn,
House made of evening light,
House made of dark cloud,

. . . .
Restore my feet for me,
Restore my legs for me,
Restore my body for me,
Restore my mind for me.

. . . .
As it used to be long ago, may I walk.
Happily may I walk.

. . . .
In beauty it is finished. (146–47)

Ben's use of the word "*Tségihi*" demonstrates that he knows at least *some* language from his culture. Ben's speech, like the title of Momaday's book, is taken from the anthropologist Washington Matthews's 1902 translation of the Navajo Night Chant (see Bierhorst). Ben's translation of this song into English for Abel, then, may be a translation of a translation rather than "authentic" speech. My point here, however, is that Ben is engaged in a process of intercultural translation and transmigration of tongues and that he attempts to teach this process to Abel. The goal again is not recovery of "pure" or "authentic" speech or an Ur-text but connection with a prior tongue which might itself be transmigrated, multilingual, or fallen but which still contains wisdom and knowledge that preexists the hegemony of Euro-American culture and language. Most important, Ben encourages Abel to join in the song: "And we were going together on horses to the hills. . . . We were going to sing about the way it always was. And it was going to be right and beautiful" (190). Benjamin argues that translation is not "the sterile equation of two dead languages" but has "the special mission of watching over the maturing process of the original language and the birth pangs of its own" (75). By translating the songs (which may themselves be translations of other songs) and encouraging Abel to sing them, Ben extends the life of the songs, allowing them to mature and grow and *change* in a new context.

Like Tosamah, Ben is not faultless; at times he seems all too willing to forget his culture, to assimilate and forget "the old ways" (148). But Ben does teach Abel the value of adapting to the present reality while keeping some hold on the "home" culture and language. Does Abel finally absorb the lessons of Ben, Tosamah, and Francisco? And so we have circled back to the starting point of this chapter, Abel's Dawn Run. It is crucial, of course, that Abel enters into this ritual, the Dawn Run, which has been described to him by Francisco. And it is crucial that he is singing: "*House made of pollen, house made of dawn. Qtsedaba*" (212). In this sentence there are words taught to him by Ben that belong to the Navajo culture and prayers ("house made of pollen, house made of dawn"), but there are also words from other languages. *Qtsedaba* traditionally marks the end of a story in the Jemez Pueblo culture, and *Dypaloh*, which opens the text, is the traditional beginning (Evers 301). Abel has incorporated the lessons he has learned from the other translators and is now moving between languages. And perhaps Abel does find revelation through this translation: "Pure exhaustion laid hold of his mind, and he could see at last without having to think. He could see the canyon and the mountains and the sky. . . . He was running, and under his breath he began to sing. . . . And he went running on the rise of the song" (212). The song sustains Abel, allowing him to see past the pain of his present reality into a future that might hold more hope.

However, I have difficulty believing that Abel has finally learned to translate. First, I am troubled by the phrase "There was no sound, and he had no voice" (212). What are we to make of this comment, placed almost as the very last words of a novel that, in excruciating detail, charts Abel's struggle for voice? I am also concerned that Abel is wounded and battered both emotionally and physically when he makes this Dawn Run. Before the run, he tells the local priest that his grandfather is dead—perhaps Abel imagines that he will be unable to bury the body. Does Abel believe he will die in this Dawn Run? The text is somewhat ambiguous, but again I believe this undercuts a reading of Abel's struggle for voice as wholly successful. Finally, and most important, I would like to know that someone *hears* Abel's song. Although Susan Scarberry-García argues that Abel is "reintegrated within his culture" (15), we never see Abel telling his story to his own people. And in a book that emphasizes the importance of passing on oral traditions in some form, it is extremely problematic that Abel has no listener for the song that he sings. So the novel concludes where it begins, with Abel alone, running in the snow, possessing only a voice with no sound, a story with no listener. The ending of *House Made of Dawn* finally suggests that Abel has not yet become a translator—an individual capable of transforming and *transmitting* his history, his memory, and his culture.[8]

Perhaps this is why Momaday returns to a number of these issues in *The Way to Rainy Mountain*. Like *House Made of Dawn*, this text emphasizes the importance of language to identity: "The way to Rainy Mountain is preeminently the history of an idea, man's idea of himself, and it has old and essential being in language" (4). Throughout this short collection, Momaday also stresses the necessity of connecting with the native culture through its tongue. For example, Momaday tells the story of two twins who are saved from a giant because they know a word taught to them by grandmother spider, "*thain-mom*" (above my eyes). When the giant sets fires around the twins, they repeat this word, and "the smoke remained above their eyes" (32). As Momaday comments, words are powerful talismans: "A word has power in and of itself. It comes from nothing into sound and meaning; it gives origin to all things. By means of words can a man deal with the world on equal terms. And the word is sacred" (33). From the example of his grandmother, who tells this story, Momaday learns that words from the Kiowan language can be used to confront "evil and the incomprehensible" (33).[9] Momaday recovers these words in his text and shows they are necessary for survival.

But in *The Way to Rainy Mountain*, Momaday does not focus only on recovery of language, as Abel does in *House Made of Dawn*. *The Way to Rainy Mountain* also shows the necessity of moving *between* languages. Momaday uses certain Kiowan words in this text, but he also tells the stories in English. He thereby translates and preserves both the stories and aspects of the language. Furthermore, he emphasizes that although the language has undergone some loss, the culture can still be preserved: "The verbal tradition by which it [the story of the Kiowan people] has been preserved has suffered a deterioration in time. What remains is fragmentary: mythology, legend, lore, and hearsay—and of course the idea itself, as crucial and complete as it ever was. That is the miracle" (4). The language may suffer deterioration ("what remains is fragmentary"), but the culture endures. Furthermore, the Kiowan culture can still be recovered by the translator's memory: "Yet it is within the reach of memory still, though tenuously now, and moreover it is even defined in a remarkably rich and living verbal tradition which demands to be preserved for its own sake" (86). The language is preserved by the translator's memory, and the culture endures, even when it is transmigrated to a new social and linguistic context.

In *The Way to Rainy Mountain*, Momaday does what Abel cannot —he translates the stories and language of his culture. Momaday thereby transmigrates the traditions, making them live and breathe in another tongue. Benjamin argues that the life of the original text attains in translation "its ever-renewed and most abundant flowering" (73). It is this flowering that Momaday sets in motion in *The Way to Rainy Mountain* through his translation of his culture's stories. And it is this flowering that Abel seems only on the verge of beginning when he sets out on his fateful Dawn Run, toward life or death, toward silence or voice.

Palimpsestic Translation in Leslie Marmon Silko's *Ceremony* and *Almanac of the Dead*

As discussed in the introduction, in an earlier era of translation readers knew multiple languages. A Roman reader therefore might translate a Greek text into Roman as a meditation on the original poem or play and its language. Consequently, as Susan Bassnett argues, "the Roman reader [who could also read Greek] was generally able to consider the translation as a metatext in relation to the original. The translated text was read *through* the source text" (45). I am interested in using this idea of languages being read *through* each other to approach the trope of translation in Leslie Marmon Silko's *Ceremony*. If translation is viewed as an exercise in allowing one text (or language) to be read (or spoken) through another, then *Ceremony*'s resolution becomes clearer. In effect, language becomes a kind of metaphorical palimpsest. A "palimpsest" is a text that has been written over and on throughout the course of history, with fragments of earlier, imperfectly erased writing still visible. "Dominant" and "marginal" texts/languages exist in a dialectical relationship—a relationship in which they are read through and against each other.

What if we view language not as a space in which one discourse (the dominant one) wipes out or perhaps writes out the "marginal" one but a space where remnants of many languages exist in a dialectical tension? *House Made of Dawn* shows the multilingualism of the contemporary world, but for Silko the translator's goal is not only speaking several languages but also showing the palimpsestic nature of language itself. In *Ceremony* Tayo's translation difficulties parallel those of Abel. Yet Silko's novel rewrites Momaday's both in its focus on linguistic hybridity (the imbrication of languages within each other) and in its concern with the role the listener or the community plays for the translator. And both *Ceremony* and Silko's more recent novel, *Almanac of the Dead*, suggest a strong connection between translation and revelation—between finding points of reciprocity and connection between "different" linguistic systems and the worlds these linguistic systems create.[10]

Like Abel, Tayo (the protagonist of Silko's novel *Ceremony*) returns from fighting in World War II and experiences great difficulty connecting to his Laguna culture and language. Tayo is an orphan of "mixed blood," as Abel is. Like Abel, Tayo has an older relative who tries to teach him the customs and language of his culture. And most important, like Abel, Tayo struggles to understand his native tongue and to reconcile it with the English-speaking world he and his friends (fellow war veterans) now inhabit. Tayo initially feels he has no voice, telling a white doctor: "He can't talk to you. He is invisible. His words are formed with an invisible tongue, they have no sound" (15). If we compare this sentence with one of the last lines of Momaday's *House Made of Dawn*—"There was no sound, and he had no voice" (212)—we can see that Silko is alluding to Abel's dilemma. Yet Silko also revises Momaday's text. For one thing, although Tayo is not fluent in his native tongue, he retains some knowledge of it: "[Ku'oosh] spoke softly, using the old dialect full of sentences that were involuted with explanations of their own origins, as if nothing the old man said were his own but all had been said before, and he was only there to repeat it. Tayo had to strain to catch the meaning, dense with place names he had never heard. His language was childish, interspersed with English words, and he could feel shame tightening in his throat; but then he heard the old man describe the cave" (34). Tayo strains to understand the elder's language, but he also struggles to express himself, even if he feels ashamed by his "childish" language. "The imperative is the telling," as Silko comments in an essay. "It is imperative to tell and not to worry over a specific language" ("Language and Literature" 61).[11] Tayo does not refuse the interlingual burdens of translation that "telling" entails. Furthermore, Tayo does not seek a pure language but rather the ability to move between languages, to mesh and mingle them. Early in the novel he makes the rather sardonic comment: "I'm half-breed. I'll be the first to say it. I'll speak for both sides" (42), but later he comes to realize that there is power in speaking for "both sides" or for many sides—there is power in a plurality of tongues.

This does not mean that Tayo has an unproblematic relationship to language. Before he can become a translator he must come to terms with the nightmarish linguistic babble that entangles him. When Tayo dreams, he hears voices in Spanish, Japanese, and Keres (the language spoken by the Laguna people), "rolling him over and over again like debris caught in a flood" (5). This flood of language threatens to overwhelm him: "He could hear Uncle Josiah calling him. But before Josiah could come, the fever voices would drift and whirl and emerge again—Japanese soldiers shouting orders to him . . . and he heard the women's voices then; they faded in and out until he was frantic because he thought the Laguna words were his mother's, but when he was about to make out the meaning of the words, the voice suddenly broke into a language he could not understand" (6). Tayo has never known much about his mother, and he longs to hear her voice, believing (like Ichiro in *No-No Boy*) that he can perhaps "refashion an identity for him and reappropriate him to himself" (Derrida, *Ear* 143) by fusion with the mother tongue. But the mother tongue is overwhelmed by "a language he cannot understand"—the babble of contemporary speech. For Tayo this babble means that "the world had come undone" (18), and he struggles to survive in this vertiginous, discursive landscape.

Silko indicates, however, that with the advent of Anglo-Americans and their language, the traditional Native American world has in fact been altered. The natural world and its names are changed by contact with English: "But the fifth world had become entangled with European names: the names of the rivers, the hills, the names of the animals and plants—all creation suddenly had two names: an Indian name and a white name" (68). Language is here configured as a tangle, but in this tangle English threatens to overwhelm the native tongue: "Now the feelings were twisted, tangled roots, and all the names for the source of this growth were buried under English words, out of reach. And there would be no peace and the people would have no rest until the entanglement had been unwound to the source" (69). Is it, then, the translator's job to untangle language, to trace it back to its source? What is the task of the translator in confronting this linguistic babble?

While some characters—such as Auntie—appear to believe their job is untangling language (69), the overall vision of the book implies something rather different. The native language is changed by contact with English, and the task of the translator is to make something positive of this change. Silko stresses that contact with other languages can lead to growth and development of a culture and its language. Oral stories, for example, are powerful medicine, as the opening poem illustrates: "You don't have anything / if you don't have the stories. / Their evil is mighty / but it can't stand up to our stories" (2). But oral stories are not static; rather, they are always growing and changing: "And in the belly of this story / the rituals and the ceremony / are still growing" (2). Thus the task of the translator is not only speaking the oral stories but also allowing the stories to "flower" (as Benjamin might put it) in another language. And the translator plays an important role in the evolution of the story, for she or he can either resist or assist the story's growth and transmigration. Betonie, a nontraditional Navajo medicine man, teaches Tayo that "things which don't shift and grow are dead things" (126), and Tayo applies this idea to stories. Looking around at the natural world, for example, he sees "a world made of stories, the long ago, time immemorial stories, as old Grandma called them," but also notes that this world of stories is "alive, always changing and moving" (95). Translation, oral storytelling, and ceremony are intermeshed in Silko's novel, and she illustrates that in all these activities, change and growth are productive and useful —a necessary part of adaptation to the contemporary world.[12]

Silko's text also implies a movement toward a hybrid discourse in which Native American languages can be heard through English and in which English is also used to further Native American stories. In explaining why his grandmother encourages him to learn English, Betonie tells Tayo: "She said 'It [the ceremony] is carried on in all languages now, so you have to know English too'" (122). There is no simple binary, here, in which Native American languages signify truth, insight, and selfhood, while English is equated with duplicity, delusion, and lack of identity. Unlike Abel, then, Tayo brings languages together so that the story, the language, the ceremony can grow and can be pushed toward revelation. Benjamin argues that "in the individual, unsupplemented languages, meaning is never found in relative independence, as in individual words or sentences; rather, it is in a constant state of flux" (76). However, according to Benjamin, translation brings languages into contact with each other so that "languages continue to grow . . . until the end of their time" (76); translation "catches fire on the eternal life of the works and the perpetual renewal of language" (76). Tayo must sometimes speak in English—this is part of the modern world, the modern ceremony. But he must also find ways of transmigrating and embodying the oral Laguna language and culture through his speaking of English; he will thereby push his own language and culture toward renewal and eternal life.

Fortunately, Tayo observes several individuals who teach him how this translation task might be achieved. Descheeny, Ts'eh, and Betonie show Tayo that cultural and linguistic hybridity are useful and indeed powerful forces in these processes of translation and transmigration. Betonie's grandfather Descheeny, for example, speaks both Spanish and Navajo (148). Descheeny's wife, who is Mexican, hears in his cabin "all these language I never heard before" (149). And both Descheeny and his wife realize that this linguistic hybridity is empowering: "This is the only way. . . . It cannot be done alone. We must have power from everywhere. Even the power we can get from the whites" (150). It is unclear if this statement is spoken in Spanish, Navajo, or English, but certainly it describes the power that can come when languages are allowed to

collide and collapse, when the discourse of the "master" is rearticulated within the spaces of another discursive domain.

Of course, Tayo's status as a "half-breed" allows him to embody the changes that occur through literal hybridity, as several
characters imply (100) and as several critics have discussed.[13] But I
am most interested in how *linguistic* hybridity becomes empowering for Tayo as a translator. The hunter Tayo meets, for example,
speaks English, but he also knows songs from the Laguna culture
and the Jemez or Zuni (207). Ts'eh, the hunter's sister or wife (this
is never made clear), has a sister married to a Navajo, another sister
who lives in Flagstaff, and a brother in Jemez (223).[14] Through these
two characters Silko points toward a kind of geographic, cultural,
and linguistic mixing that is powerful, productive, and part of the
ceremony itself—the ceremony that will, ultimately, banish "witch-
ery" from the world.

But it is only from Betonie that Tayo learns to speak palimpsesti-
cally. As James Ruppert argues, Betonie is able to "translate Western and Native discourse into the new ceremonies and ceremonial
vision," and so he is "the ideal person to effect the cure of Tayo and
to help him mediate the [Western and Native] discourses" ("Dialogism" 132). But how does this mediation and translation work on
the linguistic and even lexical level? Betonie normally speaks "good
English" (117), although he also knows Navajo (125). Yet Betonie
not only codeswitches between these languages but also allows the
Native American tongue to be heard *through* the English one. In
a crucial passage, Betonie uses an English word but signifies Native American values: "There was something about the way the old
man said the word 'comfortable.' It had a different meaning—not
the comfort of big houses or rich food or even clean streets, but the
comfort of belonging with the land, and the peace of being with
these hills" (117). Betonie gives the word a "special meaning" (117),
inflecting it with Native American values. He translates in such a
way that the "marginal" discourse is not sutured over but rather is
allowed to coexist with the dominant one. In fact, it is a bit unclear
in this sentence what is the marginal meaning of the term "comfort" and what is the "dominant" one. Certainly, in the modern
world Anglo-Americans appear to be enfranchised both culturally
and linguistically, but as Betonie points out, "This hogan was here

first. It is the town down there [in Gallup] which is out of place. Not this old medicine man" (118). While we might be tempted to say that the Native American meaning of the word "comfort" is out of place in the dominant landscape/discourse, Betonie's statement undercuts this binary.[15] We can see Betonie mastering the dominant language so that he takes up his rightful place *in* it, but also so that he can destabilize English through a practice of linguistic transmigration in which the "marginal" discourse begins to overturn the enfranchised one.

Tayo sees the value of this linguistic transmigration, which helps him make sense of (but not necessarily unwind) the linguistic babble in which he is caught. Tayo appears to believe, initially, that he must choose between languages and cultures—that he must believe *either* in the white world of science and linguistic factuality or the Native American world of ritual and oral stories. Yet what Tayo finally accomplishes is a complicated transcoding of his ethnic identities: "He knew what white people thought about the stories. . . . He had studied those books, and he had no reason to believe the stories any more. . . . But old Grandma always used to say, 'Back in time immemorial, things were different, the animals could talk to human beings and many magical things still happened.' He never lost the feeling he had in his chest when she spoke the words, as she did each time she told them stories; and he still felt it was true, despite all they had taught him in school—that long ago things *had* been different" (94–95). In a discussion of Native American literature, Cheryl Walker postulates that "perhaps the only way to avoid being captured by the reductivism of hegemony is by preserving the oxymoron: that is, the contradiction implied by two incompatible discourses within which it becomes clear there are gaps and fissures one cannot dismiss" (xv). Tayo does not choose between the white books of science and the Native American oral stories; rather, he struggles to hold on to both realms of knowledge, both cultural "stories." In so doing he begins the process of transcoding identities so that he can be both "American" and Laguna. For it is only by seeing how these linguistic and cultural identities intersect that Tayo can survive. The stories that seem dichotomous *do* fit together: "He cried the relief he felt at finally seeing the pattern, the way all the stories fit together—the old stories, the war stories, their stories—to become the story that was still being told" (246). The white stories ("their stories"), Tayo's grandmother's and Ku'oosh's stories ("the old stories"), and the new stories ("the war stories") do fit together to become a story that Tayo can build. Contact between different discursive systems allows the story to grow—but only if the translator sees, and does not dismiss, differences. Differences are, then, incorporated into the processes of transcoding identity and transmigrating tongues.

Furthermore, finding contact points, "contact zones" in/of language, enables translation and revelation. After the encounter with Betonie (which is an encounter with the multiple possibilities of language), Tayo recovers the ability to pray and find revelation: "He repeated the words [to the sunrise song] as he remembered them, not sure if they were the right ones, but feeling they were right, feeling the instant of the dawn was an event which in a single moment gathered all things together—the last stars, the mountaintops, the clouds, and the winds—celebrating this coming. The power of each day spilled over the hills in great silence. Sunrise. He ended the prayer with 'sunrise' because he knew the Dawn people began and ended all their words with 'sunrise'" (182). As Ben does in *House Made of Dawn*, Tayo speaks the prayers in some form of language so that they are not lost.

Yet Tayo cannot be a translator until he finds an audience. This is the step Abel never reaches—reintegrating the individual's story/experiences with the community's: "It took a long time to tell them the story; they stopped [Tayo] frequently with questions about the location and the time of day; they asked about the direction she had come from and the color of her eyes" (257). As Tayo tells the story of his encounter with Ts'eh and the she-elk, he knits himself back into the community and into its traditions. The community responds by incorporating his story into theirs:

> They started crying
> the old men started crying
> "A'moo'ooh! A'moo'ooh!"
> You have seen her
> We will be blessed
> again. (257)

Silko does not specify the language in which Tayo tells his story, so we must presume that, like his earlier speech, it is a blend of English and Keres. But Tayo no longer feels *ashamed* of his blended speech. Telling of his encounter with Ts'eh in English and the Laguna language does not obscure the older story but allows it to shine through. "A real translation is transparent," Benjamin notes; "it does not cover the original, does not block its light" (80). Tayo finally learns to move between discursive systems in a fluent and even fluid way—keeping the languages open so that through contact with each other they can grown and change. Thus the oral stories of the Laguna "past" continue to live and flower and *grow* in another written/spoken form, in another discursive landscape that they enter and alter.

Silko's text as a whole also points to this fluent, and even fluid, form of translation. Like *House Made of Dawn*, *Ceremony* contains numerous interspersed words with origins in other languages: Ts'its'tsi'nako (1), *Y volveré* (6, 97); mesas (6, 28, 121); Iktoa'ak'o'ya (13); arroyo (28, 230); A'moo'oh, a'moo'ohh" (33); K'oo'ko (37); Ck'o'yo (46, 54, 173, 192, 204, 247); Pa'caya'nyi (46, 47); piñons (80, 129, 146, 216, 220); cantina (86); Ka't'sina (94); *menudo* (100); piki bread (116); hogan (117, 123); chongo (117); e-hey-yah-ah-na (143); Pa'to'ch (145, 220); Kaup'a'ta (170, 174, 175, 192); heheya (174); *cerros* (185, 187); kiva (230, 256); and so on. Unlike Momaday, however, Silko rarely italicizes these words, and she frequently translates them for the reader; we are told, for example, that "*cerros*" are "gently rounded hills of dark lava rock" (185) and that "Ts'its'tsi'nako" means "thought-woman" (1). *Ceremony* aims for a sense of linguistic fluidity and fluency—a sense that the translator and reader move between cultures and languages to "write" texts that allow these cultures and languages to grow and expand in productive ways. But Silko does not render this process invisible. In fact, in *Ceremony* she emphasizes translation, as she will also do in *Almanac of the Dead*, where she gives literal translations of songs with the embedded note "[Translation]" (*Almanac* 724). In *Ceremony*, Silko similarly emphasizes the visible process of translation: "[Ts'its'tsi'nako] is sitting in her room / thinking of a story now / I'm telling you the story / she is thinking" (1). Many translators speak of foregrounding the role of the translator so that readers are made aware of the presence of another individual who is writing, and rewriting, the source text. Here and elsewhere Silko makes her readers see the translative process of linguistic and cultural modification she undertakes as the author of this written text.

Translation and revelation are also crucial themes of *Almanac of the Dead*, yet here too we can see a focus on language not as "pure" but as a contact zone between peoples and cultures. Two twin sisters named Lecha and Zeta attempt to translate the Almanac of the Dead—a collection of texts that have been handed down to Native Americans, generation after generation. Lecha and Zeta are given these texts by their grandmother, an old Native American (Yaqui) woman named Yoeme. The almanac is comprised of notebooks that appear to be in a code that the twins must decipher (128); they are also multilingual texts containing various Native American glyphs and dialects, as well as Spanish and Latin (134). Throughout much of the novel, Lecha's project is translating these notebooks: "The old notebooks are all in broken Spanish or corrupt Latin that no one can understand without months of research in old grammars. Lecha has already done translation work, and her notebooks contained narratives in English" (174). Adding English to these multilingual notebooks, as Lecha does, is seen as enhancing them (130). Like the grandmother's diaries in *The Floating World*, the notebooks form a changing, constantly evolving, multilingual text that asks the reader to meditate on language and translation. Yoeme tells her grandchildren that "you must understand how carefully the old manuscript and its notebooks must be kept. Nothing must be added that was not already there. Only repairs are allowed, and one might live as long as I have and not find a suitable code" (129). Yet when Lecha adds her own stories to the almanac (in English), Yoeme nods with approval. Thus "repairing" the almanac means not so much rewriting it but writing it. The stories Lecha adds are what Derrida would call a productive form of writing called forth by the original text (*Ear* 153). Translation of the almanac allows it to flower and evolve in a new cultural context. Translation also furthers multilingualism, enabling languages and cultures to coexist in a dialectical tension with each other. Translating and even reading these notebooks is an entry into the problematics of multilingualism, one that illustrates the need for linguistic hybridity and fluidity.

The notebooks therefore emblematize the process of translation, but they also emblematize language itself. Language seems hegemonic but is actually made up of multiple other discourses, as the notebooks illustrate:

> For hundreds of years, guardians of the almanac notebooks had made clumsy attempts to repair torn pages. Some sections had been splashed with wine, others with water or blood. Only fragments of the original pages remained, carefully placed between blank pages; those of ancient paper had yellowed, but the red and black painted glyphs had been clear. . . . The pages of ancient paper had been found between the pages of horse-gut parchment carried by the fugitive Indian slaves who had fled north to escape European slavery. . . . There was evidence that substantial portions of the original manuscript had been lost or condensed into odd narratives which operated like codes. . . . Here and there were scribbles and scratches. . . . Whole sections had been stolen from other books and from the proliferation of "farmer's almanacs" published by patent-drug companies and medicine shows. . . . Not even the parchment pages or fragments of ancient paper could be trusted; they might have been clever forgeries, recopied, drawn, and colored painstakingly. (569–70)

Composed of the language of the past and present, blood and wine, forgeries and "authentic fragments" (but are they really "authentic"?), oral and written stories, blank pages and glyphs, Spanish, English, Latin, and several Native American dialects, the almanac notebooks embody the palimpsestic nature of language itself. There is no pure, authentic text here, no pure and authentic language that can be "recovered." There are only stories that overlap with other stories, languages that overlap with other languages.[16] More insistently than *Ceremony*, *Almanac of the Dead* implies that language is broken and that we cannot recover an "authentic" story of it through translation. In *Almanac of the Dead* there is no "original" or "uncontaminated" story, no "pure language" to be "reclaimed." Rather, "pure language" and a "pure story" as such exist only in a dialectical context of multilingualism. And the translator must always attempt both to "capture" the prior text and to create something *new* that transcends the prior texts, that puts to question whether the prior text can even be accessed.

For Silko, the translator does not seek "authenticity" through his or her translations. However, he or she does seek some form of revelation, some form of "truth." This may seem paradoxical, but Silko nonetheless insists that translation of the almanac notebooks reveals truth: "The almanacs had warned the people hundreds of years before the Europeans arrived. . . . Without the almanacs, the people would not be able to recognize the days and months yet to come, days and months that would see the people retake the land" (*Almanac* 570). Encoded into the almanac is the overlapping story of the past and the future. And translation enables this story, this revelation, to occur: "Through the decipherment of ancient tribal texts of the Americas the Almanac of the Dead foretells the future of all the Americas. The future is encoded in arcane symbols and old narratives" (*Almanac* 16). Translation of these texts reveals and indeed creates the revelation of "truth." But truth is multifaceted and multilingual. And in the past as in the present, truth exists only in the web and tangle of discourse, of contradictory narratives and languages. In *Ceremony* Tayo must both connect to and expand the stories of his people, their linguistic and cultural worlds. But in *Almanac* this role is even weightier: the translator recovers and *creates* the stories that will be the future—the stories that will lead to "truth" and revelation.

Radical Bilingualism in Susan Power's *The Grass Dancer*

So far in this chapter, I have discussed a gradual movement beyond the literal meanings of "translation." Susan Power's more recent novel *The Grass Dancer* continues this expansion. Quite literally, it encourages bilingualism through a character named Red Dress. Born in the past (1846), Red Dress continues to be heard by her ancestors in the present moment. Even more paradoxically, she speaks Dakota and English, *simultaneously*: "I could swear she spoke in

English and Dakota simultaneously" (206); "Charlene couldn't be sure if the language was English or Sioux" (298); "'I have seen you dancing,' Red Dress said in two languages, two distinct voices" (331). When I teach this novel I frequently ask my students to think about whether it would be possible to speak in two languages at once without producing babble. What would such a double tongue sound like? I often get baffled looks from my students, but perhaps this is part of Power's point. Locked as we are in our unilingual ways of thinking, it is hard to imagine how one could speak two languages at once. But don't we often do this? Here I am speaking the language of the academic, but I am also trying to draw in readers less familiar with jargon, such as my students. Can I succeed in speaking two (or more) languages at once? More important, how does this attempt to speak two languages at once cause me to reflect on language itself—on its power structures and on how it is made up of imbricated and overlapping discourses that appear to be separate but are not?

On a literal level it may be impossible to imagine Red Dress's discourse, but metaphorically this radical bilingualism functions in a crucial way in Power's text. "When the words of the master become the site of hybridity—the warlike song of the native—then we may not only read between the lines, but even seek to change the often coercive reality that they so lucidly contain," maintains Homi Bhabha ("Signs" 181). In Power's text, the "warlike song of the native" (Dakota) literally becomes part of the master's discourse (English), and language becomes a space of hybridity, resistance, and change. So, as in Silko's text, language is a space that makes manifest the ambivalence of the process of linguistic colonization. Furthermore, Red Dress's radical bilingualism teaches her descendants to translate in the contemporary moment—to speak the intersignifying, intercritical stories that constitute the history of linguistic encounter and resistance in the United States. Eric Cheyfitz discusses a practice of translation that "would not be a mode of repression of languages (within a language) by a master language" because "there would be no master language" and "there would be no native speakers." Rather, "all speakers exist in translation between languages, which is where we all exist" (134). Power's novel demonstrates that we exist between languages—but also that this location can become a source of empowerment and even revelation.[17] In this text, then, a radical bilingualism that creates tension and exchanges *between* languages is a crucial aspect of any translative activity, of any power the translator might achieve to transmigrate tongues and transcode ethnicity.

The text is also attentive to how translation can actually erase indigenous languages. More insistently than either Momaday or Silko, Power illustrates that since the early days of contact between Euro-American invaders and the indigenous peoples of the Americas, translation was often used in attempts to efface the native tongue. David Murray affirms that in the early days of encounter "the great *bulk* of language learning and translation was being carried out by Indians, this reflecting, of course the wider situation, in which Indians were also the ones involved, willingly or otherwise, in *cultural* translation" (5). Power's character Charles Bad Holy MacLeod embodies this idea of an enforced translation that annihilates indigenous languages and customs. Educated at the missionary school in Carlisle, Pennsylvania, Charles returns to the reservation "with twenty books and a head full of education . . . but he didn't remember one story about his tribe. He didn't remember one honor song" (106–7). Charles has to translate himself into an "American" and into the English language; in so doing he abrogates his prior identity as a Dakota Indian and expunges his knowledge of the tribal language. In 1912, when Charles returns, there are still people who can teach him his language, but by 1981 (when the novel opens), translation of the language has become more difficult. Charlene, a teenager, listens to a Dakota song and has difficulty understanding it: "The men launched enthusiastically into the chorus, and it took Charlene a moment to translate the lyrics into English; she was becoming less proficient in the Dakota language after so many years of school" (31). For individuals such as Charlene living in the contemporary moment—when assimilation is encouraged and the native tongue is devalued—translation from the Dakota language becomes a central problem.

In the novel as a whole, then, Red Dress is an emblem of how the native tongue can be preserved in the past and the present; when she dies in 1864, she insists on becoming an instrument of both cultural and linguistic memory: "So many of [the words] slipped away, beyond recall. I am a talker now and chatter in my people's ears until I grow weary of my own voice. *I am memory*, I tell them when they're sleeping" (282). Her radical bilingualism creates a contact zone between English and the native tongue that continually remakes English, the language of colonization and conquest. It is from within this contact zone that a liberatory practice of translation might emerge. Yet Red Dress moves through several stages in her translation practices. In 1863 she learns English from a missionary, Father La Frambois, but then refuses to be baptized, to be bribed by "stories of heaven and eternal life" (239). She writes her Christian name—Esther—but fashions the *E* with dramatic flourishes, "curved into the shape of a lush bear heavy with winter fat" (250). On the lexical terrain, Red Dress insists on inscribing her own vision of nature into the letters that are supposed to reflect her conversion to the white man's religion and language. On a broader level, she continues to speak in "a voice of my own" (243). For example, when Father La Frambois asks her to translate his words to her tribe, expecting her to "be [his] voice" and the agent of "[her] people's salvation" (242), she turns his message of religious damnation into a sermon about his respect for her people. Father La Frambois's plan to secure converts is foiled by Red Dress's resistant mode of translation. Like many actual Native American translators, she is an equivocal link between the world of the whites and her people's world.[18] Lawrence Venuti notes that translation can either affirm or transgress, construct or critique, ideologies and discursive values of "foreign" cultures. The translator can, through an ethics of translation, choose to make the translated text a place where "a cultural other" is manifested and understood, or she or he can make the translated text a place where the values of the translator's own culture are narcissistically affirmed (Venuti 13, 5). Clearly, Red Dress's first translations function through a "domesticating" mode that transgresses the values of the source text, rendering it unintelligible.

But Power's text as a whole points to another method of translation that may be more useful in the long run—a method that works not through an abrogation or refusal of the oppressor's language and worldview but through an appropriation and hybridization of it, a combination of it with the language and worldview

of the Sioux. Red Dress eventually adopts a form of radical bilingualism in which she speaks both English and Dakota, allowing
their differences to remain. Translation therefore becomes a space
of productive cultural collision, a space of transculturation. Pérez
Firmat uses the term "transculturación" (*Cuban Condition* 24) to
describe an activity that emerges from the spaces of translation and
denotes a "liminal zone of 'impassioned margin' where diverse cultures converge without merging" (*Cuban Condition* 26).[19] According to Anuradha Dingwaney, "*Transculturación*, insofar as it des-
ignates the space within which the dominant language and culture
is rewritten, inflected, subverted by the 'subaltern,' functions as a
form of resistance" (8). In my understanding of this term, transculturación acts as the space where the oppressor's language and
worldview is not so much denied but rather appropriated, inflected,
subverted, and rewritten from within.

In Red Dress's translations, the trace of what is disavowed (the
Native American language and worldview) is not repressed but repeated as something different—as something still existing within
the discursive terrain. Hearing Red Dress speak English and Dakota "simultaneously," Calvin Wind Soldier notes that "the part of
the voice speaking Dakota was low, from deep in the throat, and
the part speaking English was breathy and high, the *s* sounding
like a hiss" (206). What has been repressed—the snake, the "savage," the hiss—is still contained within the discourse (within English, in fact), repeated rather than suppressed. Furthermore, a subaltern discourse—the low voice of the Dakota people—works from
within the structures of the dominant discourse to undermine it.
Red Dress's mode of discourse is therefore an example of linguistic
hybridity. According to Bhabha, colonialist discourse references a
process of splitting that can be exploited: a splitting between the
mother culture and its bastards, the self and its doubles, where "the
trace of what is disavowed is not repressed but repeated as something *different*" ("Signs" 172). Therefore, "hybridity is a *problematic*
of colonial representation and individuation that reverses the effects
of the colonialist disavowal, so that other 'denied' knowledges enter
upon the dominant discourse and estrange the basis of its authority
—its rules of recognition" ("Signs" 175). In Red Dress's speaking,

the denied, low voice of Dakota decomposes the authority of the master's discourse, of English itself.[20] In her final incarnation, Red Dress shows the interdependency between English and Dakota, the discourse of colonization and the subaltern. She neither synthesizes these languages nor domesticates one in favor of the other; rather, she lets both of them speak through her, allowing their different discursive demands to come into contact, to collide and become interdependent. The words of the Dakota language do not actually slip away but are translated into the radical bilingual discourse Red Dress creates, which "belongs" neither to the colonizer nor to the colonized.

Metaphorically, the text also presents a practice of translation that sutures English and Dakota together in syncretic formulations that allow linguistic and cultural oppositions to remain in tension with each other within new discursive configurations. In a dream Red Dress sees herself becoming "the uneasy voice of the grass" (246). The symbolism surrounding "grass" in this novel is complex, but on one level grass represents language or (more precisely) the differences but also the overlaps between languages. Speaking to another woman, Red Dress says: "Koda—*friend*—*look at this sullen brown grass, dispirited because winter is coming to punish it. This, to me, is English. It is little pebbles on my tongue, gravel, the kind of thing you chew but cannot swallow. Dakota is the lush spring grass that moves like water and tastes sweet*" (260). This passage seems to separate the two languages, yet in the earlier vision in which Red Dress becomes the "uneasy voice of the grass," each step she takes "leaves a stunted patch of pale, dry grass, struggling to grow" (246). This natural symbolism points not to a division between languages —English (dry grass) and Dakota (green grass)—but to a cycle of exchange. Green grass fades with the seasons, becoming the brown grass of fall. Yet it leaves behind seeds that eventually become new grass. The symbolism surrounding the voice of the grass suggests a process whereby languages (English and Dakota) can be syncretized and both tongues can be transmigrated. In so doing, the translator finds his or her identity and place within a multilingual world, a contact zone of language and culture.[21]

On the lexical terrain the text's discourse also mirrors this syncretism. Some words from Dakota are present in the text, trans-literated into English: *waštunkala* (22, 99, 118); Wakan Tanka (24, 60, 201); Unči (44, 328); *unšika* (57, 252); Yuwipi (61, 87, 95, 163, 201); *heyo'ka* (68, 82, 171, 244); *Yuwipi* (77, 81, 84); *Iho! (Iho!)* (85); *Topa. (Topa.) (Topa.)* (85); *wateča* (87); *winkte* (107); *Šunka Sapa* (107); *Takoja* (113, 116, 120, 328, 330); *wožapi* (104); *Tunkašida* (90, 113); *Wanaǧi Tačanku* (104, 118, 122); Čuwignaka Duta (202, 222); Ini Naon Win (216); *Atewaye* (230); *Ohan* (132, 243); *wašičuns* (141, 165, 263); *Ina* (155); *wičaǧadata* (243); *Tanke* (247, 249); Šunka Wakan Wanaǧi (243); Čanwapekasna Wi (259); mazaska (260, 318); Koda (260); Waniyetu Wi (260); *Tanke* (274); *tatanka* (275); unči (300); Tunkašida (316); *Mosquito Wičaša* (319); Tunkašida Wakan Tanka (326); *hanbdeč'eya* (326, 332); *Hau* (327, 332); *Iyotiye wakiye* (332). Most of these words are translated; for example, we are told that "Iktomi" is "the tricky spider" (61), that "*heyo'ka*" is a sacred clown (68), and that "*wožapi*" is a berry pudding (104). Power uses native words less frequently than does either Silko or Momaday. On the other hand, Power works hard to show that the language has not slipped away and to bring it to life for contemporary readers.

Power's text also contains more fused constructions and sentences—more syntactic units that actually show a hybrid discourse at work within the English language. For example, the protagonist's friend Frank Pipe has the nickname of "*Mosquito Wičaša*" —Mosquito Man (319). This nickname syncretizes language to produce a new code that is neither Dakota nor English *but both*. Red Dress, in particular, tends to use syncretic constructions. In the following sentence, for example, Red Dress moves back and forth between English and Dakota in a seamless fashion: "The warriors nodded, breathing, '*Ohan*,' and several of the women trilled the *wičaǧadata* cry of approval" (243). Red Dress also tends to embed translations of Native American words into her English sentences: "It was early October, Čanwapekasna Wi, the moon when the leaves rustle" (259), or "By November, Waniyetu Wi, the winter moon, Fanny could not be persuaded to go on long walks" (260). Even more radically, a contemporary character, Frank Pipe, actually alternates between English and Dakota:

"Tunkašida Wakan Tanka, my friend is ready for the
    [Dakota]   [English]
hanbdeč'eya. He wants to send you his voice." (326)
    [Dakota]   [English]

As explained in the introduction, linguists have argued that speakers who switch codes in a grammatically correct manner may create a third language that transcends the two discourses of which it is composed. Looking at Frank Pipe's sentences we can see that although he alternates codes, the sentence is still grammatically correct. Frank moves beyond bilingualism toward a syncretic new mode of translation that transmigrates Dakota into English and in so doing changes English itself.

In the contemporary moment, then, characters like Frank Pipe must learn to employ syncretism and the radical bilingualism of a translator such as Red Dress. Yet Frank Pipe is a peripheral character, and the principal struggle of the novel centers on whether the protagonist (Harley) can incorporate his ancestor Red Dress's lessons about translation into his own life in the contemporary moment. Harley's mother, Lydia, at first seems to be another guide in this process, someone who could teach him to translate. As a young woman, Lydia had the ability to formulate a syncretic linguistic and cultural identity. She is Christian yet she remembers the old ways; she speaks English but is also fluent in Dakota: "I was Lydia, the good girl who confessed every Wednesday and took Communion each Sunday, Lydia who spoke fluent Dakota to the elders while Evelyn stumbled through 'Hello' and a few simple phrases. As my mother was fond of saying, I was the good from both sides" (199–200). But after her husband and adopted son are killed by a racist drunk driver who believes they are "Indian ghosts" (6), Lydia becomes entirely silent: "And so I have become another person, the one who sits on her tongue. I answer to Lydia, but when I think of myself, I use another name: Ini Naon Win. Silent Woman" (216).[22] Power emphasizes that, like Abel's, Lydia's silence is not empowering. Harley, for example, feels that his mother is "being slowly erased by some spectral finger" (18). Furthermore, Lydia's silence—not her language—is being passed on to her son: "The dark silence that had blossomed inside [Harley] as a small child had both expanded and compressed, become a leaden weight branching everywhere, even to his fingers" (319). Lydia's silence functions as a metaphor for the silencing of her people by Euro-American culture. And the silence—not the story—grows inside the people.

Lydia's silence causes Harley to be somewhat disconnected from the traditions of the Dakota; he appears to associate his ethnicity with something from the past that honors his relatives, but not with something that might be useful to him in the present as he struggles to take his place within a modern, "American" cultural context. Lydia does not help Harley to understand how his ethnicity might be useful, how it might be transcoded in such a way that it serves him in the present moment. Like Abel and Tayo, Harley teeters on the verge of alcoholism and self-destruction. And like Abel and Tayo, at times Harley appears to see the traditions as hollow, performing them in such a way that they are undermined: for example, he performs a grass dance but he is drunk, his makeup is smeared, and he barely remembers the steps (324).

Therefore it is no coincidence that Harley learns to translate and transcode his ethnicity only when he recovers the legacy of his great-great-great aunt, Red Dress. Toward the end of the novel Harley agrees to go into the vision pit—to engage in a three-day ritual of fasting and prayer designed to give the individual ancestral help. At first, Harley feels that he cannot pray, but he does make the effort: "'I don't know how to pray,' Harley mumbled, but he dismissed the idea. *I will learn*, he told himself. . . . But now he was alone on Angry Butte, beneath the face of the sky. 'I have to stand up for myself,' he said aloud. He tried a tentative prayer: 'Tunkašida Wakan Tanka, you know everything, you made my heart. Let me look into it for the first time.' Harley taught himself to pray from a hole in the ground" (326). Interestingly, Harley prays in English and Dakota: "Tunkašida Wakan Tanka, you know everything." While this is not actual bilingualism (the words of the Dakota language are not written in Dakota in the text but transliterated into English), this metaphorical bilingualism does move Harley beyond his previous monolingualism and enables encounters with a number of his dead relatives, including his grandmother, his father, and the brother he has never known.[23] Finally, Red Dress visits Harley, who actually hears (and understands) her two tongues: "*Iyotiye wa-kiye,* echoed in Harley's ears. *I am sad*" (332). The vision pit concerns reconnecting with the ancestors but also with the ancestors' ability to translate and make a place between languages. When Harley's ancestors ask him if he is ready for an adventure, he answers in Dakota but then translates: "'*Hau,*' Harley answered in Dakota. Yes" (327). Harley allows languages to coexist in a dialectical tension with each other—a tension that translation embodies but does not destroy.

Harley also finds revelation through such methods of translation. Earlier, other characters had this experience. Frank Pipe, for example, eventually learns to speak fluently in Dakota and to be "in the spirit": "Frank Pipe expressed himself in Dakota, finding the words so effortlessly his grandfather nodded. Harley's pulse quickened. His friend was in the spirit, and the sight of it moved Harley, gave him a spark of hope" (326). Yet for Harley revelation is not only about speaking Dakota "effortlessly." It entails finding his place in his history and community and in the languages that constitute his identity. And it also involves transcoding ethnicity, for Harley must eventually demonstrate not only that he understands the traditions but that he can perform them as well. When Harley's ritual in the vision pit concludes, his mother and friends return singing a song "supported by the voices of the community" (332). Like Silko, Power emphasizes the translator's reintegration into the community. But Harley also hears a "powerful new voice that was unfamiliar." At first this voice upsets Harley: "Who was this unknown singer? He became a little angry, thinking to himself that after such an ordeal as the *hanbdeč'eya,* it wasn't right to bring outsiders into the circle" (332). Then Harley realizes who is singing: "Harley listened carefully, his hands curled into fists, and it was only as the song neared its end that he realized the truth: What he heard was the music of his own voice, rising above the rest" (332–33).

It is crucial in this final scene that Harley finds "the music of his own voice" and participates in this ritual. And it is crucial that he now seems familiar with the Dakota tongue, as evidenced by his use of the word *hanbdeč'eya* and his singing of what is (in all probability) a Dakota song. Yet Power finally does not specify what language is spoken, what discourse enunciates "the music of his own voice." Aided by Red Dress and his community, Harley has finally learned to transcode his ethnicity and transmigrate his tongue. The hybridized, transliterated discourse that Harley eventually speaks engenders the collision and collusion of worlds and words that is translation. Translation therefore becomes a space where one nation does not write another "out" but rather is written and rewritten from within.

Violence as Voice in Sherman Alexie's *Reservation Blues* and *Indian Killer*

Like those of Silko and Power, Sherman Alexie's novels *Reservation Blues* and *Indian Killer* continue to move beyond literal concepts of "translation." The earlier novel, in fact, implies that the language itself is not necessary for preservation of the culture. In *Reservation Blues* almost no one speaks the language of the Spokane tribe, but certain individuals embody the linguistic values of the culture by transmigrating them into spoken English and into music. In this novel Alexie suggests that the indigenous language is *not* the point—what matters is transmigration of the cultural values into English, into new songs and stories. "Y'all need to play songs for your people. They need you" (23), one character tells Thomas Builds-the-Fire, and Thomas proceeds to turn his stories into a music that transmigrates his people's culture.

Yet *Reservation Blues* does not end happily. Perhaps this should lead us to question whether Alexie is satisfied with the idea that one can "translate" without knowing the language. Alexie's next novel, *Indian Killer*, illustrates more darkly the problematics of linguistic dispossession through John Smith, an orphaned Native American deprived of any knowledge of his culture and language. As an adult John Smith becomes violent and dreams of killing a white man. *Indian Killer* raises the question, then, of what happens when an individual is completely unable to translate. In *Lost in Translation*, Eva Hoffman comments that "linguistic dispossession is a sufficient motive for violence, for it is close to the dispossession of one's self. Blind rage, helpless rage is rage that has no words—rage that overwhelms one with darkness. And if one is perpetually without words, if one exists in an entropy of inarticulateness, that condition itself is bound to be an enraging frustration" (124). *Indian Killer* posits chillingly that for the voiceless, violence may become a way of brutally transmigrating a kind of cultural voice.[24]

In *Reservation Blues* three young Spokane men (Thomas Builds-the-Fire, Junior Polatkin, and Victor Joseph) team up with two Flathead women (Chess and Checkers Warm Water) to form a band. Aided by a guitar from the legendary blues singer Robert Johnson and Big Mom, a local Spokane semideity who has helped many rock stars, the band, Coyote Springs, is almost successful. But after a disastrous recording session in New York City, the group returns to the Spokane reservation in disgrace. Eventually, Junior kills himself, Victor goes back into an alcohol-induced haze, and Chess, Checkers, and Thomas leave the reservation for jobs in Seattle. As they leave, however, they take their cultural traditions with them, as exemplified by the shadow horses accompanying them: "In the blue van, Thomas, Chess, and Checkers sang together . . . with the shadow horses: we are alive, we'll keep living. Songs were waiting for them up there in the dark. Songs were waiting for them in the city" (306).

This passage and the novel as a whole imply that the culture and traditions of Native Americans can be translated only when they are transformed and transcoded. Thomas is the reservation storyteller, but no one listens to him: "Thomas shared his stories with the pine trees because people didn't listen" (28). Thomas's stories—told in English because only a few elders on the reservation remember the tribal language (36, 263)—have both a physical and a linguistic presence: "Thomas Builds-the-Fire's stories climbed into your clothes like sand, gave you itches that could not be scratched. If you repeated even a sentence from one of those stories, your throat was never the same again. Those stories hung in your clothes and hair like smoke, and no amount of laundry soap or shampoo washed them out. Victor and Junior often tried to beat those stories out of Thomas, tied him down and taped his mouth shut. . . . But none of that stopped Thomas, who talked and talked" (15). The stories transform the languages of others, so that "your throat was never the same again." And they creep into people's dreams and minds.

But Alexie is careful to indicate that despite their power, Thomas's stories do not heal: "More than anything, [Thomas] wanted a story to heal the wounds, but he knew that his stories never healed anything" (6). Thomas and the other members of his tribe devalue his stories, seeing them as useless in the modern world.

The translation problem of this novel, then, revolves around how Thomas can transform his stories so that they do heal—and whether these stories can be effective without any connection to the indigenous language. Splashed across the backdrop of the novel is the history of the linguistic colonization of the Spokane: "My braids were cut off in the name of Jesus / To make me look so white / My tongue was cut out in the name of Jesus / So I could not speak what's right" (131). However, enunciated here in music—in the song "My God Has Dark Skin" that the band Coyote Springs sings—is also a story of linguistic resistance:

> I had my tongue cut out by these black robes
> But I know I'll speak 'til the end
> I had my heart cut out by the black robes
> But I know what I still feel
> I had my eyes cut out by the black robes
> But I know I see what's real. (132)

This song speaks to the need to recover the language—not to let the tongue be cut out by the black robes (or priests). A kind of resistance inheres in this refusal to stop speaking the indigenous language.

But in the contemporary moment this form of resistance does not operate. The parents are mostly dead, gone, or alcoholics, so they cannot pass on the language and traditions. Moreover, the dominant culture has denied Native Americans their language. Three commandments from Thomas's ironic "The Reservation's Ten Commandments as Given by the United States to the Spokane Indians" explicitly mention this subject of linguistic colonization:

> 5. Honor your Indian father and Indian mother because I have stripped them of their land, *language* and hearts. . . .
> 6. You shall not murder, but I will bring FBI and CIA

agents to your reservation and into your homes, and the most intelligent, *vocal*, and angriest members of your tribes will vanish quietly. . . .

9. You shall not give false testimony against any white men, but they will tell *lies about you*, and I will believe them and convict you. (154–55, emphasis added)

The (potential) translator has not fallen into silence, as happens to Lydia in *The Grass Dancer*. Rather, the translator has been brutally stripped of her or his own language and simultaneously deprived of any empowered presence within the dominant discourse, within the language of hegemony.[25]

Furthermore, in the contemporary moment the translator appears to have lost contact with the indigenous tongue that *might* offer an alternative basis for linguistic empowerment. Thomas, for example, recalls that his mother sang "traditional Spokane Indian songs" (22). Yet he himself cannot find the words to save his people: "He knew the words to a million songs: Indian, European, African, Mexican, Asian. He sang 'Stairway to Heaven' in four different languages but never knew where the staircase stood. He sang the same Indian songs continually but never sang them correctly. He wanted to make his guitar sound like a waterfall, like a spear striking salmon, but his guitar only sounded like a guitar. He wanted the songs, the stories, to save everybody" (101). Here Alexie offers a possible "solution" to the translation problem: transmigration of the Spokane stories into music as an alternative form of "language" that undercuts the dominant discourse. Alexie also points to a hybrid multilingualism—Thomas can sing in four different languages, he knows the words to a million songs. Yet he does not know how to sing the Indian songs "correctly." And he cannot save his people through his multilingual songs and stories. In the end he does not transmigrate the native tongue into English through his music. Why?

To answer this question we must look closely at how Thomas's multilingual, musical stories are received and at the band's own motivation. When Thomas hears Robert Johnson singing the blues, he realizes that the blues are an "ancient, aboriginal, indigenous" language (174). Yet the Spokane refuse to claim this language: "Those blues created memories for the Spokane, but they refused to claim them. Those blues lit up a new road, but the Spokane pulled out their old maps" (174). Symbolically, the Spokane refuse to hear the alternative possibility offered by the indigenous language. Similarly, Coyote Springs is described as singing "a tribal music" that "might have chased away the pilgrims five hundred years ago" (79–80). Their music is a blend of Native American, Spanish, and English words, a fusion of blues, country, and rock styles. Like the blues, it calls upon sources of power that are lodged in the communal past. The music functions as a trickster that can both free and empower. According to Gerald Vizenor, the "tribal trickster is a liberator and healer in a narrative, a comic sign, a communal signification and a discourse with imagination" (187).[26] Yet, as Vizenor goes on to suggest, the trickster can liberate only when the audience materializes its relationship with it: "The trickster narrative situates the participant audience, the listeners and readers, in agonistic imagination: there, in comic discourse, the trickster is being, nothingness and liberation" (196). In Alexie's novel, music is a trickster that can liberate, but the listeners must be a participant audience, actively contesting the discourse, creating and constructing it as they listen. Yet finally, the audience does not receive the music's message. Instead, Thomas is ostracized from his tribe for associating with individuals from another tribe (Chess and Checkers). As with the blues, then, the Spokane people do not follow the "new road" lit up by the music.

Another problem lies in the band itself. Victor and Joseph want to become famous so that they can sleep with white women, and even Thomas says that he sings because he wants "all kinds of strangers to love me" (213). When he is invited to New York, Victor makes clear his goal: "We're going to be rock stars. . . . And we won't have to come back to this reservation ever again. We'll just leave all of you [jerks] to your [awful] lives" (227). Perhaps the band fails, then, because it has no larger goals; as Thomas says in a dream, perhaps they need to have "*something better in mind*" (72). A music that is of the people and for the people, such as Big Mom's, "created and recreated the world daily" (10). But Coyote Springs' goals of leaving the reservation and obtaining wealth, fame, and the love of white women are in conflict with their need to sing songs "for their people"—their need to create a tribal music that can both endure and transmigrate native stories into the English language.

Finally, though, the most difficult problem with the new music Coyote Springs creates is that it is all too quickly co-opted by the dominant culture. When the aptly named Phil Sheridan and George Wright, of Calvary Records, lure Coyote Springs to New York for an audition, the band self-destructs. By using the names of two generals from history who destroyed the Spokane and other Indian tribes (Sheridan and Wright), Alexie connects the contemporary context with that of the past. In both time periods the indigenous language/voice is co-opted and destroyed. Coyote Springs exits the record studio in shame, leaving their instruments behind. When they return to the reservation, they find themselves ostracized and impoverished. Overall, then, the band's music is destroyed by individualistic problems but also by larger social concerns: the inability of the people to appreciate the music, and the way the dominant culture all too quickly co-opts and undermines the music's power of subversion.

But is the music and the possibility of transmigration that it offers destroyed altogether? As I suggested earlier, although Thomas, Chess, and Checkers leave the reservation, they leave with the music, with the shadow horses to which they are singing. They thus preserve the possibility of the transmigration of the native tongue in music. In a dream the three learn a new song taught to them by Big Mom: "Big Mom taught them a new song, the shadow horses' song, the slaughtered horses' song, the screaming horses' song, a song of mourning that would become a song of celebration: we have survived, we have survived. They would sing and sing, until Big Mom pulled out that flute built of the bones of the most beautiful horse who ever lived. She'd play a note, then two, three, then nine hundred, nine thousand, nine million, one note for each of the dead Indians" (306). Revelation—such as it exists in this novel —is achieved only through respect for Big Mom and the song she teaches. Big Mom knows the tribal language and songs, and she functions as a linguistic and cultural link to the past, ensuring that "none of the Indians . . . would forget who they are" (306); in short, she is a positive figure of translative activity. She is not, as Louis Owens claims, "a cartoonish character" (*Mixedblood Messages* 78) but rather an important source of cultural knowledge, an important link to the Spokane community that existed in the past and that might continue in the present.[27] Those who disregard her advice—as do Victor and Junior—cannot survive. But those who connect with the linguistic and musical legacy of resistance that she represents survive to sing new songs, to tell new stories that transform and transmigrate the language and stories of the past. As Chess, Checkers, and Thomas leave the reservation, they cling tightly to the manes of the shadow horses running alongside the blue van. Alexie implies that the language and the legacy of the past will not be lost but will become part of the present-tense story these characters will transmigrate into the modern, urban world.

IN *Reservation Blues*, Thomas maintains a tenuous connection to the native language through Big Mom. He thereby preserves a potential ability to translate stories and an ability to sing songs and prayers in the Spokane language or hybridize these songs and prayers with English. *Indian Killer*'s ironically named Native American protagonist, John Smith, has no such link, for he is an orphan who does not even know what tribe he is from, let alone this tribe's language. He therefore can only dream of translating between a native tongue and English. John eventually commits an act of violence to find voice, but he is probably not the novel's title character, the so-called Indian Killer. The Indian Killer appears to be a Native American ritualistically scalping white men in Seattle. Whites retaliate by staging their own acts of violence against Native Americans or other dark-skinned individuals. Violence is present in all the novels I have discussed in this chapter, but *Indian Killer* is certainly the bloodiest. Does this blood originate in a translation problem? How can the ripped roots of the Native American tongue shed so much blood? And at what point does this blood itself become a kind of language? John Smith considers these questions as he contemplates killing a white man: "Which white man had done the most harm to Indians? [John Smith] knew that priests had cut out the tongues of Indians who continued to speak their tribal languages. He had seen it happen. He had gathered the tongues in his backpack and buried them in the foundation of a bank building. He had held wakes and tried to sing like Indians sing for the dead.

. . . He wanted to see fear in every pair of blue eyes" (29–30). John does not know the language of his tribe, yet he wants to "sing like Indians sing for the dead" (29). His act of violence and the violence of this novel as a whole translate the silence of the past into something that can bleed and yet *bloom* in another cultural moment.

In the contemporary moment, however, the native language exists only in vestigial and tenuous forms. For example, Native Americans greet each other with the phrase, "What tribe you are?" (31, 128, 251, 279). Although spoken in English, this sentence appears to be inflected by another syntax, another grammatical system. In a discussion of the use of nonstandard English by Native Americans, Guillermo Bartelt argues that "non-standard English monolingualism does not necessarily imply total acculturation to mainstream American values" (39), a point that Alexie's novel aptly reflects. English is broken here, but in a way that is consistent and conscious—a way that reflects the presence of other linguistic traditions sutured over by the dominant discourse. The indigenous language also continues in the elder generation who has not quite lost touch with it. For example, an older character—Sweet Lu—appears to know the Navajo language (129). The Indian Killer (whoever he is, which is never made clear) also appears to know some Native American language; he is described as silently singing an "invisibility song" (152) and as teaching other Native Americans songs and dances from the past (420).[28] And finally, Father Duncan, a Spokane who has become a Jesuit priest, sings "traditional Spokane songs and Catholic hymns" (13) as he rocks John to sleep. Father Duncan also tries to create a syncretic identity but is torn apart by this attempt. Pointing to stained glass windows that depict Jesuits being slaughtered by Native Americans, he tells John: "You see these windows? You see all of this? It's what is happening inside me right now" (15). I will return to Father Duncan's role as a translator, but it is significant that although he knows both Spokane and English and inhabits both the dominant and the marginalized culture, he is unable to translate between them or transcode his ethnicity. The novel as a whole indicates, then, that although indigenous native languages persist in vestigial forms, very few people are actively translating them in the contemporary moment.

Into this discursive landscape comes John Smith, an individual who never had the opportunity to learn his native tongue. And yet, John is no more comfortable speaking English. Like Abel, English almost seems to be a foreign language to John. Unlike Abel, John continually struggles—and fails—to express himself in English: "John . . . wanted to talk, to finally speak. To tell them about Father Duncan and the desert, the dreams he had of his life on a reservation. . . . But there was no language in which he could express himself" (377). Over and over, the text dwells on John's silences, on his inability to find his place within English.[29] In several fascinating passages, however, John dreams of learning a native language. In a chapter titled "How He Imagines His Life on the Reservation," John has the following fantasy: "John's grandparents are very traditional people and are teaching John the ways of his tribe. Ancient ways. John is learning to speak his tribal language. Sometimes, the whole family plays Scrabble using the tribal language. This is much more difficult and John always loses, but he is learning. There are words and sounds in the tribal language that have no corresponding words or sounds in English. John feels the words in his heart, but it is hard to make his mouth work that way" (44). Here John appears to be understanding the worldview implicit in the tribal language—he is feeling the language in his heart. This gives him a certain power: "John is too young for school, but is smart enough to read books. . . . John sometimes pretends that all of the difficult words, the big words with their amorphous ideas, are simple and clear. A word like democracy can become rain instead. That changes everything. John can read a phrase from his history book and change it to 'Our Founding Fathers believed in rain'" (44). John uses his knowledge of both tongues to create resistant translations of English, translations that undermine and critique hegemonic values. Our founding fathers, it seems, did not believe in democracy, and John's imagined mastery of both English and the indigenous language allows him to aggress this idea in English.

This chapter also contains a scene in which John's imagined family plays Scrabble in English, but since there are no *E* tiles left in the set they let any other letter fill in for *E*." This works well, according to John: "It has worked well. It is diplomatic. Near the end of a game, when John's rack is filled with difficult letters, *Q, Z, K,* he can always pretend they are all *E* tiles" (44). On a very basic lexical level, Alexie shows John's family taking control of English, bending its rules and syntax to support their own meanings. Cheyfitz argues that in the "revolutionary situation," as opposed to the colonial one, "the native speaker masters the master's language . . . to take possession of it, or more precisely, take up his rightful place in it. . . . The revolutionary native speaker demonstrates that the master's language has its origin not in the master but in the political needs of any people who *must* speak it" (126–27). By quite literally changing the rules of the "language game," John's family assert their place within the discourse that has attempted to silence them but that they still *must* speak. In another passage John tells stories to his imagined family that both transcode and transmigrate native culture: "He invents ancestors. He speaks the truth about grandfathers and grandmothers. He convinces his family that Shakespeare was an Indian woman" (48). John finds ancestral strength by speaking the truth about his relatives and by *reinventing* ancestors (as Kingston does in *The Woman Warrior*). But John's translation fantasy also usurps the authority of English, convincing his family that Shakespeare "was an Indian woman." In these passages John's ethnicity is also transcoded, in that it functions assertively to create sources of strength and wisdom that preexist Euro-American imposition of hegemonic values.

Yet this is a fantasy. In the "real world" of Seattle, John feels increasingly remote from any ethnicity or tribal tongue, and so his anger intensifies: "All the anger in the world has come to my house. . . . I can feel it between my teeth. Can you taste it? I hear it all the time. All the time the anger is talking to me" (200). John's anger is something he can feel in his mouth, between his teeth: quite literally, it has become his tongue. Dispossession of language is an enraging situation, as Hoffman points out, but the muteness might trans-mute, translate itself into a kind of bloody voice. Indeed, John does finally "solve" his translation problem through an act of violence. He selects as his victim a white novelist—Jack Wilson—who has claimed to be Native American and has published novels about a detective known as Aristotle Little Hawk. Throughout the text, Wilson is posited as an individual who steals the voice of Native Americans and in so doing commits a kind of transgression against them. As a Spokane woman named Marie Polatkin comments: "Books like Wilson's actually commit violence against Indians" (264). John responds to Wilson's violent voice with a violence of his own: "John slashed Wilson's face, from just above his right eye, down through the eye and cheekbone, past the shelf of the chin, and a few inches down the neck" (411). Through this action John finds a mode of voice, telling Wilson: "No matter where you go . . . people will know you by that mark. They'll know what you did. . . . You're not innocent" (411). In inscribing Wilson with this mark, John Smith turns him into a walking text recording white linguistic aggression against Native peoples.

This action frees John, but it does not save him. He hurls himself off a skyscraper just moments after saying these words. So the translation problem of this novel is not "resolved" by John's aggression against Wilson. Does the novel offer any other resolution of this problem? *Indian Killer* is a bleak and violent text, and I am uneasy with the idea that it might suggest a "resolution" to linguistic dispossession. But it does show that John's act of finding voice through violence is not an isolated event. As a Spokane man, Reggie Polatkin, comments: "Maybe the question should be something different [from whether the Indian Killer is an Indian]. Maybe you should be wondering which Indian wouldn't do it. Lots of real Indian men out there have plenty enough reasons to kill a white man" (184). The Indian Killer, Reggie implies, is not an isolated phenomena. The novel's end also suggests that such gruesome violence will grow: "The killer sings and dances for hours, days. Other Indians arrive and quickly learn the song. . . . The killer dances and will not tire. The killer knows this dance is over five hundred years old. . . . The killer never falls" (420). This image unites the killer's violence with the five-hundred-year history of linguistic dispossession in the United States and suggests that other Indian Killers will emerge if no steps are taken to restore the language that was taken away. This image also implies that such actions of violent voice will spread and in fact become the only hope of revelation: "A dozen Indians, then hundreds, and more, all learning the same song, the exact dance. . . . With this mask, with this mystery, the killer can dance forever. The killer plans on dancing forever. The killer never falls" (420). Unlike John Smith, the Indian Killer communicates his violent voice to others, teaching others the dance and the songs of the indigenous culture that will eventually destroy the whites. The Indian Killer, then, is one of the few individuals who actually *can* transcode ethnicity and transmigrate tongues; in so doing, he finds a voice of revelation—albeit a violent one.

The novel also rejects several other, less violent potential translators. One of John's friends, Marie Polatkin, attends school in Seattle and critiques courses on Native American literature taught by Anglo-American instructors who fail to understand the group of people they claim to represent. Marie wields her tongue quite handily in English, but she has never learned her tribal language, Spokane. Her parents refuse to teach her Spokane because "they felt it would be of no use to her in the world outside the reservation" (33). Since Marie does not dance or sing traditionally and she cannot speak the language, she feels "less than Indian" (33). Although Marie is a very strong character, she seems caught in a binary in which one speaks English and adapts to the dominant culture (but becomes "less than Indian") or one speaks the native language and remains isolated on the reservation. She cannot be a translation figure who draws on the strength of the ancestral language because, like John Smith, she never learns this language.

Father Duncan's problem is more complex. He is a Jesuit priest of Spokane descent who one day vanishes mysteriously in the desert. As mentioned earlier, before his disappearance he was able to translate. Indeed, the text implies that Father Duncan is seeking revelation through translation when he disappears: "Father Duncan must have been on a vision quest in the desert when he walked to the edge of the world and stepped off. Did it feel good to disappear? Perhaps Duncan, as Indian and Christian, had discovered a frightening secret and could not live with it. Perhaps Duncan knew what existed on the other side of the desert. Maybe he was looking for a new name for God" (17–18). This passage appears to imply that translation actually destroys Duncan; when he finds a new name for God, he cannot live. Furthermore, the text portrays his multilingualism as disempowering: "Father Duncan kneeled in the sand and prayed, or laughed, or cried, or maybe he did all three simultaneously. Duncan, wanting to be heard by every version of God, prayed in English, Latin, and Spokane, a confusing and painful mix of syntax, grammar, and meaning" (125). In *House Made of*

Dawn, Ceremony, and *The Grass Dancer,* multilingualism is positive —a way of breaking English apart and inflecting it with other values. But Father Duncan's multilingualism is a "painful mix of syntax, grammar, and meaning." Like John Smith, Father Duncan remains debilitated by language—even though he can translate. In the end, then, only the Indian Killer finds revelation through translation. In rejecting every other translator figure and every other instance of positive bilingualism, Alexie strongly rewrites the prior texts I have discussed as well as his own novel *Reservation Blues.* Alexie suggests that in the past as in the present, translation and violence are irrevocably linked. For those who have been dispossessed of their language, violence may be the only effective way of translating experiences. And this violence will reach out into the dominant culture, destroying whatever lies in its path. Wilson, the white novelist who has found his voice by usurping a Native American identity, is harmed by John Smith, and the Indian Killer kills several white men. The violence will grow, and the voice will become stronger.

Yet by suggesting that both whites and Native Americans are implicated and interlinked by a history of linguistic violence, *Indian Killer* presents a cautionary lesson about our past and about our future. "The killer can dance forever" (420), the novel tells us in its closing lines. But it is our responsibility to see that the killer *does not* dance forever, that the killer "finds bread and blood in other ways" (420). Kurt Spellmeyer reminds us that when we speak about the politics of language, what is *really* at stake is "a dialectic of loss and recovery, concealment and awareness, powerlessness and power on a scale so intimate and ordinary that our 'politicized' profession characteristically overlooks it" (260). But we must not overlook this—nor should we allow our students or colleagues to overlook this. We must speak this history of linguistic and cultural genocide. We must teach this history. Above all we must ensure that it is not forgotten. By recognizing the history of linguistic genocide that is the legacy of the United States, we may begin to alter this legacy, counteracting or at least amending the cycle of violence and silence. Alexie insists that the reader render this painful and violent story into a lesson about our own world and about how we as a culture have achieved our sanctioned social voice.

4

Learnin—and Not Learnin—
to Speak the King's English

Intralingual Translation in the Fiction
of Toni Morrison, Danzy Senna,
Sherley Anne Williams, and A. J. Verdelle

*When Missus Pearson talk, sound to me like some other
language. . . . She tell me . . . that I live in a country where English
is spoke and I don't know how to speak it. . . . If I could learn to
speak English, I could become more important. . . . Nobody will
ever understand you, nobody who can help you rise, unless you can
speak the language of the nation. . . . Missus Gloria Pearson say
the only thing she want me to think about is learnin to speak
the king's English.* —A. J. Verdelle, *The Good Negress*

*So you ask, why does the vernacular persist? It is because it feeds
into a whole alternative set of identities and purposes that speakers
find rewarding and valuable.* — "Holding on to a Language
of Our Own: An Interview with Linguist John Rickford"

IN DECEMBER 1996 controversy erupted when the Oakland, California, school board unanimously passed a resolution requiring all schools in the district to participate in the Standard English Proficiency (SEP) program. Begun in 1981, SEP was a statewide educational initiative that had been used effectively at Prescott Elementary School. The program emphasizes that Black English is a rule-governed form of communication and that this language can be used to help children learn to read and write in Standardized English.[1] Contrary to media assertions, then, the Oakland school board was not recommending the teaching of "Ebonics" per se, nor were they claiming that students should be encouraged to use Ebonics in all situations.[2] The SEP program emphasized the need to understand and teach the differences between African American Vernacular English and Standardized English—and the need to encourage students to move between these discourses in appropriate situations.

Although the ensuing debate in the media concerned many complex educational issues, part of this debate entailed the subject of translation: whether (and how) African American children should be taught to translate between African American codes and a more standardized and formal English. In reading over accounts of this controversy, I have noticed that numerous teachers who were involved specifically described the movement between "Ebonics" and Standardized English as one of translation. For example, in discussing her teaching practices, Carrie Secret explains that "when writing, the students are aware that finished pieces are written in English. The use of Ebonic structures appears in many of their first drafts. When this happens I simply say, 'You used Ebonics here. I need you to *translate* this thought into English'" (81, emphasis added; see also 82, 83). In discussing the use of African American literature in the classroom, Hafeezah AdamaDavia Dalji similarly states: "This is what I love about African and African-American writers. They write in Ebonics and Standard English, so students learn to *translate* the Ebonics to Standard English and the Standard English to Ebonics. They learn too that the African language is beautiful and that no language is superior or inferior. Language is just a vehicle for you to learn and get around in your environment and to express yourself" (108, emphasis added; see also 110). It is not my purpose in this chapter to discuss the Oakland controversy in detail, but I do want to suggest that the shift between African American discourses and Standardized English is a translative activity.[3] A translation perspective on African American literature examines how texts manipulate codeswitching (the movement back and forth between different dialects or languages within the same linguistic unit), but also how thematically and formally these texts fuse discourses to create a new mode of language.[4]

The novels examined in this chapter—Toni Morrison's *Tar Baby* (1981), Danzy Senna's *Caucasia* (1998), Sherley Anne Williams's *Dessa Rose* (1986), and A. J. Verdelle's *The Good Negress* (1995)—all emphasize the complex linguistic situation of contemporary African Americans and the need for translation between African American discourses and the dominant language (Standardized English).[5] In these novels, many characters are encouraged to give up the vernacular, "improper" language they speak. Some characters make this transition, but often dire consequences result, such as the loss of family, community, love, or home. Other characters learn Standardized English but also retain the vernacular tongue. They thereby move beyond binarisms and codeswitching toward a third language, a translative discourse in which aspects of the vernacular and the dominant discourse are both incorporated. In these texts, then, ethnicity is transcoded, and the ethnic language is transmigrated through the generation of linguistic hybridity. These novels also indicate that *both languages* undergo significant change and revision when they are brought together by translative activities.

All the contemporary novels discussed in this chapter are by women writers, and most feature female characters who struggle to become translators and to speak a syncretic discourse that fuses Standardized English and African American Vernacular English, the written and the oral, the language of mastery with a "minority" discourse. Of course, texts from an earlier time period by male writers—such as Charles Chesnutt's *The Conjure Woman* (1899) and Langston Hughes's "Jesse B. Simple" stories (1950–65)—also employ vernacular speech. And some more recent texts—such as Claude Brown's *Manchild in the Promised Land* (1965), John Edgar Wideman's *Damballah* (1981), and Charles Johnson's *Middle Passage* (1990)

—allude to struggles between an enfranchised language and a disenfranchised, vernacular code. Although these texts (and many others) foreground the role of the vernacular, they do not emphasize the role of the translator or the question of translation, and so I do not discuss them here. For example, in Charles Johnson's novel *Middle Passage*, the African American narrator, Rutherford Calhoun, embarks on a kind of reverse middle passage to Africa on board a slave ship. In Africa the captain of the ship buys a group of Africans known as the Allmuseri who speak a language described as "not so much like talking as the tones the savannah made at night, siffilating through the plains of coarse grass, soughing as dry wind from tree to tree" (77). They also have a written language, Rutherford tells the reader, "of such exquisite limpidity, tone colors, litotes, and contrapletes that I could not run my eyes across it from left to right, without feeling everything inside me relax" (77). To understand this written language (which consists of pictograms), you have to "look at the characters . . . as you would an old friend you've seen many times before, grasping the meaning —and relation to other characters—in a single intuitive snap" (78). To comprehend the language, in short, one has to take on the full role of the translator—to understand not just denotative meanings but also connotative and contextual ones. This would seem to be a difficult project, yet Rutherford and the rest of the crew communicate easily with the Allmuseri. How does Rutherford learn to translate? What difficulties does he encounter as a translator? Although Johnson raises the issue of linguistic difference in the text, he does not confront what might be lost in translation and what might be gained.

On the other hand, the female writers I discuss in this chapter dwell almost obsessively on the difficulties of translation. I would hypothesize that there are several reasons contemporary African American women writers foreground this struggle more than male writers. First, as discussed in the introduction and Chapter 1, women are more frequently figured as translators, as mediators between divergent and often contradictory languages and cultures. African American women writers use their status as translators to undermine disabling binary oppositions such as white over black; empowered, Standardized English over disempowered, vernacular dialect; and *also* male over female. Second, African American women, by virtue of their race *and* their gender, have a doubly dispossessed relationship to the dominant discourse, to Standardized English. Indeed, in two out of the four texts discussed below, women struggle with men who want to translate their stories and their identities *for* them—who want to claim power over a "text" that is "silent" because of both its feminine and its racialized status. A powerful trope is written into African American literature from its very beginnings in which to seize the word is to claim "manhood" and an identity as a "free man."[6] But what does the woman who seizes language become? I suggest here that the trope of translation replaces the trope of seizing the word to claim "manhood." Lastly, for these women writers, translation sometimes offers an alternative to hierarchical formulations of linguistic conflict present in many texts by male writers, formulations in which a self finds voice by "othering" a nonsubject of a different (and presumably lesser) racial or gendered status. In the texts I examine, translation can create, instead, a space in between self and "other," male and female, black and white, Standardized English and African American discourses—a space where these terms can be undermined, hybridized, or re-created. The trope of translation is prevalent in contemporary African American women's writing, then, because "the imperative to translate" is doubly inflicted on, and inflected for, these women writers and the characters they create.

Translation Themes: Toni Morrison's *Tar Baby* and Danzy Senna's *Caucasia*

The two novels I discuss in this section feature light-skinned heroines who can and do pass in various ways (socially or linguistically or both) for white. Both texts therefore employ translation between Standardized English (SE) and African American Vernacular English (AAVE) as a substantive trope integral to their main character's formulation of an identity and voice. I begin with a novel that explicitly questions whether African American languages can be preserved for individuals who inhabit a modern, urbanized, Anglocentric world. Although Morrison's *Tar Baby* is somewhat pessimistic on this subject, it is worth examining because it tells us much about why individuals give up vernacular speech. As linguist John Rickford indicates, the vernacular is crucial to preserving unconventional subject positions: "So you ask, why does the vernacular persist? It is because it feeds into a whole alternative set of identities and purposes that speakers find rewarding and valuable" (65). So what does it mean when the vernacular is lost?

Jadine, of Morrison's *Tar Baby*, appears to be quite comfortable inhabiting the modern world and speaking the dominant discourse, SE. She is a light-skinned fashion model educated in Paris; her aunt and uncle work for a wealthy white man who has funded her career. She is fluent in French as well as in Standardized English. In short, Jadine represents the fully assimilated African American woman. Perhaps her lover Son is too harsh when he calls her a "little white girl" (121), but his statement has a ring of truth. In her way of speaking, acting, and thinking, Jadine has become "white." But Jadine admits to being "run out of Paris" by the sight of a beautiful, dark-skinned African woman who makes Jadine feel "lonely and unauthentic" (48). Morrison suggests through this incident that Jadine has abandoned, rather than transcoded, her blackness and that negative consequences result from this rejection of racial identity.

Jadine's inability to translate between African American languages and Standardized English emblematizes this conflict over the transcoding of racial identity. In a crucial scene in the novel, Jadine goes to Eloe, Florida, with Son. In this rural town in the South, she discovers that she cannot speak the language: "She said yes . . . but she didn't understand at all, no more than she understood the language he was using when he talked to Soldier and Drake and Ellen and the others who stopped by . . . no more than she could understand . . . the news that some woman named Brown, Sarah or Sally or Sadie—from the way they pronounced it she couldn't tell—was dead. . . . Jadine smiled, drank glasses of water and tried to talk 'down home' like Ondine" (248, 250). Here Morrison sets up a stark contrast between the "white" world of urban sophistication that Jadine usually inhabits and Son's southern black world, and she sets up a stark contrast between the languages that are used in each domain. Jadine leaves Eloe, finally, because she considers it "rotten and more boring than ever. A burnt-out place" (259). In Eloe there is a past but no future, and Jadine needs "air, and taxicabs and conversation in a language she understood" (259). Jadine does not value AAVE or the world it embodies, and she therefore abandons it.

As the linguists Ralph Fasold and Walt Wolfram point out, there are many African Americans "whose speech is indistinguishable from others of the same region and social class" (49). In other words, not all African Americans speak AAVE, nor am I suggesting here that they must or should. Yet in *Tar Baby*, Morrison clearly uses Jadine's employment of SE, of "white" English, to suggest that the identity she has adopted is also white. And Morrison also illustrates that there are grave social consequences to this linguistic/social identity: isolation, displacement, and the inability to find a community. Morrison also establishes that Jadine chooses not to translate between languages or to create a third code that syncretizes them. Throughout the novel, Jadine mocks African American Vernacular English and the world it represents; she refuses, in short, to disarticulate it from the discourse of racism. When Son tries to explain Eloe's values to her, she mockingly sings, "Ooooo, Ah got plenty of nuffin and nuffin's plenty fo meeeeeee" (171). She associates the vernacular with poverty, with a life that goes nowhere, that is uncultured and even unlettered. In the above passage, she does attempt to "talk 'down home,'" but this attempt is rather halfhearted. Eventually Jadine returns to the world of high fashion, to the white world of cloisonné and money in which she was at ease, if not entirely contented.[7] And she reverts to the language she loves: Standardized English, a language that (from Morrison's formulation of this conflict in this particular novel) appears to cut her off from her "ancient properties" (305), leaving her adrift in the modern world.

Set in opposition to Jadine is Son, who initially appears to be somewhat more flexible in his choice of language and identity and also more capable as a translator. Son is allied with the possibilities of AAVE to remake and undermine Standardized English. He often uses AAVE, especially when he wants to manipulate whites. In the following conversation with a white man—Jadine's patron Valerian Street—Son uses AAVE to explain how he came to be in the bedroom of Valerian's wife late at night, hiding in a closet: "Yes, sir.

I uh thought I smelled oyster stew *out back* yesterday. And it got dark early, the fog I mean. They *done left* the kitchen and I thought I'd try to *get me* some. I couldn't run out the back door so *I run* through another one. It was a *dinin* room. I ran upstairs into the first room *I seen*. When I got in *I seen* it was a bedroom but thought it belong to the one *y'all* call Jadine. I *aimed to hide* there till I could get out" (147, emphasis added). I have italicized parts of speech that employ typical AAVE linguistic features such as dropped word endings ("dinin room"); pronouns used in apposition to the noun subject of the sentence ("get me some food"); use of "done" for completed action ("they done left"); doubled present-tense verbs to emphasize a continuous state ("aimed to hide"); present verb tense used to emphasize a progressive ("I seen"); and irregular but consistent conjugations of past-tense verbs ("I run through another one"). These are all features of AAVE, but one suspects that here Son is playing into Valerian's idea of him as illiterate and perhaps stupid. To use terms researched by Thomas Kochman, Son may be "shucking and jiving," which refers to "transactions involving confrontation between blacks and 'the Man.' . . . It is language behavior designed to work on the mind and emotions of the authority figure to get him to feel a certain way or give up something that will be to the other's advantage" (153). Through this linguistic performance Son convinces Valerian that there is a logical reason he has been hiding in Valerian's house for several weeks; further, he convinces Valerian to give him food, clothing, and shelter and to avoid reporting him to the police. Roger Abrahams comments that in African American communities "the ability with words is as highly valued as physical strength" (*Deep Down* 62), and one can certainly here see why. Son uses vernacular language to gain Valerian's trust and financial support and to talk his way out of a difficult situation.

Son also appears to speak a less vernacularized discourse with Jadine ("Hey. I was saying good morning to you" [117]) and an even deeper version of AAVE when he is in Eloe, Florida ("Old Man, you one crazy old man" [248]). Morrison illustrates, as numerous linguists have pointed out, that AAVE is not one language but many and that each of its dialects can be used in different situations and different contexts to communicate and empower speakers.[8] Son is fluent in the many dialects of AAVE, and he can translate between them. Yet he is not fluent in SE and at times needs Jadine to translate it for him. In fact, Jadine and Son's first sustained encounter concerns her translation of a written French text—a magazine article about her modeling career—into Standardized English for Son. But Jadine also has to translate the parts of this article written in SE before Son understands:

> "What does it say?" He put the magazine flat on the desk turned at an angle so she could read and *translate the text*. . . .
> Jadine leaned over and *translated* rapidly the important parts of the copy. . . .
> "Right here it says 'fast lane.' What's that about?" [Son asks].
> "Oh, they're trying to be hip. It says, 'If you travel as Jadine does in what the Americans call the fast lane, you need elegant but easy-to-pack frocks.'" (117, emphasis added)

Morrison illustrates that Son is a foreigner within not only French but also English—he does not know the meaning of "fast lane." In this scene of translation, Jadine appears to take on the role of translator, helping Son to master the master's language.

And yet this passage also bespeaks a struggle between Jadine and Son over who will control their relationship and whose language will be utilized—in other words, who will translate whom. The novel sets two translation figures and two discourses in opposition to each other and narrates the destruction that results. Son, in fact, expects Jadine to learn his language—and he expects to teach her to translate herself into a "black" woman. He rejects an elder's advice about Jadine and about "yellow" women: "Yallas don't come to being black natural-like. They have to choose it and most don't choose" (155). Son only responds: "She's not a yalla, . . . just a little light" (155). But the advice that the older man, Gideon, gives Son has little to do with skin color per se and more to do with racial identity: Gideon suggests that individuals like Jadine (light-skinned, urban, educated, and schooled in SE) must actively *choose* to be African American and that many do not. Son first denies this advice and then later believes he can force Jadine to embrace her "blackness": "He saw it all as a rescue: first tearing her mind away

from that blinding awe. Then the physical escape from the plantation" (219). Son believes he will rescue Jadine from the white man's
world, from mental and emotional slavery, from "the plantation."
He believes he will enable her to transcode her ethnicity so that it
signifies something positive and empowering.

Son also believes he will rescue Jadine from the language of the
whites. He wants to "blow with his own lips a gentle enough breeze
for her to tinkle in" (221). He wants to give her, in short, a language
that will move her, that will cause her to "tinkle" like a wind chime.
Yet as the continuation of this quote makes clear, Son teaches Jadine
his language to keep her within his control: "He would have to be
alert, feed her with his mouth if he had to, construct a world of
steel and down for her to flourish in" (221). What is this "world
of steel and down"? Isn't this a cage where Jadine, like a pet bird,
will be lovingly fed by Son's language, his mouth, his tongue even,
but also kept imprisoned so that she cannot fly away? So Son "insists on Eloe" (225)—he insists that this small southern town is the
center of the world. And "regarding her whole self as an ear," Son
"whispered into every part of her stories of icecaps and singing fish,
the Fox and the Stork, the Monkey and the Lion, the Spider goes
to Market" (225). Obviously, many of these stories are Afrocentric;
for example, the tale of the monkey and the lion is the story of the
Signifying Monkey, and Spider is a traditional trickster figure in
West African culture.[9] Yet by pouring these stories into Jadine's ear
and into her "whole self," Son attempts to forcibly transcode her
ethnic identity from "yalla" or "white" to "black" and to transform
her into a woman who knows her "ancient properties" (305) and
speaks the vernacular.

But Son fails, and Jadine returns to New York alone. Eventually, their relationship disintegrates. What is apparent, then, is that
Morrison's novel sets up a number of binary oppositions, such as:

Euro-American languages (SE, French)	*versus*	AAVE *and its dialects*
Jadine		Son
Individualism, isolation		Community, fraternity
Sterility		Fertility

Money	Poverty
"Success"	"Failure"
The present or future	The past
"White" identity	"Black" identity
Education	Illiteracy

As discussed in Chapter 2, these are the kinds of binarisms present in John Okada's *No-No Boy*, and like *No-No Boy*, *Tar Baby* refuses to mediate these binarisms. Part of the problem lies in Jadine and Son themselves. Neither character is willing to compromise, to move between worlds, or to move between languages and identities.[10] So these two figures remain on opposite sides of a linguistic and cultural divide. Each seeks to annihilate the other's differences, to be an abrogating translator who refuses the other's worldview. Alan Rice has explicated how Morrison's novel uses signifying and the vernacular to reclaim a "'tainted' language" (157), but I do not think Morrison's inquiry ends here. Through the linguistic contest between Son and Jadine, she indicates that both the "tainted" language (SE) and the vernacular tongue must be reclaimed, combined, and hybridized to produce something that changes both codes. Neither Son nor Jadine is willing to translate between their favored language and the disenfranchised code in order to produce something new. So when the text ends, Jadine flees back into the urban, "white" world of modeling, while Son appears to flee back into the world of his ancestors, the African American rural world of the "past."[11]

Interestingly, Morrison sets a large part of the novel on a small Caribbean island called Isle des Chevaliers, which is off the coast of Dominique (or Dominica). Jadine's patron has a home there, and it is on this island that Jadine and Son first meet. Perhaps in setting part of the action in a space that is neither African nor American, in a world between cultures, Morrison intends to introduce the possibility of an intermediary discourse that can transcend some of these binarisms. After all, many Caribbean countries have a pidgin or a creole language created by the fusion of different languages (such as African and French or English and French). In fact, the official language of Dominica today is English but a French-based creole is still spoken, especially in outlying villages. Yet in the novel none of the indigenous characters speak this creole. Thérèse Foucault, for example, has lived in Dominica all her life, and she speaks some English as well as the "the French of Dominique" (108), an uncreolized French. The novel's setting, then, gestures toward the idea of an "in-between" space where languages could be revised or reinvented, but none of the characters in the novel appear to realize the potential of creolized or hybridized languages.

As mentioned in the introduction, other novels by Morrison touch on issues of translation, although she does not investigate these issues as extensively as in *Tar Baby*. In these other novels there is, as well, some hope that individuals can create new, hybridized languages or find the "word shapes" (*Beloved* 99) to translate and tell their stories, to cross linguistic divides. For example, in *Song of Solomon*, Milkman learns how to fly—to transcend materialism and "whiteness"—only when he goes to the South, recovers the vernacular, oral story of his African ancestor Solomon and the songs of the flying Africans, and fuses them with his history in the present-tense moment, as an African American. And in *Beloved*, Paul D. and Sethe do share their stories, or parts of their stories, despite the "forest" (165) that springs up between them. Sethe is also finally rescued from the past by the women of her town, whose song searches "for the right combination, the key, the code, the sound that broke the back of words" (261). Like Bull's cry at the end of *No-No Boy*, the women's song suggests a return of language to its roots in pure sound and a rebirthing that perhaps offers the potential for a new language. Such a rebirth is never achieved by Son or Jadine in *Tar Baby*. Ultimately, they fail to become translators between AAVE and SE, and they fail to transcode themselves out of their enclosed, limited, monolingual worlds.

Like the others examined in this chapter, Morrison's novel depicts translation as an intralingual and even an intracultural problem. *Tar Baby* does not, on the face of it, enunciate a conflict between a white society that tries to force its language down the throat of the "other" and an ethnic tongue, as has been the case in many other texts discussed in this book. Rather, this conflict occurs between two individuals *within* the African American community —Jadine and Son—and between the languages that this community *might* speak. *Tar Baby*, like *Caucasia*, also raises the question of what race/language the lighter-skinned individual will choose. In such works discussed in Chapter 3 as *Ceremony* and *House Made of Dawn*, it is the "mixed-breed" individual who inhabits a middle ground between languages and cultures and who therefore has more need to become a translator and (perhaps) more facility at bridging languages and cultures. I suggest here that the light-skinned African American individual sometimes takes up a similar role. She or he can choose to "be" white and speak in SE; sometimes she or he can even choose to pass. Or the individual can refuse SE and embrace a "black" identity. But texts such as *Tar Baby* and *Caucasia* impute that there needs to be a third option—a way the light-skinned individual can be *both* black and white and can hybridize SE and AAVE to produce a new code that moves beyond the notion of the "separation" and compartmentalization of languages and racial identities.

These issues are foregrounded in Danzy Senna's *Caucasia*, which concerns two sisters—Birdie and Cole Lee—who are separated when their white mother flees Boston because she fears she will be implicated in a political crime. The father, Deck, who is African American, keeps the darker-skinned daughter (Cole) with him, and the mother (Sandy) takes Birdie (who is light enough to pass for white) with her. After a number of years of passing as a white, Jewish girl named Jesse Goldman, Birdie resolves to find her sister, and the novel ends with their reunion. As we will see, Birdie is extremely skillful at adapting herself linguistically and socially to the environments she inhabits. But is Birdie perhaps too good at translating? Does she eventually lose her own voice? Birdie is very aware of subtleties of language—of accents, dialects, and vernaculars. She struggles to connect this knowledge to herself as a racial individual and to understand the link between "self" and discourse.

I alluded above to the fact that in *Tar Baby*, many languages are present (French, English, slang, African American vernaculars, and so on) but that Son and Jadine seem to reduce this number to only two. Birdie is more aware of what Werner Sollors calls the multilingualism of America, and she pays careful attention not only to the various dialects she hears but also to the way these dialects *sound*—to the various accents present in English. She learns this skill from her mother, who "was prejudiced against three accents in the world: the German accent, the white Southern accent, and the Boston accent. All three made her suspect a person of great evil" (295). Accent is here somewhat humorously correlated with identity, although Sandy's statement is meant to be read as slightly paranoid, a feature of her personality in the novel in general. In the United States, however, anyone with a "white" or Euro-American accent appears to feel that he or she has the right to claim "American" identity. Irish American girls from Roxbury, for example, tell Cole to *"go back to the jungle, darkie. Go wash your ass. Go, you little culahd biscuit"* (40). By italicizing these words, Senna clearly indicates they are spoken in an accent, in a kind of "foreign" dialect. Yet in the hierarchy of accents in the United States, it appears the Irish American individual's accent is marked (or rather in this scene marks itself) as "American," whereas the African American individual, even one who speaks standardized, unaccented English, is construed as foreign, a "darkie" from the "jungles" of Africa.[12] Interestingly, one of AAVE's most distinctive and frequently commented-on features is its patterns of accent, stress, and pronunciation (for example, *"po*lice" rather than "po*lice"*; "truf" instead of "truth"; "axe" for "ask"; and so forth). Senna here overturns a common binary about accents: AAVE (and other ethnic discourses) are accented, marked, stressed, and emphatic, while "white" English is unaccented, unmarked, unstressed, and unemphatic.[13] Through Birdie, Senna notes the discursive and pronunciation diversity that exists *within* white English.

Senna also uses her character to indicate how accents inscribe social identities as "American" or "foreign," as "empowered" or "disempowered," as "literate" or "illiterate." Chameleon-like, Birdie becomes very adept at imitating accents in order to fit in. When she wants to be accepted as a "WASP," she speaks in an imitation of this dialect: "Sometimes, when I was with the Marshes, I would secretly imagine I was the daughter they never had. And sometimes I got carried away with my fantasy and would start talking differently, affectedly, trying to imitate Libby's long nasal drawl, and using expressions I had heard Nicholas use, as if they were my own" (194). Accent here allows Birdie to "pass" into a new identity, a new version of herself. And with the "townie" girls Birdie meets in New

Hampshire, she uses language as a badge of power but also a mask of her "true" self: "I talked the talk, walked the walk, swayed my hips to the sound of heavy metal, learned to wear blue eyeliner and frosted lipstick and snap my gum. And when I heard those inevitable words come out of Mona's mouth, Mona's mother's mouth, Dennis's mouth—nigga, spic, fuckin' darkie—I only looked away into the distance" (233). She remains calm about racist jokes and remarks because she believes that her real self is "hidden beneath my beige flesh," "preserved, frozen solid" (233).

Earlier in her life, when Birdie was at an Afrocentric school called Nkrumah, she learned to speak AAVE and to translate between AAVE and SE. Here, too, Senna indicates that Birdie is a careful observer of languages but also that these languages, and the identities that go along with them, must be learned and performed. For example, in the following scene, Cole teaches Birdie and herself how to translate between SE and AAVE:

"We talk like white girls, Birdie." She picked up the magazine she had been reading, and handed it to me. "We don't talk like black people. It says so in this article."

I glanced at the article. The heading read, "Black English: Bad for Our Children?"

The magazine was *Ebony*. . . .

Cole continued: "They have examples·in here. Like, don't say, 'I'm going to the store.' Say, 'I'm goin' to de sto'.' Get it? And don't say, 'Tell the truth.' Instead, say, 'Tell de troof.' Okay?" (53)

As we will see, this scene reverses many episodes in *The Good Negress*, where the young heroine is instructed *out of* AAVE. Here, Cole and Birdie must be instructed into what is supposed to be "their" language. Cole's father also tries to teach Cole his version of Black English—a politicized black power dialect. But only Birdie picks this up: "'Salaam Aleikum,' I greeted my father one afternoon as I clambered into his car. Another time I kissed him good-bye on the check, saying, 'Stay black, stay strong, brotherman'" (75). Birdie excels at picking up new dialects and the new identities that she believes these dialects confer. Like Olivia in *The Floating World* (discussed in Chapter 2), Birdie possesses a translating consciousness that "exploits the potential openness of language systems" (Devy, "Translation and Literary Theory" 185).

To be a social success at Nkrumah, Birdie must speak AAVE and change herself into someone who is "black." This is not easy for a child who looks so "white" that her father is once almost arrested for "kidnapping" her (58–61). Birdie wears her straight hair in a tight braid to mask its texture, buys hoops for her ears, and dresses like her "black" sister. But to translate herself into a "black" identity, she also must master the language: "I stood many nights in front of the bathroom mirror, practicing how to say 'nigger' the way the kids in school did it, dropping the 'er' so that it became not a slur, but a term of endearment: *nigga*" (63). Later in her life Birdie thinks about speaking AAVE to an audience of Nkrumah students and has even decided on a series of titles for her talk: "What White People Say When They Think They're Alone," "Honkified Meanderings: Notes from the Underground," or "Let Me Tell Ya 'bout Dem White Folks" (189). Birdie considers herself both a linguist and a translator—she carefully studies dialects ("what white people say") but also the power dynamics correlated with specific languages and linguistic identities. Wahneema Lubiano comments that the African American "vernacular is perfectly constituted to undermine ironically whatever dominant language form it employs. In other words, it stands in deconstructive relation to the dominant language whether by using the dialect and syntactical structure of 'black English' or by subverting standard English dialect" (96). Whether Birdie uses AAVE or SE, she subverts the power dynamics implicit within these languages by moving back and forth between them, and Senna is clearly signifying on and mocking the white tradition of linguistic empowerment *through* SE.

At times Birdie is also a translating link between "whiteness" and "blackness." For example, when Cole grows closer to her father and does not want to speak to her mother, Birdie acts "as the go-between, shouting out messages between them like a translator of foreign tongues" (84). Interestingly, in this construction Birdie marks herself as a "foreigner" in both tongues—the "white" tongue of the mother and the "black" tongue of the sister. The translator is a link between divergent tongues and cultures, but this is frequently an uncomfortable position; Birdie appears to be homeless, a foreigner lacking a language of "selfhood." She asserts that she learns the art of "changing" at Nkrumah, a skill that would later become second nature to her: "There I learned how to do it for real —how to become someone else, how to erase the person I was before" (62). Senna asks us to consider what identity—if any—the translator has. As she translates herself to a new language/identity, does she disappear?

It could be argued that, like *Tar Baby*, Senna's text constructs a number of binarisms:

AAVE	*versus*	*SE*
Father		Mother
"Black" identity		"White" identity
Cole		Birdie

Yet Senna's text continually undermines such oppositions. Birdie's African American father, Deck, for example, is a Harvard-educated professor more comfortable speaking SE than AAVE. And Cole, as illustrated above, actually has to learn AAVE, a language in which the "white" Birdie becomes more fluent. Furthermore, Birdie's ability to continually master and adapt herself to new languages and identities suggests that such a binary separation of language and identity is arbitrary rather than real or absolute. Most radical, however, there is also a language in this text that the two girls speak together which might undermine the binary division of AAVE versus SE and which might combine these languages. Called "Elemeno," Cole and Birdie invent and speak this language when they are young. Senna suggests that Elemeno has the ability to cross thresholds between languages and cultures and to be (at least imaginatively and in private) a hybrid language which allows for "transculturación," a zone of "impassioned margin" where diverse cultures converge without merging (Pérez Firmat, *Cuban Condition* 26).

This language is described at the start of the book, and it is constantly associated with Cole: "Before I ever saw myself, I saw my sister. When I was still too small for mirrors, I saw her as the reflection that proved my own existence. . . . The face was me and I was the face and that was how the story went. . . . We even spoke our own language. Cole insists that it began before I was born, when I was just a translucent ball in my mother's womb" (5). Initially, this seems to be a preoedipal language associated with an undifferentiated stage of infantile oneness. Later, however, after Birdie has learned to distinguish herself from Cole, the language continues to grow: "Later we perfected the language in our attic bedroom. . . . It was a complicated language, impossible for outsiders to pick up—no verb tenses, no pronouns, just words floating outside time and space without owner or direction. . . . My father described the language as a 'high-speed patois.' . . . My grandmother said . . . we spoke in tongues. Cole and I just called it 'Elemeno' after our favorite letters in the alphabet" (6). But Elemeno is not merely a language; it is also a culture, a place, and a people. Cole tells Birdie that the Elemeno people "could turn not just from black to white, but from brown to yellow to purple to green, and back again. She said they were a shifting people, constantly changing their form, color, pattern, in a quest for invisibility" (7). Like Birdie, then, the Elemenos can change color and language. In a book highly sensitive to language and what it represents for particular formulations of ethnic identity, we might say that Elemeno initially represents a language of camouflage, one that allows the subject to assume a new identity but in so doing to perhaps "disappear" into this new identity and surroundings.

Yet once Birdie is separated from Cole, Elemeno becomes a way of preserving the "old" identity Birdie once had as a sister to an African American sibling, Cole. As the novel progresses, Birdie comes to associate Elemeno with Africanness, and with an identity as an African American. Birdie is fascinated by a West African god, Exu-Elegba (which Gates speaks of as the "Signifying Monkey"), who represents, Birdie says, "potentiality and change" (242). From a book on Candomblé (a Brazilian/West African religion), Birdie learns that this god is "a trickster, always shifting his form, always at the crossroads" (242), and his face seems to Birdie "amorphous, unfinished" (242). Exu-Elegba is clearly an analogy for Birdie's own constantly unfinished, constantly transforming, constantly in-process identity. Like the Elemenos, Exu-Elegba may disappear into his surroundings, as Birdie sometimes seems to. No wonder, then, that Birdie prays to this god in Elemeno: "I whispered under my breath a little prayer that I made up. A prayer in Elemeno. A prayer to Exu, the God of Change, the God of Potential" (244).[14]

Elemeno starts as a language of transformation of self, then, yet it eventually becomes a language of self and racial reclamation, a language that allows ethnicity to be transcoded. Elemeno is also a language that allows for the self to be continually shifting, but still located or perhaps "placed" by familial and racial bonds. Speaking Elemeno connects Birdie to "the real story of my father and sister" and means that Cole can remain "clear as sunlight" in Birdie's memory (191). When Birdie finally decides to find her sister, to stop being Jesse Goldman and return to being Birdie Lee, she repeats a pattern of words under her breath, words she no longer understands but whispers just the same, words in Elemeno: "*kublica marentha doba. lasa mel kin*" (289). Elemeno, then, appears to be the tentative link to her sister as well as a link to a racial (and not invisible) subject position Birdie might inhabit.

When Birdie and Cole are reunited, it is not surprising that Cole speaks in "broken Elemeno," which Birdie at first does not understand. But, gradually, Senna tells us:

Then it began to come back to me.
simapho. nooli stadi. beltin caruse mestiz jambal. kez wannaba. fello mao-tao burundi. simapho. ki wo fela.
We talked about where each of us had been. (405)

Elemeno is no longer a pure, preoedipal language: it is now broken and fractured by knowledge and loss. But it can still speak where each woman has been—metaphorically and actually. And, finally, the language allows Birdie to claim her own face, her own racial identity—to make a choice at last about what she will "be." Shortly after this reunion with Cole and Elemeno, Birdie sees a "cinnamon-skinned girl with her hair in braids" looking out a bus window and is able to say that "she was black like me, a mixed girl" (413). Birdie is able to claim her status as both "black" and "mixed" specifically through a reunion with Elemeno and with her sister Cole (who, it should be noted, is also described as "cinnamon-skinned" [5]). Like many works of passing by African American writers, *Caucasia* finally suggests that racial identity is not biological or essential but a choice one makes.[15] Birdie chooses to be "black" and to claim this as a somewhat stable identity, even as she enunciates that she is also "mixed." Birdie claims, then, an identity-in-process, but also one that sees her race as more than a fiction. Birdie's father, Deck, insists that "race is a complete illusion, make-believe. It's a costume" (391), to which Birdie responds: "If race is so make-believe, why did I go with Mum? You gave me to Mum 'cause I looked white. You don't think that's real? Those are the facts" (393). Somewhere between the theory that race is a total social fiction and the idea of essentialism (race as biological), Birdie claims that race does matter, it does count, it does signify. And Elemeno symbolizes a language that allows Birdie to claim a self-in-process that is also, still, a racial self.

I have suggested that Elemeno is a language that finally allows Birdie to reconnect with and transcode her "blackness." And yet what are we to make of the fact that the very name itself—Elemeno—is composed of letters from the *English* alphabet? Furthermore, many of the words spoken by the girls in Elemeno sound like a corruption of Standardized English: "wannaba" could be "wannabe" or "want to be"; "simapho" could be "simple"; "mel kin" could be "my kin." Therefore, although Elemeno is associated with Cole, with Africa, and with a racial identity, it may also be created by a corruption, bastardization, or creolization of English. Elemeno may be a language that transmigrates both an African tongue and English; symbolically, it may be the hybrid discourse located somewhere between hegemonic, standardized language and ethnic discourse. Elemeno may be the language of translation, mediation, and transformation that Son and Jadine were unable to find. Perhaps Elemeno brings English into contact with other cultures so that it can be transformed. And perhaps it creates, in Homi K. Bhabha's notion, a "third space," a space in between where Birdie and Cole may "elude the politics of polarity and emerge as . . . [their] selves" (*Location of Culture*, 38–39). What is clear, however, is that it is a private and familial language that eventually allows Birdie to claim a public racial identity. Through the semimythical language of Elemeno, she translates between her blackness and her whiteness, finally creating a self that takes account of *both* racial heritages.

Hybrid Translation Forms: Sherley Anne Williams's
Dessa Rose and A. J. Verdelle's *The Good Negress*

I turn now to two novels that embed the topic of translation into the very form and languages the texts speak: Sherley Anne Williams's *Dessa Rose* and A. J. Verdelle's *The Good Negress*. Both novels are, quite literally, novelistic hybrids. Mikhail Bakhtin argues that "the novelistic hybrid is *an artistically organized system for bringing different languages in contact with one another*, a system having as its goal the illumination of one language by means of another, the carving-out of a living image of another language" (361). For Bakhtin, hybridization is a contestatory activity, having as its goal the setting of different voices against each other so that authoritative discourse can be unmasked. *Dessa Rose* and *The Good Negress* set SE and AAVE against each other to undermine the power of the dominant discourse, but they also indicate the difficulty of separating the "language of mastery" from the "marginal," oral, vernacular discourse. Both texts translate SE, then, not only to contain or undermine its power but also to show that the power of *both* SE and AAVE must be harnessed to create individuals who can navigate the multiple linguistic terrains of their worlds, transcode ethnicity, and renovate the language of hegemony.

In *Dessa Rose*, Williams takes two separate historical incidents and unites them to create "the other history" (x). In 1829 a pregnant African American woman helped lead an uprising on a coffle (a group of slaves chained together for transport); she was sentenced to death, but her hanging was delayed until after the birth of her baby. In North Carolina in 1830, a white woman was reported to be giving sanctuary to runaway slaves on her isolated plantation. These two women never met, but Williams's novel is a fictional rendering of what might have happened if they had. The novel begins when the slave woman, whom Williams names Dessa Rose, is interviewed by a white man, Nehemiah Adams, for a book he is writing on slavery called *The Roots of Rebellion in the Slave Population and Some Means of Eradicating Them* (or *Roots*). Nehemiah is a parody of the white, male, racist historian, determined to get his "story" by any means. But Dessa tells her story in a roundabout fashion that Nehemiah (called Nemi) cannot follow, and she is lib-

erated by other slaves before he can get "the facts" (34). Dessa takes
shelter with a white woman named Miss Rufel (or Ruth), and eventually she and Dessa become friends and engineer a permanent liberation of the slaves who have sought refuge on Ruth's plantation.
Dessa's son is born during the course of the narrative, and at the
end Ruth goes east and the slaves find safe haven in the American
West.

The novel's primary linguistic questions center on who will
translate Dessa's story: the white, male historian (who would like
to write it in SE, in "factual," direct English) or Dessa herself or her
representative (who would like the story to contain elements of oral,
vernacular expression). Yet Williams constantly undermines such
a separation of languages. This is apparent even from the opening
"Author's Note," in which Williams speaks of feeling "outraged by
a certain, critically acclaimed novel of the early seventies that trav-
estied the as-told-to-memoir of slave revolt leader Nat Turner" (ix).
Williams and many other critics believe that the novel spoken of
here (William Styron's *The Confessions of Nat Turner*) served as a
false translation of the "original" Nat Turner narrative. But Williams's point also concerns written Standardized English: "Afro-
Americans, having survived by word of mouth—and made of that
process a high art—remain at the mercy of literature and writing;
often, these have betrayed us. I loved history as a child, until some
clear-eyed young Negro pointed out, quite rightly, that there was
no place in the American past I could go and be free" (ix–x). History, language, "fact," and writing often betray and imprison African Americans, who survive by orality, by word of mouth, by
the vernacular. However, this formulation is quickly undermined
by Williams's own writing of a novel that is "fiction" but also "as
true as if I myself had lived it" (x). The writing of the novel allows
Williams to claim a summer in the nineteenth century (x), that is,
to recover a piece of African American history. Since parts of the
novel are written in SE, SE and writing do not always betray African
Americans. When combined with other forms of language, SE and
written language can help speak "the other history" (x).

How is it that Williams's use of SE and writing can speak African American history, while Styron's betrays it? Perhaps this has
something to do with the different kinds of translations—of the

past, of history, and of language—that each writer employs. I read Williams's text as endorsing a mode of translation that is flexible, multimodal, and dialogic, and Styron's text (as read by Williams) as employing an abrogating, colonizing, univocal mode of translation. These contrasts between modes of translation are also thematized by the struggle between Dessa and Nemi with which the novel opens. Nemi constantly attempts to contain and reduce Dessa's voice and story. He sees her as a "nigger wench" and wants to get the "facts of the darky's history" (34) out of her by whatever methods are necessary, including punishment, torture, and starvation. But he fails to understand that Dessa's "loquacious, round-about fashion" (16) of telling her story is actually part of the story's meaning.

Certainly Dessa avoids responding directly to Nemi's questions to shield those who have escaped, yet she also has another agenda. In these early encounters, Dessa struggles to be a resistant translator of her experience rather than a translated text. By narrating her story, she attempts to translate it out of silence and into meaningfulness: "She saw the past as she talked, not as she had lived it but as she had come to understand it. . . . She had lost Kaine, become a self she scarcely knew, lost to family, to friends. So she talked" (56). Although Nemi thinks he controls the situation and the terms of the translation, he does not. Dessa answers in a roundabout way, sings and hums when asked a direct question, and constantly makes the translation practices serve *her* purposes. She exercises a great deal of critical literacy, even playing with Nemi and signifying on him: "Talking with the white man was a game; it marked time and she dared a little with him, playing on words, lightly capping, as though he were no more than some darky bent on bandying words with a likely-looking gal" (59). Dessa's ability to signify grants her a kind of power over the white man and enables her to turn Nemi's questions back upon themselves so that no factual information is obtained. As Geneva Smitherman and many other linguists have shown, signifying, playing the dozens, and language games are integral to African American communities. Such games are not "mere" entertainment; they also confer power and status.[16] Smitherman argues that indirection and ambiguous meanings were also a way that slaves spoke in the oppressor's language but still maintained their own identity ("Black Language" 104). Dessa gains power and control over Nemi through signifying, but she also retains her own mode of voice through this linguistic practice. But Nemi only sees Dessa's indirection as a flaw in her speech.

Nemi also fails to understand another aspect of the African American vernacular—the call-and-response messaging sometimes contained in songs. So Nemi thinks that Dessa's singing is mere entertainment when in fact she uses songs to ask and get answers to her questions about when she will be liberated from her jail cell (67). Nemi is totally surprised by Dessa's escape, for example, but Dessa has been forewarned in a song the white man hears but fails to understand, a song that tells her that "the Lawd have called you home" (64).

The initial scenes of the novel, then, appear to undermine expected binarisms:

SE	versus	AAVE
Nemi		Dessa
Power		Powerlessness
Written discourse		Spoken, oral discourse
Direction		Indirection
Speech		Songs, chants
Fact		Dreams, emotions, "fiction"

But I am most interested in how the actual language and form of the novel also undermine such binarisms. Williams seeks a language like Senna's Elemeno—one that can translate between black and white, past and present, oral and written, SE and AAVE. But, more realistically than Senna, Williams illustrates how such a language might sound and what it might look like, as well as how it might undermine oppositions.

First, it must be noted that in Williams's novel both whites and blacks appear to speak various vernacular dialects; for example, Ruth and Hughes (a white slave driver) speak in a southern, vernacular discourse.[17] So the opposition of "proper," Standardized English = white and "improper," vernacular English = black is complicated. Second, a number of oral elements of language are added into the written text of the novel, such as songs (2), call-

and-response (62), and choruses of voices rather than one speaker (3). The binary of SE = written and AAVE = oral is therefore also undermined. Further, there is a constant and fluid switching back and forth between SE and AAVE and, moreover, slippage between who speaks what discourse. In the initial scenes of the novel, for example, Nemi mainly employs SE and Dessa uses AAVE. Yet his recounting of these incidents in his journal shows Nemi actually codeswitching between SE and AAVE: "'I kill white mens,' her voice overrode mine, as though she had not heard me speak. 'I kill white mens cause the same reason Masa kill Kaine. Cause I can.' [says Dessa]. It had been an entrancing recital, better in its way than a paid theatrical [comments Nemi]" (13). The subtle intertwinement in this passage of SE and AAVE, and of Nemi and Dessa's discourse, speaks to Williams's larger thematic message: the disempowered voice sometimes does speak for itself, overriding the dominant discourse. Interestingly, it is probable that Dessa never makes these statements, that Nemi has misconstrued her words. But even in his misconstrual Nemi mixes his discourse with Dessa's, and his language is not pure and uncorrupted; even in the white man's fantasy of blackness, of otherness, and of what blackness "speaks," the vernacular, minority discourse cannot be separated from Standardized English.

Later in the novel, it becomes apparent that Nemi's SE has slipped into the vernacular discourse and, further, that at times Dessa manipulates the dominant discourse *better* than Nemi does. In a crucial scene toward the end of the novel, Nemi finds Dessa and wants to prove she is an escaped slave by having her disrobe and show her scars. "Ware the goods!" (which translates as "Beware of the goods!") shouts Dessa to the sheriff, knowing that this is what is said on a coffle when a pretty woman is being protected from rape so that she can be sold as a "fancy trade" (243). Dessa here manipulates and employs the discourse of slavery, but in the scene as a whole her language is at least as "proper" as Nemi's, as the following conversation shows:

> "*I belongs* to Miz Carlisle," I said, "staying down to the hotel. I *takes care* of her baby, Clara—. . . ."
> "That's all a lie, sheriff. . . . When I caught up with her she

swore she belonged to some Suttons. *This a* dangerous criminal
and I want her held."

"Master, I never *seen* this master before in my life."

"The one *I wants* got scars all over her butt. . . . Let's have
that dress off; let her prove she *ain't* the one." (243, emphasis
added)

As indicated by my italics, both Dessa and Nemi speak vernacular
English; moreover, as the scene goes on, Nemi's language becomes
less and less "proper" (245). It seems, then, that rather than translating Dessa's story, Nemi has been translated by her. Crucially, his
speech, the discourse of the "master," has also been changed, translated, transmigrated, by its encounter with the vernacular, "improper" dialect. Nemi is no longer the empowered, white subject
who speaks SE but is, quite literally, a half insane, deranged, dirty,
unkempt white man who speaks a language that even the white
sheriff finds confusing.

There are many other examples of how the novel constantly
shifts discourses and undermines the binary of empowered, SE
speech over unempowered, AAVE dialect. But I wish to stress that
not all these examples are negative. Ruth and Dessa, for example, mingle words and languages at the end of the novel: "Maybe
we couldn't speak so honest without disagreement, but that didn't
change how I feel. 'Ruth,' 'Dessa,' we said together; and 'Who was
that white man—?' 'That was the white man—' and stopped. We
couldn't hug each other, not on the streets, not in Acropolis, not
even after dark; we both had sense enough to know that. The town
could even bar us from laughing; but that night we walked the
boardwalk together and we didn't even hide our grins" (246). Dessa
narrates this passage but, most crucially, her narration not only
moves back and forth between SE and AAVE but also represents
Ruth's voice; Ruth's language, in other words, is not translated into
Dessa's. A mode of translation is employed here that is polyvocal
and dialogic—a mode of translation that does not contain the story
but releases it.[18]

I have been discussing how *Dessa Rose* is a novelistic hybrid on
the level of its speech patterns, but I now want to turn briefly to
two other aspects of its formal hybridity: its genre, and its final nar-

ration of the creation of the text as text. I have already noted that the novel is composed of both SE and AAVE, songs, chants, dreams, choruses of voices, and multiple points of view (Ruth's, Nemi's, Dessa's, and so forth). There is a kind of bricolage of narrative discourses here, as well as a bricolage of genres. The novel employs and makes references to aspects of the slave narrative genre. At times it also reads like a classic tale of female bonding and even a romance (a "bodice ripper"). At other times it reads like a "road novel," especially when the slaves go "on the road" to earn the money that will allow them to go west by selling themselves into slavery and then escaping. The novel reflects a strange fusion, or even stew, of genres. But how exactly does this novel come to be "told"? Initially, we know, Nemi is determined to write Dessa's story, but his book falls to pieces when he waves it in front of the sheriff to "condemn" Dessa:

> "Here," he say, shaking it in my face. Clara reached for the book and knocked it out his hand. The pages wasn't bound in the cover and they fell out, scattering about the floor. Nemi started grabbing the papers. . . .
> "Nemi, ain't nothing but some scribbling on here," sheriff say. "Can't anyone read this."
> Miz Lady was turning over the papers in her hand "And these is blank, sheriff," she say. (255)

Quite literally the master's book, the "master's pieces," are undermined, deconstructed, rendered impotent by this scattering. In this scene Dessa clutches some of Nemi's pages in her hand. I hypothesize that when Dessa does finally tell her story, she incorporates Nemi's translation of her story into the narrative that she creates. Therefore, the final text that is *Dessa Rose* is told by Dessa but it contains the master's voice, Nemi's "facts," the master's forms and language, even as it undermines them.

Even more important, Dessa's oral narrative is preserved within the confines of written discourse. The book narrates its own construction as a text on its final pages, when Dessa states: "*I hopes I lives for my people like they do for me, so sharp sometimes I can't believe it's all in my mind. And my mind wanders. This why I have it wrote down, why I has the child say it back. I never will forget Nemi trying to read me, knowing I had put myself in his hands. Well, this the childrens have heard from our own lips"* (260). Dessa never learns to read and write, so she does not have the written language to record her own story. But she does want her tale to be preserved as an antidote to "Nemi trying to read me." So she has her child Mony write it, but she also has him read (or rather "say") it back to her: "This why I have it wrote down, why I has the child say it back." Certainly, as Marta Sánchez argues, Dessa "critically appropriates the language of the dominant culture to subvert its power" (33). But does Dessa's "black English become the very center of culture" (Marta Sánchez 33), and does Williams therefore dismiss "the legitimizing power of official discourse," as Andrée-Anne Kekeh claims (225)?[19] Which is privileged here: the oral telling of the tale in AAVE, or the literate writing of it in a variety of languages? The oral, vernacular story and the written discourse that is Dessa's history exist in a tenuous balance *together* in the text that finally is *Dessa Rose*.[20]

Hybridity here is not only (or not exclusively) contestatory; rather, literary hybridity becomes a way of taking power from different sources. I think it is important that Williams finally refuses to choose *between* SE and AAVE but suggests that they can exist together, in something like a peaceful coexistence, in a person, in a text, and perhaps even in a world. "Linguistic differences cannot be dealt with in the same manner in which Americans have come to terms with racial or religious differences," comments Joseph Magnet (298). Linguistic differences should not simply be annihilated or translated out of existence. Texts such as Williams's recoup the "other" stories and the "other" languages that are overwritten by the dominant narrative, the dominant language. Yet such texts also show the flowering and growth of the oral and vernacular language within written English. The language of hegemony is therefore both undermined and re-created through transmigration of the ethnic tongue.[21]

The best translators, it seems, both undermine the dominant discourse and utilize the power of *all* the languages to which they have access. This is clearly the case in A. J. Verdelle's novel *The Good Negress*. After the death of her father, Denise, the young African American heroine of this novel, is transplanted from Detroit to her grandmother's house in Virginia so that her mother can work full-time. After five years in the South, Denise is moved back to Detroit when her mother needs help caring for the baby she is having with her second husband. By this time Denise has fully adopted AAVE, and in terms of the linguistic conflicts she faces, she almost seems to have come from a foreign country: "When [my teacher] Missus Pearson talk, sound to me like some other language" (123). Denise continues: "She tell me . . . that I live in a country where English is spoke and I don't know how to speak it. . . . If I could learn to speak English, I could become more important. . . . Nobody will ever understand you, nobody who can help you rise, unless you can speak the language of the nation" (122–23). Intralingual translation struggles are foregrounded in the text, as Denise attempts to move from her southern, "cakky-lakky" (112) language—which is not considered to be English—to the language which is supposed to be spoken in the North ("the king's English"). Furthermore, as in the other novels discussed, translation also takes on metaphorical significance as a valence or register for ethnic identity. In a discussion of the Ebonics controversy, James Collins claims that "standard English is perceived as 'the language of business,' and as acquirable stuff that allows the possessor to advance in the great chain of being; it has no memory of group, no burden of history. Like a state church, it is open to all, requiring only of the heretofore non-standard speaker that she come alone, with no group and no history" (216). Denise initially attempts to translate between her teacher's social identity for her (in which she forgets her group history as an African American) and her own sense of who she is. In *The Good Negress*, however, a true intralingual, syncretic, transmigrated voice is eventually enacted; Denise does not simply pick between the languages available to her but, like Dessa, creates a new code through hybridization and translation. And certainly this new code enables the renovation of ethnic identity, the disarticulation of blackness from the discourse of racism.

In *Siting Translation*, Tejaswini Niranjana argues that translation can produce "strategies of containment. By employing certain modes of representing the other—which it thereby also brings into being—translation reinforces hegemonic versions of the colonized" (2). Applying this idea to Verdelle's novel, we might say that Denise is initially expected to learn Standardized English because only through its mastery can she obtain a status as an individual who is no longer (or at least not entirely) colonized. Translation also initially entails assimilation to hegemony and hegemonic language. Denise's African American teacher, Missus Pearson, tells her that "learning to speak proper English is absolutely necessary for all Americans. . . . People come to America thousands at a time, and they would give an arm to have the opportunity to learn rules of English grammar and pronunciation, to learn to speak proper English" (118). Denise is here portrayed as an immigrant who must give up her own language in order to become an empowered citizen of the new nation.

Missus Pearson also continually refers to Denise's need to learn "the king's English" (119). Of course, in the United States there has never been a king, so what does this phrase mean? If Denise masters "the king's English," will she become a royal subject—part of the colonizing nation, rather than the colonized? This seems to be Missus Pearson's logic. So over and over again, she tells Denise that her southern dialect is atrocious (104), not English (161, 192), and just plain "Wrong. Wrong. Wrong" (189). Pearson also claims that Denise's "separate speech" is "difficult . . . to understand" (160)—conveniently ignoring the fact that members of Denise's family and speech community seem to have little problem with it. Mastery of SE also means conformity to a white norm of African American identity. Missus Pearson tells Denise that "if [she] could learn to speak English, [she] could become more important" and that "nobody who sounds dumb will ever be important" (123). "Sounding dumb" and speaking the vernacular are equated. More problematic, transcending the vernacular is equated with transcending one's racial position. Pearson has very specific ideas about what kind of life Denise will make for herself, and she disapproves of Denise's afterschool job at a store, telling her: "You will never get over being colored. You have no business down to that store. . . . They got you in there cleaning toilets, making you a good little negress" (209). In another context, the psychiatrist Frantz Fanon argues that "the negro of the Antilles will be proportionately whiter . . . in direct ratio to his mastery of the French language" (18), adding, "In every country of the world there are climbers, the ones who forget who they are and, in contrast to them, the ones who remember where they came from" (37). Pearson is clearly a "climber" who wants to forget who she is and who wants to make Denise forget where she came from (a rural, southern, African American community). In Pearson's formulation, ethnic identity (being "colored") is something one "gets over" if one wishes to succeed within hegemonic discourse and culture.

Yet the above passage suggests that Pearson has not transcended her race (as she would like to believe she has) or the "improper" speech of her race. "You have no business down to that store" she states, and Denise notes that "the fault in her English was like a chasm in the ground" (209). When Pearson is upset, the "improper" speech she thought she had eradicated returns, like a "chasm in the ground," along with the improper ethnic self. Another way of reading this scene is that Denise's "improper" vernacular discourse has infected and inflected Pearson's "proper" English. So while the master discourse attempts to assert control, it finds that it is controlled and changed by its progressive and continuing struggle with the "minority" discourse. Unconsciously, Denise may use her improper language to resist the master's mastery and infect Pearson's discourse with unruly vernacular elements.

Consciously, however, Pearson's ideology holds sway over Denise throughout the early sections of the novel, and language becomes, in effect, her religion: "Gloria Pearson has given me ten years' worth of spelling words—I go from one set to the next, and I am never idle. I am so grateful that she taught me to try to match the English language to what I was trying to say. Making a match between what I wanted to say and what is permitted in English is the closest thing I had then to religion" (190). Collins reminds us that "standard English is available to many only through a complex reworking, a struggle, a cultural transformation, a personal disorientation and remaking of self" (223), and here we can see Denise struggling to remake her language and transform her ethnic identity. Denise also begins using SE in the same way that Missus Pearson uses it: to contain the power of nonhegemonic discourses. For example, she listens to her friend Josephus (another individual from the South) and translates his discourse into Standardized English, thereby losing its meaning: "In my head I repeat after him the way I repeat after Missus Pearson, and I make the words have beginnings and endings in my head on account a Josephus don't say them. So then I realize that I'm not really paying attention to what Josephus say" (124). The culture of Standardized English, argues Michael Silverstein, is "aggressively hegemonic" (287). In making Josephus sound just like Missus Pearson, Denise dominates his language with the language of the standard, the language of hegemony.

However, Denise ultimately refuses to be dominated by the language of the standard and moves toward a more disruptive concept of translation. For example, when Pearson tells her that the other kids are making fun of her southern dialect, Denise thinks to herself: "I don't know why they say southern Negroes don't know how to talk. They may not talk North-like but they—we—talk" (112). Denise sees the validity of the vernacular as a form of speech not accounted for by the standard. She also comes to see the limitations in Pearson's way of looking at the world, as the following passage illuminates:

> "Denise, why do the two of you run away every day?"
> "We ain't run *away*, Missus Pearson," I say. "We jes runnin."
> She doesn't correct me, but I hear in my English where I'm
> wrong. Not only that but I ain't said much a nothing. Her
> authority and corrections a my English all the time make me
> tend not to say what I might say from my head, since I know
> she probably won't let me finish my thought. She dismisses us,
> and I think to myself that her question ain't answered. *Children
> just run, where there's space to*, is how I answer her question
> in my head. Me and J, we are careful not to run that day. But
> this and her later noise about Clara let me know that children
> are not what she knows about or really cares enough about to
> understand. (125)

Initially Denise thinks that she "ain't said much a nothing," but she then realizes that Pearson's schooling actually means that she cannot "say what I might say from my head." Furthermore, Denise can answer Missus Pearson's question for herself, and in answering it she begins to see that Missus Pearson does not really know—or care about—children. What begins as a statement of her own linguistic flaws, then, ends as an indictment of the teacher's flaws and those implicit in this "language of mastery" (181). Kenji Hakuta's research has demonstrated that bilingual children seem to be superior in "metalinguistic ability": the ability to "think flexibly and abstractly about language" (49).[22] In the above passage, Denise clearly demonstrates metalinguistic ability by questioning Pearson's language and (more important) the social and educational ramifications of this language. Denise also notes that "Miss Pearson is very particular bout whitepeople and they ways" (175). Denise comprehends that Pearson is not only trying to make her speak Standardized English but also trying to transcode her racial identity so that she "gets over being colored." In a very real sense, Denise resists becoming the person Pearson wants her to become, an individual like Jadine in *Tar Baby* who forgets the black vernacular and the alternative subject positions it offers.

Between this language of mastery, this language of "being someone" that Pearson encourages, and her own "cakky-lakky" dialect (which is dismissed), Denise eventually finds a hybrid language that allows the disempowered discourse—the vernacular—to enter upon the dominant discourse and renovate it. Bhabha defines hybridity as "a *problematic* of colonial representation . . . that reverses the effects of colonialist disavowal, so that other 'denied' knowledges enter upon the dominant discourse and estrange the basis of its authority" ("Signs" 175). Verdelle's text is structured as a novelistic hybrid, containing as it does both the dominant discourse (as presented by Pearson) and a vernacular one (as presented by Denise and characters from the South). The novel sets these different discourses against each other to unmask the authority of the dominant discourse. As in *Dessa Rose*, however, Verdelle's novel formally works toward an uneasy, but peaceful, coexistence between "the king's English" and the "minority" discourse.

There are three ways in which hybrid languages operate in this text. First, hybrid languages operate on the lexical level—on the level of words. We notice quickly that Denise is a creative manipulator of language. For example, Denise describes leaving the breakfast table in the following vernacular and very creative mode: "I tore away from the table, my arms heavy like they *was* wet and wrung out. They swung very late behind my *hurly-burly* hurt" (3, emphasis added). Yet just a few sentences later, she switches into more standardized English: "Disbelief is an emotion, you know. Like an ocean and its major pulse, it can overtake. It can blind your eyes and block your ear canals. It can knock you to a depth" (3). This page is certainly an artistic hybrid in terms of how it moves between dialects, meshing elements of colloquial, oral speech with written and formalized literary codes. Denise also continually invents words, such as "sliver-wigglers" (139), a term she uses to describe people who come late to church and must slip into the pews without disturbing anyone. Denise evokes a performative, visual, poetic language. Her description of her grandmother's "beetlebug wig" (129), for example, is one many of my students claim they can actually "see" in their mind's eye.

Denise also continually introduces oral elements—such as call-and-response—into the written speech of the book. For example, she says: "Sometimes God just bring you (clap) exactly what you need" (43). And in a longer description of a sermon, we see this call-and-response in greater detail: "Sit down and linger with Your Lord and Savior. He (clap) gave everything for you. Rest your feet, and talk (clap) with Jesus. . . . Sit down with Your Father, *sit down*, with Your Father. Sit (clap), down (clap, clap) in Your Father's House" (138). We can hear the rhythms and sounds of the minister, of the African American church, enclosed as they are in claps, in calls-and-responses, in parentheses that (as my students also point out) actually look like a pair of clapping hands. Denise also lets us listen to the songs of the African American church through typographical keys and cues about their sound: "Eventually the organ man . . . leads the flock back to the quiet from the heat of the interlude. *Hush, now hush. (This is my story, this is my song)*" (137).

Yet when it suits her narrative purposes, Denise codeswitches to a language that is grammatical and standardized. In describing her family's reaction to their father's death she employs a mature and almost lyrical voice. This is a voice Missus Pearson would certainly be proud of, though it is stamped with Denise's own imprint: "We all stood at the graveside where my daddy's coffin lay. Oh, the postures of children at the graves of their father! They make small hooklike outlines—thin bodies, bent heads. They think they are like soldiers because they give so superhumanly to stand there, but anyone can see their hearts and shoulders flutter, their little wills shake" (150). On the lexical level itself, then, this book constantly migrates back and forth between vernacular speech forms and more standardized ones, as well as between inventing languages and manipulating the language that is already enfranchised. Smitherman comments that currently an emerging sense of bilingual consciousness is apparent among middle-class African Americans who employ "a developing level of linguistic experimentation as they incorporate the Ebonics flava into dialogue and discourse" (*Talkin That Talk* 38). Smitherman calls this "a new linguistic form, reflecting a dynamic blend of traditional and innovative language patterns" (38). Denise experiments imaginatively with language, incorporating AAVE but also creating a new linguistic form, a hybrid oral-poetic-vernacular-yet-written translative discourse that is her own.

Second, like *Dessa Rose*, the novel is hybridized in genre. On the surface, Verdelle's novel can be read as a standard literary form—a bildungsroman detailing a young girl's growth into maturity. Yet Verdelle introduces a number of nonstandard elements into this standard literary genre such as a recipe for making a pie (31), letters (170), hymns (136), sermons (138), poems (111), and even Denise's sentence-parsing diagram (172), which takes up almost a full page of the text and (quite literally) shows Standardized English being deconstructed, broken down into its component parts. The book's form indicates that the world is made up of multiple kinds of texts that coexist in something like an uneasy tension. Furthermore, traditional concepts of a bildungsroman's temporal sequence are violated by this novel, which is nonlinear, achronological, and pieced together out of bits and fragments of memory. In fact, the form of the book does not mirror a Euro-American concept of time as linear and straightforward but rather the piecing together of meaning through storytelling that is more traditional in oral, African, and African American cultures. Denise comments that memory does a "circle dance—steadily, deviously, protectively—in the head" (115), and this description is the best we are given of the book's form and of why it is structured as it is. Denise also states that she has to listen "to get the pieces of the story . . . so that if I told the story myself, it would be as full as thick soup" (141). The genre of the book, then, dialogizes the standard literary form of the bildungsroman by introducing the oral and nonlinear structures of memory, storytelling, and even improvisational cooking. Thus Verdelle's text is quite literally double-voiced in the sense that Henry Louis Gates uses this term: Its "literary antecedents are both white and black novels, but also modes of figuration lifted from the black vernacular tradition. . . . It speak[s] in standard Romance or Germanic languages and literary structures, but almost always speak[s] with a distinct and resonant accent, an accent that Signifies (upon) the various black vernacular literary traditions" (xxiii). Verdelle signifies on the form of the bildungsroman, but she also signifies on the black vernacular tradition—a tradition that might not acknowledge the importance of a voice such as Missus Pearson's. While this book is clearly a speakerly text—a text that privileges "the representation of the black speaking voice" (Gates 112)—it also dialogizes this voice, incorporating other voices into it so that the final voice and form of the novel are heterogeneous and multivocal.

Finally, hybridity also exists on the level of the main character and the voice she manifests and achieves as a translator and storyteller. At times Missus Pearson appears to be Denise's role model, her "voice." Yet Denise has a stronger role model/voice in her maternal grandmother, who lives in the South and teaches her a powerful kind of critical literacy. Denise's grandmother tells her the story of her own grandmother, a woman called Gibraltar Jones who emphasized learning to "watch and remember . . . to witness" (113). Gibraltar was a respected griot and was also apparently gifted with foresight. She has certainly not mastered written Standardized English, but she is still empowered. Through the story of Gibraltar, Denise learns a lesson about the value of other kinds of critical literacy. Denise also describes her grandmother's folk, vernacular instructions as "the bedrock" that is "under her skin" and as powerful "lectures" (200) that propel her:

Learn verses from the Bible and say them over meals. Sweep the house from front to back every other day, and sweep the room from ceiling to floor if you walk through a web. Wash all windows and walls in spring. Honor your grandmother and respect your elders,

*period. Go to sleep giving thanks to the Lord. Rise with
humility, anticipating service. Do your schoolwork, read when
asked—letters, news, instructions that came with packages.
Be a good child, be a good daughter, never lie or steal. Come
home before dark, don't track dirt in the house. And always,
always close the gate.* (200)

These lectures and the story of Gibraltar are contrasted in this book
with the more formal "lectures" of Missus Pearson, and all these
voices become components in the identity and voice Denise eventually articulates, the translative discourse she eventually employs.

But in the end, Verdelle indicates that neither the grandmother
nor Missus Pearson is sufficient as a role model. Missus Pearson,
for example, tolerates prejudice against darker-skinned African
Americans (198), while the grandmother sometimes imitates whites
and sees them as superior to most African Americans (235). So Denise must dialogize and hybridize these role models to produce a
new mode of voice and practice of translation. Denise finally realizes that she possesses a composite identity created from the world
around her, but also from her own imagination: "There was a big
window at the end of the school hallway. It was tall and wide. It
was big enough for me to stand in. I ran down the hall toward the
pale gray of that window light, my feet clap clapping on the dark
and polished wood. I thought it was school that had made me, but
it wasn't. It wasn't Miss Gloria Pearson either. It wasn't Margaret
[her mother] with all of her controls. I was made by the insistence
that I cut the teetering pumpkin. Just by that sliver of window
in the wide building of the days" (179–80). Denise is made by the
power of memory to preserve images from the past ("the teetering pumpkin") and create new images for the future (the "sliver
of window in the wide building of the days"). But to create a "window" tall enough to stand in, an identity that expresses rather than
compresses self, she must exercise her own imaginative powers. She
must "make" herself by moving *beyond* the identities and voices
that surround her.

Since the novel is told after Denise has "mastered" standardized,
written English and gone on to study at the Hampton Institute to
become a teacher (284, 286), Denise could presumably have chosen

to speak, narrate, or write it in SE. Or as a form of resistance to the language of the standard, to Missus Pearson, and to getting "over" being "colored," she could have employed AAVE. But what Verdelle shows Denise doing is combining and hybridizing languages, SE and AAVE, as well as the oral and the written. The use of oral, vernacular forms within Denise's written text reflects, then, not vestigial "imperfections" but an accomplished literary-linguistic style. Furthermore, this is a deliberate choice Denise makes and a deliberate construction of her identity. As Donald Rubin claims, "rhetorical choices help writers construct the social identities they wish to project in given writing episodes. . . . Written language *reflects* and conveys a writer's social identity, but it also *constructs* or instantiates it" (4). Verdelle depicts Denise meshing languages to produce a new mode of language that mirrors, even as it creates, her new version of selfhood, of a transcoded ethnic identity as an African American.

In the fertile and cross-pollinated space of translation, Denise formulates a mode of language that allows her to transmigrate the vernacular and renovate Standardized English. This new mode of language is not the language of the "nation," but it is one that can be understood clearly—a poetic and oral language: "I have to take my mind to think on something soothing. Even as I stumble up the road. I recall myself learning. I remember when that sky opened up. . . . I reach to where the freedom is" (299). Denise has not eliminated all aspects of southern dialect, as the first sentence illustrates. But she has also mastered—and moved beyond—the king's English: "I remember when that sky opened up. I feel the new sensation of lightness over my head. I explore this endlessness that seems to be a part of the whole thing" (299). Denise has shaped a new mode of language, yet she has also demarcated a new identity for herself. She will not be a "good negress" continually swabbing toilets, nor will she "get over" being "colored," being Southern and African American. Language, as Ludwig Wittgenstein has said, is a "form of life" (23). Denise eventually finds a language not of mastery or assimilation to the dominant norm but one that intermeshes discourses in order to adapt and remake them. Translation is a trope for the way a monologic view of language or identity can be transcended by a hybrid and syncretic language. But translation also produces an identity or a voice or even a work of art that represents something entirely new. Like Denise's window of light, translation allows us to see the selves and voices we are made up of, as well as to move beyond them into the wide building of the days, into voices and identities that are uniquely our own.

I HAVE ARGUED throughout this chapter that a translation perspective makes visible the innovative ways that African American writers manipulate the multiple discourses present in the world, enabling us to see the creation of new languages. In an essay on code-switching in Dakar, linguist Leigh Swigart makes a similar point, in a different context. She describes "a fluid and unmarked switching between Wolof and French" (83) that she calls "Urban Wolof." Swigart argues that this is a new language with distinct purposes and uses and a particular and powerful social status. She also contends that this language must be taken seriously by linguists and the dominant society.

The idea of the "seriousness" of hybrid discourses returns me to the Ebonics debate in the United States with which I began this chapter. The media reduced this controversy to a binary choice: either students are taught Ebonics or Standardized English; either they are prepared for life by mastery of the dominant discourse or left in illiteracy and poverty. But such writers as Morrison, Senna, Williams, and Verdelle teach us that Standardized English is just one code, among many, that African American individuals must speak and master. Furthermore, Standardized English is not separate from African American Vernacular English—they are both contained within our discursive system, within this thing we call "English." The works discussed in this chapter also illustrate that when diverse languages intersect and commingle, the language of both the "minority" and the "majority" may undergo significant transformation. "This is the oppressor's language / yet I need it to talk to you," bell hooks entitles one of her essays.[23] But is English the oppressor's language, after all? Just who has mastered whom, and at what cost? For all these writers, English is a multilingual space of both contestation and copresence—a space in which AAVE and SE mingle, translate, and, perhaps finally, re-create each other.

The Reader as Translator

Interlingual Voice in the Writing

of Richard Rodriguez, Nash Candelaria,

Cherríe Moraga, and Abelardo Delgado

Chicanos do not function as constantly choice-making speakers;
their language is a blend, a synthesis of the two into a third.
Thus they are interlingual, not bilingual. The codes are not separate,
but intrinsically fused. —Juan Bruce-Novoa, *Chicano Authors*

IN PREVIOUS CHAPTERS of this book, I have examined writers
who employ the trope of translation to transcode cultural and ethnic identity and characters who move toward new formulations of
voice that transmigrate languages and transcend binary conceptualizations of the relationship between the ethnic and the American.
Chicano/a (Mexican American) literature, on the other hand, engages in a more radical translational enterprise because it asks, and
at times even forces, not only the character or writer but also *the*
reader to assume a primary role in these processes of translation.[1]
In the other texts discussed, of course, a reader sometimes encounters "foreign" words that she or he must decipher. Many Chicano/a

works, however, contain sentences, paragraphs, and even entire sections written in Mexican Spanish; quite literally, then, a non-Spanish-speaking reader *must* become a translator if she or he hopes to gain meaningful access to these texts.[2] Moreover, while a writer such as Maxine Hong Kingston tells her readers at the end of *The Woman Warrior* that the story of Ts'ai Yen "translated well" because she has done much of the work of translation and even re-creation for us, Chicano/a writers ask the reader to do more of the arduous metaphorical work of translation: to struggle not only with words we do not know but also with textual dilemmas of social and cultural identity that are sometimes left purposefully unresolved.

Yet these writers do not indicate that the readers, or the characters themselves, must understand only Spanish to become adept at this translational enterprise. Finally, both readers and characters are asked to move toward an interlingual voice. According to Juan Bruce-Novoa, interlingualism is the mixing of two languages so that they "are put into a state of tension which produces a third, an 'inter' possibility of languages" ("Dialogical Strategies" 245 n. 15). For Bruce-Novoa, bilingualism implies moving from one language code to another, while interlingualism implies the constant tension of two (or more) languages at once. I will illustrate that in Richard Rodriguez's autobiographical trilogy—*Hunger of Memory* (1982), *Days of Obligation* (1992), and *Brown* (2002)—and in Nash Candelaria's *Memories of the Alhambra* (1977), interlingualism is created primarily through the linguistic matrix of English. In Cherríe Moraga's *Loving in the War Years* (1983) and Abelardo Delgado's *Letters to Louise* (1982), on the other hand, both Spanish and English are used to create an interlingual discourse that moves toward a new mode of voice and a renovated sense of ethnicity.

I will also argue something that critics such as Bruce-Novoa and others have not: that interlingualism is created specifically within, and by, a discourse of translation.[3] One reason these writers turn to the trope of translation is because of the long and complicated history of the relationship between English, Spanish, and indigenous languages and cultures in Spain, the United States, and Mexico. Mexican Spanish speakers in the United States (as discussed in the next chapter) have remained a somewhat stable bilingual community; Chicano/a authors could therefore use an ethnic language (Spanish) and still have a readership. Indeed, many of the foundational texts by Chicano/a writers have strong bilingual and Spanish-language roots.[4] Nevertheless, for many of these writers Spanish is not a pure, untainted mother tongue; in fact, it was brought to Mexico by Spanish conquerors and eventually used to displace indigenous languages and peoples. Thus, as Oscar Zeta Acosta phrases this in *The Autobiography of a Brown Buffalo* (1972), "My father is an Indian from the mountains of Durango. Although I cannot speak his language . . . you see, Spanish is the language of our conquerors. English is the language of our conquerors." But then Acosta states, "Now what we need is . . . a name and a language all our own" (198).

I contend that one way to produce this new language is through translation and linguistic fusion, rather than simply choosing one language over another or codeswitching between them.[5] Even writers who seem to be somewhat uninterested in presenting Spanish in their texts employ the trope of translation and create interlingual texts that translate Mexican Spanish into English and English into Mexican Spanish. Rodriguez uses English oppositionally, dialogizing it so that its faults, as well as its fault lines, are uncovered. Candelaria uses English but suggests that Mexican Spanish must be brought back into the linguistic matrix. Moraga codeswitches and fuses languages, indicating that her "mother tongue" is a syncretic blend of Spanish and English that exceeds the languages of which it is comprised. And Delgado produces a new tongue that is more than the sum of the parts—a *mestizaje* discourse in which terms are neither Spanish nor English but both, simultaneously. In the texts, both English and Spanish are transmigrated through the trope of translation. All these works also insistently employ translation practices and metaphors to draw both Spanish-speaking and non-Spanish-speaking readers into an interlingual zone of meaning where languages can be fused, syncretized, and re-created.[6] Finally, these texts insist that we become writerly translators within their interlingual zones of meanings so that we can write our way to a future in which multilingualism and linguistic diversity are the valued norm rather than the abrogated exception.[7]

English as the Matrix of Interlingualism: Translation Struggles
in the Writing of Richard Rodriguez and Nash Candelaria

In an essay on Chicano/a prose style, Willard Gingerich asks, "How
does one represent honestly, authentically, and fully a Spanish or
bilingual experience only in the alien language of the dominant social and economic class? *What compromises are inevitable and what
stylistic strategies can be employed to minimize or outwit those compromises?* How does one manipulate the matrix language (English)
to express the experience of the core language (Spanish) especially
considering that the latter is itself often a dialect (caló, 'border'
Spanish, regional dialect, etc.) deeply buried within the matrices
of Mexican and Castilian Spanish?" (210, emphasis added). As discussed in Chapter 3, a character such as Betonie in Leslie Marmon
Silko's *Ceremony* uses English in such a way that it *does* express
Native American values and ideals. Do writers such as Candelaria
and Rodriguez illustrate that the matrix of the English language
can be dialogized, can be undermined and subverted by an oppositional voice that uses hegemonic discourse against itself and transmigrates Spanish values into the English language? And what role
does translation play in this process?

Rodriguez has been attacked as the minority spokesperson for
conservative political interests in the United States (Flores 85, Saldívar 158), and many literary critics have commented negatively on
his stance toward language and identity, his writing style, his views
on Americanization, and his attitude toward his community.[8] The
persona he presents in his writing certainly seems at times to be an
individual who, like Jadine in *Tar Baby*, turns away from the alternative language and the possibilities of nonhegemonic subjectivity
it might offer.[9] Yet in both *Hunger of Memory* and *Days of Obligation* there is a subtext that constantly subverts this hegemonic message from *within* its own ideological and lexical boundaries, and in
his recent work, *Brown*, this subtext is foregrounded as Rodriguez
accepts American English's multilingualism. In fact, in all three
works Rodriguez uses English oppositionally so that it is dialogized. Mikhail Bakhtin comments in *The Dialogic Imagination* that
"a word, discourse, language or culture undergoes 'dialogization'

when it becomes relativized, de-privileged, aware of competing definitions for the same things. Undialogized language is authoritative or absolute" (426). English, as it is written by Rodriguez, is not authoritative or absolute. Indeed, in *Brown* he asserts that there is power in language that "forms at the border of contradiction," in language that has the ability to "express two or several things at once" (xi). Rodriguez's works dialogize English by incorporating aspects of a "minority" language and voice.

Rodriguez is also not the complacent, colonized subject.[10] Alfred Arteaga remarks that "autocolonialism, in the extreme, requires the other's adoption of the hegemonic discourse. . . . The other assimilates both discourse and the relationships it systematizes, so to the degree the discourse suppresses, the autocolonist effaces or denigrates him/herself from within. In the endeavor to mimic the monologue of power, the other *harmonizes with it and suppresses difference*" (77, emphasis added). In his dominant text, Rodriguez attempts to suppress difference, but in his subtext he continually reasserts and reinstates difference. He describes himself not as an autocolonized subject but as a Caliban figure who has "stolen their books" and now "will have some run of this isle" (*Hunger* 3). Rodriguez's first two works, in particular, contain a dialogue between a complacent, colonial, English-speaking, assimilated subjectivity and a postcolonial, unruly, and multilingual one.

Turning, then, to Rodriguez's first two works, it is apparent that the dominant text does attempt to assimilate discourse (English) and the relationship it systematizes (power over an ethnic "other"). In particular, Rodriguez emphasizes that Spanish is a disempowered, private dialect that must be abandoned in order to formulate an empowered, public, "American" voice; furthermore, ethnicity is not transcoded but discarded as one becomes "American." He discusses this many times in *Hunger of Memory* and *Days of Obligation*, so here I will simply give two examples:

> The social and political advantages I enjoyed as a man result from the day I came to believe that my name, indeed, is *Richeard Road-ree-guess*. . . . I celebrate the day I acquired my new name. (*Hunger* 27)

Women, usually women, stood in front of rooms crowded
with the children of immigrants, teaching those children a
common language. For language is not just another classroom
skill, as today's bilingualists would have it. Language is *the*
lesson of grammar school. And from the schoolmarm's achievement came the possibility of a shared history and a shared future. To my mind, this achievement of the nineteenth-century
classroom was an honorable one, comparable to the opening of
the plains, the building of bridges. Grammar-school teachers
forged a nation. (*Days* 163)

In these passages Rodriguez accepts English, but he also accepts its
ideology, one in which to be named in English is to attain subjectivity, one in which the genocide of millions of indigenous people
can be euphemized as "the opening of the plains." The common
language of the United States, Rodriguez appears to believe, must
be English, taught in the classroom, where it displaces Spanish and
all other languages in order to create "culture" (*Days* 167). And like
Missus Pearson in *The Good Negress* (discussed in Chapter 4), Rodriguez articulates the idea that speaking English, being an American citizen, and "getting over" one's race are fundamentally and in-
herently interconnected.

Mexican Spanish, on the other hand, represents the language of
ethnicity, the family, and the home. The sounds of Spanish mean his
parents are recognizing him as "*someone special, close, like no one outside. You belong with us. In the family. (Ricardo)*" (*Hunger* 16). When
Rodriguez and his family speak Spanish, they can play with language: "Excited, we joined our voices in a celebration of sounds. . . .
Some nights, no one seemed willing to loosen the hold sounds had
on us. . . . We pieced together new words by taking, say, an English
verb and giving it Spanish endings. . . . Tongues explored the edges
of words, especially the fat vowels. And we happily sounded that
military drum roll, the twirling roar of the Spanish *r*. . . . Voices
singing and singing, rising, straining, surging, teeming with plea-
sure that burst syllables into fragments of laughter" (*Hunger* 18).
This is one of the few truly joyful passages in Rodriguez's first two
works, and Spanish clearly represents an Edenic realm of familial

bonding and pleasurable linguistic and social interaction. The family also exercises a power over English here ("We pieced together new words by taking, say, an English verb and giving it Spanish endings") similar to the fantasy of power over English present in Sherman Alexie's *Indian Killer* when John Smith dreams of his life on the reservation. Yet, like John Smith's, this fantasy of power over English is only an illusion. As soon as Rodriguez and his brothers and sisters master English, they appear to assimilate to the oppressive and colonialist logic with which it is so often imbued.

Further, as Rodriguez becomes an "American citizen" and masters English (while simultaneously losing his Spanish), the special feeling of closeness he had with his family diminishes. Worse yet, a new quiet grows in his home: "The family's quiet was partly due to the fact that, as we children learned more and more English, we shared fewer and fewer words with our parents. Sentences needed to be spoken slowly when a child addressed his mother or father. . . . The young voice, frustrated, would end up saying, 'Never mind' —the subject was closed" (*Hunger* 23). Yet, as Rodriguez later comments, this is more than a "literal silence" (*Hunger* 25). In becoming "American" the child has left behind the Mexican parent and the possibility of transcoding ethnicity, of formulating a Mexican American identity. He or she has also left behind the possibility of bilingualism, of maintaining *both* languages, or of interlingualism (preserving a tension between languages). Rodriguez forgets his Spanish, or rather, he becomes unable to speak it: "I'd know the words I wanted to say, but I couldn't manage to say them" (*Hunger* 28). In accepting his subjectivity as an assimilated, English-speaking American, then, he appears to lose his ability to translate between English and Spanish.

Yet is the ability to translate Mexican Spanish lost? In fact, the subtextual themes of the first two books articulate another strategy of identity and voice. In *Days of Obligation*, Rodriguez meditates on Cortés, Mexico, and the indigenous population, making the following comment: "Postcolonial Europe expresses pity or guilt behind its sleeve, pities the Indian the loss of her gods or her tongue. But let the Indian speak for herself. Spanish is now an Indian language. . . . In something like the way New York won English from London after World War I, Mexico City has captured Spanish. . . .

I take it as an Indian achievement that I am alive, that I am Catholic, that I speak English, that I am American" (*Days* 23–24). This passage suggests that both the Mexican and the Indian ingest the language of the colonizer not to be overtaken by it but to overtake or assimilate it to his or her own subjectivity and ideology. In Mexico City, Rodriguez learns that Europe has been lying when it claims to have conquered the indigenous "other": "Europe's lie. . . . Each face looks like mine. . . . Where, then, is the famous conquistador? *We have eaten him*, the crowd tells me, *we have eaten him with our eyes*" (*Days* 24).[11] Ingesting the conqueror and his language and then using it in one's own way, for one's own ends and goals, is a strategy that resists assimilation. Like Francisco in *House Made of Dawn* (discussed in Chapter 3), Rodriguez expresses the idea that one takes in the oppressor's language yet keeps one's own soul/persona/culture.[12] This passage suggests that the ideology of the ethnic culture can be transmigrated into the English language and into an American subjectivity.

If we look more closely at how Rodriguez translates in these two books, then, we can see traces of this subversive transmigration. In *Days of Obligation*, when his Mexican driver asks (in English) whether he speaks Spanish, he does not respond (21). His goes to Mexico to make a film for the bbc in which he will be a "presenter," not a translator. He does not want to take on the role of the "Indian guide, a translator—willing or not—[who] facilitates[s]" conquest—the role of someone like Marina/La Malinche, Cortés's Aztec mistress who aided in the conquest of Mexico (*Days* 22).[13] In both works he comments that people tell him how bad his Spanish is: "*Pocho* then they called me. . . . (A Spanish dictionary defines that word as an adjective meaning 'colorless' or 'bland.' But I heard it as a noun, naming the Mexican American who, in becoming an American, forgets his native society)" (*Hunger* 29); "The Mexican American who forgets his true mother is *pocho*, a person of no address, a child of no proper idiom" (*Days* 58). On the surface, passages such as these indicate that Rodriguez cannot translate, that he cannot find the words (in Spanish or in English) to express his consciousness as a Mexican American. Yet the fact that he has here provided excellent, writerly, thoughtful translations of the word "pocho" should alert us that perhaps he is protesting too much.

Rodriguez can translate, but he retains control over his translations by insisting that they do not function as translations often function —to facilitate the oppressor's conquest of a nation or a tongue. He translates, then, by seeming not to translate.

Another, more intimate example of this translation-by-not-translating is present in *Hunger of Memory*, when Rodriguez's grandmother scolds him for playing with a *"gringo"* friend. When the friend wants to know what his grandmother says, he does not explain: "I started to tell him, to say—to translate her Spanish words into English. The problem was, however, that though I knew how to translate exactly *what* she had told me, I realized that any translation would distort the deepest meaning of her message: It had been directed only to me. The message of intimacy could never be translated because it was not *in* the words she had used but passed *through* them. So any translation would have seemed wrong; her words would have been stripped of an essential meaning" (31). The grandmother's words are protective, a warning against the Anglo boy, a drawing close of Richard (Ricardo) in her own proper idiom. But how do we, the readers, know this? Rodriguez has not translated his grandmother's words in a literal, readerly way to his friend, but he has translated them in a writerly, contextual way for the attentive reader. So we do understand the message of intimacy that passes "through" the Spanish words and into the reader's consciousness.

Two other examples of Rodriguez's writerly translations display his oppositional use of English. Both are from *Days of Obligation*, suggesting that Rodriguez has more fully developed his translation methodologies by the time he writes this second book. On the level of national politics, Rodriguez provides a translation/meditation on the meaning of the border in which the word undergoes dialogization (in Bakhtin's terms) because it becomes relativized, deprivileged, and aware of competing definitions for the same things. In San Diego, Rodriguez states, "people speak of 'the border' as meaning a clean break, the end of us, the beginning of them" (84). Yet "in Mexican Spanish, the legality takes on distance, even pathos, as *la frontera*, meaning something less fixed, something more akin to the American '*frontier*'" (84–85). *La frontera* is not a firm break but a new realm of cultural and linguistic mixing. As Gloria Anzaldúa comments, "The U.S.-Mexican border *es una herida abierta* [is an open wound] where the Third World grates against the first and bleeds. And before a scab forms it hemorrhages again, the lifeblood of two worlds merging to form a third country—a border culture" (25). Which concept does Rodriguez endorse: the border as firm division, or the border as new, miscegenated frontier? Rodriguez actually chooses both, infecting the English concept of the border with the Mexican Spanish meaning of frontera and the Mexican meaning of frontera with the American idea of border. As he says, "The border is real enough; it is guarded by men with guns," but Mexicans "incline to view the border without reverence, referring to the American side as el otro cachete, the other buttock" (*Days* 85). Finally, the meaning is neither purely Spanish nor purely American but both, and also more than both— Rodriguez has formulated a new concept of the border that transcends the sum of its parts, the two discourses of which it is comprised. In short, he has transmigrated the meaning of *both* terms. As he says elsewhere, "The border is a revolving door" (*Days* 91). Rodriguez's writerly translation of this term is not meant to clarify or resolve its meaning but to create a dialogue between its multiple and sometimes contradictory aspects. The differences between Mexico and the United States and their politics and languages intersect in this term (border/la frontera) but then are left in tension with each other in the new, syncretic construction that Rodriguez creates.

Similarly, on a more personal level, when Rodriguez translates the different versions of "you" in Spanish—*tú* versus *usted*—into English his goal is not so much resolution between his Anglo and Mexican cultural inheritances but "irresolution, since both sides can claim wisdom" (*Days* xvii–xviii). As in many romance languages, in Spanish there are two forms of the pronoun "you." "*Tú*," as Rodriguez explains, is "the intimate voice—the familiar room in a world full of rooms. *Tú* is the condition, not so much of knowing, as of being known; of being recognized" (*Days* 54). *Usted*, on the other hand, is "the formal, the bloodless, the ornamental you . . . spoken to the eyes of strangers. . . . *Usted* shows deference to propriety, to authority, to history. . . . *Usted* is the language outside Eden" (*Days* 54). This distinction between an Edenic, close, fam-

ily language (what we might call the tú world) and one of alienation and formality (the usted world) may sound familiar; indeed,
in *Hunger of Memory* this is the exact differentiation made between
Spanish (the world of the family and closeness) and English (the
world of public yet isolated individuality). What was a difference
between languages has, in Barbara Johnson's terms, become a difference *within* languages (*Critical Difference* 102). For English too
contains the possibility of intimacy, of closeness, as Rodriguez elsewhere asserts: "I began to distinguish intimate voices speaking
through *English*. . . . I began to trust hearing intimacy conveyed
through my family's English" (*Hunger* 31). Either language can become a realm of both usted and tú.

But Rodriguez chooses to use English to express a possible reconciliation between the Edenic language world and the world outside the garden: "If one could learn public English while yet re-
taining family Spanish, *usted* might be reunited with *tú*, the future
might be reconciled with the past" (*Days* 67). Tantalizingly, Rodriguez appears to suggest that in the United States it might be possible to reach a compromise between tú and usted, the language
of the private and the public, of the ethnic and the American, of
the self and the "other." Yet such a reconciliation is not reached in
this work, and he is left with irresolution: "I end up arguing about
bilingualism with other Mexican Americans. . . . I play the heavy,
which is to say I play America" (*Days* 67).

This does not mean that Mexican Spanish disappears in *Days of
Obligation* but rather that English becomes miscegenated, "besotted" (in Rodriguez's own terms [*Days* 73]) with specks, linguistic
flecks, of the "other." Mexicans have forced Anglo-Americans to
use their language, "to speak Spanish whenever they want their
eggs fried or their roses pruned" (73). By force of numbers, Rodriguez also tells us, "Mexicans have taken over grammar-school classrooms" (73). Thus the Southwest is now "besotted with the culture
of *tú*" (73). The tú, Mexican Spanish–speaking world is no longer
a product or export of Mexico—it has become part of the United
States. We have seen the "other," and it is U.S. (US).

Mexican Spanish also keeps returning to Rodriguez as an entity
that he would reject yet cannot completely deny. Perhaps this is why
he begins *Days of Obligation* with a graphic image of his persona

vomiting out the Spanish he has ingested: "I am on my knees, my mouth over the mouth of the toilet, waiting to heave. It comes up with a bark. All the badly pronounced Spanish words I have forced myself to sound during the day, bits and pieces of Mexico spew from my mouth, warm, half-understood, nostalgic reds and greens dangle from long strands of saliva. I am crying from my mouth in Mexico City" (xv). Although Rosaura Sánchez claims that Rodriguez here attempts to "expurgate the Spanish texts that he had been force-fed during his stay in Mexico" (162), the image is more complicated. Indeed, he has not been "force-fed" the language but has fed it to himself: "All the badly pronounced Spanish words I have forced myself to sound." This suggests that Rodriguez still wants the language—he is crying both for and from the mother tongue, Spanish. Yet in this book he cannot keep the language down—it constantly rises in his throat, threatening to choke off his American English.

Finally, then, the linguistic/social identity he shapes for himself through translation in these first two works must be read as neither Mexican nor American but an uneasy dialectic between both.[14] In *Hunger of Memory* Rodriguez claims he is American (5), but in *Days of Obligation* he sees the world with "Mexican Eyes" (99). When these two works are read in coordination, as mediations on each other, he becomes Mexican American. Yet in becoming Mexican American he does not lose the distinctive and disjunctive aspects of either his identity or the two seemingly oppositional cultures and languages from which he derives. Instead, he opts for a constantly shifting argument between self and "other," and for a hunger of loss and memory that refuses to disappear into the English he has marshaled to suggest his assimilation.

In the last work in this trilogy, *Brown*, Rodriguez's contradictions have not disappeared, but he does narrate a compromise between Mexican Spanish and American English in which he accepts his role as a multilingual subject and translator. The book's title is a meditation on race and the meaning of his "brownness," yet he notes that brown "is not a singular color . . . but a color produced by careless desire, even by accident; by two or several [races]." Brown, he tells us, "bleeds through the straight line, unstaunchable—the line separating black from white, for example. Brown confuses." Brown undoes binary oppositions between self and "other," colonizer and colonized, the subject and the object. What does it mean then, he wonders, to "write brownly" (xi)? A brown voice will undermine the separation between the ethnic tongue and the assimilated discourse. Furthermore, this brown voice will exist within the interlingual, miscegenated terrain that is American English itself.

In his earlier two works, Rodriguez often separates the ethnic tongue (Spanish) from the "American" one (English), but in *Brown* Rodriguez accepts that this separation is an illusion. African Americans, he notes, "took the paper-white English and remade it," just as the Irish and the Welsh took English and "wadded it up, rigmarolled it, rewound it into a llareggub rap, making English theirs" (18). A brown voice must take note of this ethnicization of English —and also be aware that the assumption of public English, a public voice/persona as an "American" writer, does not necessarily entail denial of the ethnic tongue. Rodriguez cannot imagine himself as a writer "without the example of African slaves stealing the English language, learning to read against the law, then transforming the English language into the American tongue, transforming me, rescuing me" (*Brown* 31). His public persona as a speaker and writer is not only indebted to the nuns described in *Hunger of Memory* who force him to learn English but also to African and African American writers who help him conceptualize how the ethnic tongue (in this case, Spanish) could be remade specifically from within the parameters of English itself.

Thus by the time Rodriguez writes the third work, American English is not "pure." It is also not a "common language" that displaces all the other tongues and cultures it comes into contact with, as it was at times in *Days of Obligation*. Rather, English itself is multilingual, as Rodriguez comments in a stunning metaphor about the American tongue:

> Americans do not speak "English." Even before our rebellion against England, our tongue tasted of Indian—*succotash, succotash*, we love to say it; *Mississippi*, we love to spell. We speak American. Our tongue is not something slow and mucous that plods like an oyster through its bed in the sea, afearing of taint or blister. Our tongue sticks out; it is a dog's tongue, an organ

of curiosity and science. . . . Our lewd tongue partook of everything that washed over it; everything that it washed—even a
disreputable history. (*Brown* 111–12)

American English is a radically miscegenated "dog's tongue" changed
by its interaction with other languages and dialects. It stands between worlds and is constantly remade by an interaction between
languages, between tongues. It cannot and should not be kept
pure: "Those Americans who would build a fence around American English to forestall the Trojan burrito would turn American
into a frightened tongue, a shrinking little oyster tongue, as French
has lately become." English itself is omnivorous and so is always
inflected and infected with the "other," with the voices of many.
Furthermore, the country, like its language, is bilingual or even trilingual and has learned to "communicate in at least two voices . . .
three in Eurasian San Francisco" (112), where Spanish, English, and
Chinese are spoken. The United States is, then, multilingual both
within its "official" language (American English, the omnivorous
"dog's tongue") and within its semiofficial communications: "*Press
ONE if you wish to continue in English*" (114).

In *Brown*, Rodriguez's conceptualization of English has clearly
changed; he now understands it to be a curious, miscegenated,
transmigrated, multilingual discourse that coexists with other multilingual and transmigrated discourses in the United States. Translation between languages is not, then, such a heavily inflected issue
for Rodriguez, although he does occasionally take it up as a subject. For example, he comments that the word "culture" in American English "means exactly the opposite of the Spanish word"
(130). Culture, in American English, "pivots on a belief in the individual freedom to choose, to become a person different from her
past" (130). In Spanish, however, culture means something more
like blood. Culture unites rather than separates people: "Culture
in Latin American Spanish is fated. Culture in American English
yields to idiosyncrasy" (131). As in his earlier works, Rodriguez
translates these terms in oppositional and contradictory ways but
then refuses to shape a resolution between these divergent translations. In all three works, then, translation is an oppositional methodology for dialogizing English.

Yet by the time he writes the third book, Rodriguez has resolved some of the questions he raised in the earlier books about translation and his own mode of voice, as well as about his linguistic and cultural inheritance. In *Hunger of Memory* Rodriguez attempts to be purely "American" and to speak an untainted English that cuts him off from his Spanish tongue and the realm of the home and family. In *Days of Obligation* he narrates an uneasy dialectic between English and Spanish, most clearly alluded to in the many metaphors of the ingestion and vomiting out of both Spanish and English. Finally, in *Brown* he resolves this dialectic by suggesting that there are many ways to translate and to speak "brownly." Certainly one of these ways is by using, yet also refashioning, English, so that English becomes interlingual, miscegenated, brown, and inflected by Mexican Spanish, by ethnicity itself.

LIKE RICHARD RODRIGUEZ, Nash Candelaria uses English as the primary instrument of translation and interlingualism, as his primary linguistic matrix. But unlike Rodriguez he validates—both textually and through his characters—the ability to speak the parent tongue. Candelaria's text also contains more words and conversation in Mexican Spanish, and the non-Spanish-speaking reader is therefore brought more directly into the struggle to translate and to be interlingual. In many works discussed in this book so far, the translation struggle was manifested thorough discursive and linguistic conflicts between a mother and a daughter, and in many texts women carried the heaviest burdens as translators. Interestingly, then, in Candelaria's novel the translation struggle is split between two men—a father and his son; the father maintains the ethnic tongue but lacks a viable sense of ethnic identity, while the son eventually transcodes his ethnicity as a Chicano but must find the language to translate and articulate this knowledge. I will argue, then, that the father's problem of ethnic definition is played out through the son's struggle for linguistic identity and that only literal and metaphorical acts of translation can enable growth and survival of the ethnic culture.

Memories of the Alhambra tells the story of Jose Rafa and his son, Joe. (No Spanish-language accent marks and punctuation are used in Candelaria's novel.) Jose, the father, speaks Spanish fluently and is able, on a literal level, to translate between Spanish and English (160, 161). Yet on a cultural and metaphorical level he is unable to translate—to transcode his Spanish, Mexican, and American heritages and formulate a viable sense of ethnic identity and a transmigrated voice. Jose constantly struggles, instead, to define himself as ethnically "pure." "I'm glad I'm not a Mexican" (126), he comments to his wife after a roundup of illegal Mexican immigrants. He repeats the phrase many times throughout the novel: "'No soy Mejicano [I am not Mexican]'" (177, 180). Since the Rafa family originally came from Spain and has been living in Albuquerque, New Mexico, for over three hundred years, Jose considers himself Spanish or American but not Mexican or Indian. He eventually embarks on a long voyage to Mexico and then to Spain to "prove" his racial purity. However, in Spain he discovers that Spaniards do not look like him ("dark complexioned") but like Anglos (144). Later he has a dream in which he takes the role of Don Quixote, ridding the countryside of "Indian dogs" (167), only to realize that the people he murders have his family's faces and his own. Unconsciously, then, Jose recognizes that he cannot separate himself from the Indian and the Mexican. In another dream he is told by a Spanish man, "You have the chance in the New World to bring them together—Spanish, Indian, Anglo" (162), yet when he awakens, he insists: "I am Spanish. A son of conquistadors. Maybe we can get together with the Anglos, but with the Indian dogs—never" (163). Consciously, he still tries to claim a "pure" identity and abandon the taint of Mexican or Indian ethnicity.

Such a claim is difficult, of course, given the actual history of conquest, invasion, and miscegenation between Spain, Mexico, and the United States, a history that Candelaria integrates into the novel. Mexico's Aztec and Indian populations were conquered by Spaniards such as Cortés in 1519–21. Cortés and his men, however, consorted with Indian women (such as Marina, an Aztec woman also known as "La Malinche") to father a mestizo race of individuals; often the children and fathers of the original Indian race were murdered, and mestizo individuals were preserved.[15] Mexico revolted from Spain in the early nineteenth century (1810–21) and then was colonized again just a few years later, this time by the

United States. With the 1848 Treaty of Guadalupe Hidalgo, areas of what we now call the United States (including California, Nevada, Arizona, Utah, New Mexico, and half of Colorado) went from being Mexican territories to being part of the United States.[16] Thus in various times in its history, Mexico has been Indian, Mexican, Spanish, and Anglo controlled, and many different racial groups have fought and mingled within its geographic spaces.

Furthermore, even Spain itself was never a pure ethnic region, as Jose discovers when he converses with Senor Benetar, who is Spanish but of Moorish descent. The song, "Memories of the Alhambra," or "Recuerdos de la Alhambra," which Senor Benetar hears while conversing with Jose, reminds Benetar of when "his people ruled this country [Spain]" (157). This song—from which the novel takes its title—represents a possible indoctrination for Jose into a more sophisticated and multilayered, not to mention multilinguistic, concept of ethnic identity. As A. Robert Lee argues, the song illustrates that "Spanish racial purity, quite as much as its Hispano-American off-shoots, has been an illusion from the start" (330). In one of his final reflections, Jose appears to accept multiracialism and that he might be a "Mestizo child of the Old World and the New" (173). But then "a heavy weight seemed to sit on Jose's chest" (174) and he dies of a heart attack. It is easier for Jose to perish than to accept himself as mestizo, multiracial, or Mexican.

Like his father, the son initially appears to be unable to engage in either the literal or metaphorical work of translation and also unable to transcode his ethnicity. For example, in the following passage (narrated when he is a young boy), Joe is quizzed in Spanish by his more fluent cousins in Los Rafas, New Mexico, and is unable to respond:

> "Es verdad que no puedes hablar espanol? [Is it true that you can't speak Spanish?]" the oldest boy asked.
> Joe flushed. Here it came. The outsider. The one who was different. When Joe did not answer, the boys elbowed one another in the ribs and smiled knowingly. The anger was hot in Joe's chest.
> "Es verdad? [Is it true?]" another continued. "No puedes? [You can't?]"

"I thought you were going swimming," he finally said. They all laughed and jeered. It was the wrong answer.

"No puedes. No puedes [You can't. You can't]," came the singsong taunt.

"Some kind of Mexican you are," his oldest cousin said. "Can't even speak the language."

"It's Spanish," Joe said. "Not Mexican. . . . Whatever I am, I'm the same as you!" Joe said.

"Oh, no you're not," they taunted. "You're from California and you can't speak Spanish. No puedes." (80–81)

Joe is unsure whether he is Spanish or Mexican or American or all three, and his language reflects this confusion. Could he answer his cousins in Mexican Spanish, even with a simple "Sí" or "No"? Could he codeswitch between the languages, as they do? What is clear is that Joe is unable, or perhaps unwilling, to translate. Just a moment before this he has heard his father and uncles debating their ethnic status. "Tell me," says one brother to another, "are you a Mexican or aren't you?" This uncle finally concludes that the family is "a new race. Not Mexican. Not Spanish anymore. More than just American. We're New Mexicans" (80–81). But what language does the "New Mexican" speak? In college, Joe feels like a "betrayer of la raza [the race]" because he speaks "pidgeon Spanish" and is an "Anglicized Chicano—which was almost nothing at all" (96).

Nevertheless, Joe eventually claims his status as Mexican and Chicano and accepts the intercultural burdens of both literal and metaphorical translation; in so doing he transcodes his ethnicity and finds an interlingual, transmigrated voice. At a crucial turning point in his life, Joe is approached by a Chicano man on his college campus who asks: "Eres Mejicano? [Are you a Mexican?]" (92). Joe's initial impulse is to respond, "Hell no! I'm an American," but then, seeing the "nervous brown hand clasping and unclasping around a textbook," Joe responds, "Sí" (92). Joe translates this man's question not as a literal one about where he is from but as a more metaphorical attempt to ascertain filiation, brotherhood. With this translation, which is a writerly interpretation of the question, Joe feels that "the bogeyman that had hung over his father for his entire life, and over Joe for so many years, had disappeared with that simple word: yes" (92). Further, by answering this question in Spanish, Joe allies himself with "El Chicano" (92), though this does not mean he cannot have other affiliations: "Yes, he thought. American. Mexican. Human. Ape descendent son of God. Yes. Yes. Yes" (92). Metaphorically, Joe's three "yeses" reflect his acceptance of the three parts of his ethnic heritage: the Anglo, the Spanish, and the Mexican/Indian. Joe is no longer "agringado" (94), as his father and others have called him, but multiracial.

As Joe comes to accept his multiracial heritage, his ability to translate expands. For example, he struggles to decipher his father's notebooks, to translate their Spanish (177). And when he goes to Spain to take home his father's dead body, he speaks Spanish, as becomes apparent only after a conversation with a Spanish bookseller has gone on for some time:

> "Senor Gomez?" The man nodded. "I am Joe Rafa."
> . . . "I'm sorry, senor. You look familiar, but—"
> "You may have spoken to my father, Jose Rafa."
> "Ah . . . 'Passengers to the Indies.' We were to meet in Seville. But where is Senor Rafe?"
> "He's dead."
> . . . "I'm sorry, senor. It must be a terrible shock for you and your family. . . . You resemble your father very much. I was confused when you walked in."
> Joe nodded. Embarrassed, he said, "Senor Gomez. Could you speak slower. My Spanish is not too good." (178–79)

Senor Gomez and Joe continue their conversation in Spanish. At an earlier age Joe refused or was unable to translate and to answer Spanish questions in the Spanish language, but here he does both, if a bit hesitantly. So unlike Jose, who dies with his ethnic conflict unresolved, Joe appears to resolve—or at least come to terms with—his ethnic identity through both literal and metaphorical acts of translation. He finds the language to translate between Spanish and English, but more metaphorically he also learns to mesh the different parts of his cultural and racial heritage—the Anglo, the Mexican, and the Spanish. In so doing he translates himself into a multiracial, multilingual individual.[17]

Candelaria's text also indicates lexically that for characters and readers, translation—both within English and between English and Spanish—is crucial to ethnic identity and voice. Candelaria's text includes many Spanish words, and although Candelaria sometimes translates phrases for the non-Spanish-speaking reader ("'Eres Mejicano?'" "'Are you a Mexican?'" [92]), he often uses contextual translation, asking the reader to decipher the meaning of terms from their context.[18] For example, when a man keeps crying out in pain "Mi cabeza! . . . Mi cabeza!" (46–47) and is finally offered some "aspirina" for his "chingada of all headaches," an attentive reader will likely translate "cabeza" as "head" and "chingada" as the swear word it is. Furthermore, Candelaria includes linguistic constructions that fuse English and Spanish, such as "mexicatessen" (19), "Frijoles Flats" (16), "senor Headache" (48), "grandfather-chingada of all headaches" (47), and "El Chicano" (92). Both Spanish-speaking and non-Spanish-speaking readers must work to explicate the meanings of these unusual, creative terms, but Candelaria does encourage us to do the work, to translate.

English is, then, Candelaria's main linguistic matrix, but to make sense of the text's discourse, the reader must grapple with another linguistic matrix. Candelaria also transmigrates Spanish into English, where it begins to renovate the language of hegemony; both languages undergo change as new terms are invented. Through contextual translative situations and through his inclusion of Mexican Spanish words, Candelaria asks his readers to enter into a zone of interlingualism and translation. In *Memories of the Alhambra*, then, we have not yet found the new language to which Oscar Zeta Acosta alludes, but we are clearly on our way *toward* this language.

Mestizaje Discourse as the Matrix of Interlingualism: Translation Struggles in the Writing of Cherríe Moraga and Abelardo Delgado

In *Borderlands/La Frontera: The New Mestiza*, Gloria Anzaldúa comments on a desire on the part of Chicano/a individuals to find a language that transcends the sum of its parts: "For a people who are neither Spanish nor live in a country in which Spanish is the first language; for a people who live in a country in which English is the reigning tongue but who are not Anglo; for a people who cannot entirely identify with either standard (formal, Castilian) Spanish nor standard English, what recourse is left to them but to create their own language? A language . . . with terms that are neither *español ni inglés*, but both. We speak a patois, a forked tongue, a variation of two languages" (77). I have already alluded to the appearance of this forked tongue in the brief discussion of Candelaria's fused constructions ("grandfather-chingada of all headaches," "mexicatessen," and so forth), but Moraga and Delgado include a great deal more of this new tongue. Furthermore, they consistently employ what I term "mestizaje translation strategies" so that both languages become the site of interlingualism.

I am using the term "mestizaje" here instead of "mestizo/a" to indicate that this translative discourse is both something new and something that is always evolving and changing. In "Cut Throat Sun," Jean-Luc Nancy elucidates this term: "*Mestizaje* is always a very long, vast and obscure story. It is such a slow process that no one can see it happening. A single *mestizo* does not make for *mestizaje*. It takes generations. . . . For the end result is as new and as different as if another 'raza,' another people had been produced out of thin air. . . . So in the end, what we call '*mestizaje*' is the advent of the other. The other is always arriving, and always arriving from elsewhere" (122–23). In both Moraga's *Loving in the War Years* and Delgado's *Letters to Louise*, there is a hybrid, mestizaje discourse that mirrors a kind of formal innovativeness, a refusal to fulfill readers' expectations of the text. And by encouraging the reader to actualize the text, to make meaning of it as writerly translators, both Moraga and Delgado push the reader into the category of the mestizaje, someone who, as Jean-Luc Nancy says, is "on the very border of *meaning*" (123).

In *Memories of the Alhambra* Joe learns to translate, but we are never told the details of this linguistic transition. In *Loving in the War Years*, on the other hand, Moraga details the pain of learning to translate, as well as the anguish of confronting her denial of sexuality, which Moraga allies with her Chicana language and her mother's body. Like Rodriguez, Moraga ultimately views translation as a way of setting up a dialogue, an argument, between the various sides of herself: the Anglo and the Mexican, the white and the Spanish, but also the male and the female, the straight and the gay. "What is my responsibility to my roots: both white and brown, Spanish-speaking and English?" she asks, and then responds: "I am a woman with a foot in both worlds. I refuse the split. I feel the necessity for dialogue. Sometimes I feel it urgently. But one voice is not enough, nor two, although this is where dialogue begins" (58).[19] Ultimately, she refuses to be simply bilingual (two voices are *not* enough), instead finding through translation a mestizaje voice. She therefore demonstrates what Gingerich has argued: that in Chicano texts voice is found not through the calculated mastery of two separate and distinct languages but by "the inventive and often precarious spanning of an officially disparaged, linguistic free-fire zone between them" (206). I will argue that translation is a primary metaphor and practice for moving beyond "the split" between Spanish and English which Moraga experiences—and that translation allows her to fuse and mesh discourses so that a new mode of voice can be birthed from this linguistic struggle.

In the various poems, essays, and stories that comprise *Loving in the War Years*, Moraga describes a poetic persona who is initially stripped of her Spanish language and Chicana color. As the white-looking ("la güera" or "fair-skinned") daughter of a Mexican American mother and an Anglo American father, her family attempts to "bleach me of what color I did have" (51). A great deal of this bleaching has to do with language, for Moraga's mother refuses to teach her daughter Spanish (51). As much as possible, ethnicity and the ethnic language are to be cast off, not transcoded. As evidenced in several of the texts I have analyzed in this volume, this trope in which a parent refuses to teach an ethnic language to the child for fear it will hinder the child in the Anglo world occurs frequently. Yet Moraga adds to this trope by suggesting that in being deprived of her mother's tongue, she is also cut off from her sexuality and her emotions: "I am 'born American.' College English educated, but what I must admit is that I have felt in my writing that the English was not cutting it. ¿Entiendes? [Understand?] That there is something else, deep and behind my heart and I want to hold it hot and bold in the hand of my writing and it will not come out sounding like English. Te prometo. No es inglés [I promise you. It isn't

English]" (141). Spanish, sexuality, and true emotion—the ability to "hold" what is "hot and bold in the hand of my writing"—are interconnected.

Yet it is not Spanish per se that allows Moraga to recover her sexuality and proper idiom but the possibility of birth and rebirth of language, voice, and body that she uncovers in her attempts to speak and translate Spanish. Moraga then takes this possibility of rebirth into the interlingual zone—into a syncretic, transmigrated tongue composed of both Spanish and English. She describes a rebirth of language through translation in poems such as "It's the Poverty" and "For the Color of My Mother" and continues it in her essay "A Long Line of Vendidas [Traitors]." In these stanzas from "It's the Poverty," for example, she fears a monstrous rebirth of her mother's ethnic voice in herself:

> Words are a war to me.
> They threaten my family.
>
> To gain the word to describe the loss,
> I risk losing everything.
> I may create a monster,
> the word's length and body
> swelling over my *mother*, characterized.
> Her voice in the distance
> *unintelligible   illiterate.*
> These are the monster's words. (63)

Reading these stanzas in terms of a dilemma of translation, we might say that Moraga wishes to recover her mother's tongue, which will allow her to describe how she originally lost this tongue—she wishes "to gain the word to describe the loss." But she fears recovery of this mother's tongue, this mother's voice, which has been called "illiterate" and "unintelligible" by the dominant Anglo society. She fears translation, in short. She risks "losing everything" to gain the ability to translate the creative and aleatory voice of the mother, of the mother tongue. No wonder, then, that words are "a war" to her.

"For the Color of My Mother" alludes to this creative yet fearful rebirth of the mother's original tongue in the daughter's translated voice even more strongly. Here Moraga describes how her mouth splits open:

> at two
> my upper lip split open
> clear to the tip of my nose
> it spilled forth a cry that would not yield
> . . . the gash sewn back into a snarl
> would last for years. (60)

This is an arresting image of the deconstruction of the mouth/voice that recurs in later sections of the text. But perhaps more interesting, she allies this split in the mouth/voice with a split in her mother Elvira's abdomen:

> at forty-five, her mouth
> bleeding into her stomach
> the hole gaping growing redder
> finally stitched shut from hip to breastbone
>> an inverted V
>> *Vera*
>> *Elvira*
> *I am a white girl gone brown to the blood color of my mother*
> *speaking for her.* (60–61)

Since the daughter's and mother's experiences of being split open are constantly allied and paralleled, Moraga will both speak *for* her mother and speak *as* her mother. The daughter will translate the mother's story, and translation might metaphorically heal the split in the mother's belly, the gash in the daughter's voice/mouth. Other women come to Moraga and cradle the mother's silence, even as they nod to her as if to say, "Speak for us, speak of us." But still she fears this bloody process of birthing and rebirthing one's "own" language, of learning how to translate and transmigrate a language of the mother/self.[20]

It is not until almost the end of the book that she confronts this issue, in the last words of the essay "A Long Line of Vendidas," and it is not coincidental that she comes to terms with this struggle through an actual practice of translation.[21] Here, once again, Moraga imagines her mouth splitting open: "In recent months, I have had a recurring dream that my mouth is too big to close; that is, the *outside* of my mouth, my lips, cannot contain the inside—teeth, tongue, gums, throat. I am coming out of my mouth, so to speak. The mouth is red like blood; and the teeth, like bones, white. The skeleton of my feelings clattering for attention. . . . La boca [the mouth] spreads its legs open to talk, open to attack" (142). This is a striking image that combines the linguistic, the ethnic, and the sexual aspects of Moraga's struggle to translate. Quite literally the tongue (the mother tongue?) appears to be breaking free from, and birthing itself out of, the prison of the body, the white teeth and bones, which are also clearly meant to emblematize the prison of white language. But here Moraga refuses the fear of translation —of speaking both the mother's story and the daughter's, of speaking both the Anglo text of assimilation and asexuality and the Chicana text of subversion and lesbianism. She ends this essay in the following way:

> "My mouth cannot be controlled. It will flap in the wind like legs in sex, not driven by the mind. It's as if la boca [the mouth] were centered on el centro del corazón [in the middle of the heart] not in the head at all. The same place where the cunt beats.
> *And there is a woman coming out of her mouth.*
> *Hay una mujer que viene de la boca.* (142)

The last two lines of the essay are translations of each other and puns on the several senses (sexual and otherwise) of the word "come." Yet because both are in italics, it is difficult to tell which is the enfranchised text or language and which the disenfranchised one. This final passage also blurs the boundary between mind and body, intellect and emotion, voice (which is supposed to be controlled and rational) and sexuality (which is supposed to be uncontrolled and emotional). Furthermore, by stating in this essay that "the Mouth is like a cunt" (142), Moraga both sexualizes her voice and vocalizes her sex. As Yvonne Yarbro-Bejarano comments, "'mouth' and 'sex' merge, both represented as organs of speech and sex" (6). Both organs speak the mother's and the daughter's story, the Anglo and Chicana narrative that constitutes Moraga's linguistic and ethnic inheritance. Both organs, in short, become instruments of translation.

Numerous critics have argued that Moraga's "true voice"—her true tongue—is Spanish.[22] Yet I contend that Moraga's text depicts not only a recovery of the mother's tongue but also a rebirthing of language through the process of translation so that its binarisms are undermined. Hegemonic and "minority" discourses become imbricated within each other through linguistic fusion and through translation; her true tongue, then, is a transmigrated, syncretic, translative discourse. Moraga recalls that she has disowned the language of her mother—"the sound of my mother and aunts gossiping—*half in English, half in Spanish*—while drinking cerveza [beer] in the kitchen" (55, emphasis added). So what her translations recover is this mélange, this mixture, this mestizaje discourse. In her own speech, "the Spanish sounds [are] wrapped around the English like tortillas steaming in flour sacks" (128). In this image, it initially seems that the tortillas would be analogous to the Spanish sounds and the English would be the flour sacks, but the Spanish sounds are actually described as being wrapped around the English, so it is finally unclear which is the external, wrapping discourse and which the internal, intrinsic one. This is something more than "simple" codeswitching, for the codes have become metaphorically fused so that it is impossible to tell where one leaves off and the other begins.

Fluid and grammatically correct intrasentential (within the sentence) codeswitches indicate, as research by linguists has shown, that Chicano/a bilingual speakers who codeswitch utilize not two separate languages but one in which the grammars of the different languages are functionally and intrinsically meshed and integrated.[23] Some linguists have argued, in fact, that such codeswitching shows the presence not of two separate tongues but rather the creation, through fusion, of a new language.[24] In Moraga's text, such a meshing of tongues to create a new syncretic voice can be seen in the book's final poem. I will quote it in its entirety (with my translations in brackets on the right side of the page) so that the reader can see its codeswitches:

¿qué puedo decirte in return   [what can I tell you in return]
stripped of the tongue
that could claim lives
de ostras perdidas?   [of the others we have lost?]

la lengua que necesito   [the tongue I need
para hablar   in order to speak
es la misma que uso   is the same I use
para acariciar   to caress[25]

tú sabes.   you know.]
you know the feel of woman
lost en su boca   [lost in her
    amordazada   muzzled mouth]

profundo y sencillo   [profound yet simple
lo que nunca   what never
pasó   passed
por sus labios   through her lips]

but was
    utterly
    utterly
    heard. (149)

This poem is clearly preoccupied with finding voice—with free-ing the tongue, the muzzled mouth. However, the poem reaches toward an "unmuzzled tongue" that is not entirely in Spanish or in English but in *both* linguistic realms. Donna Haraway calls Mora-ga's language a "self-consciously spliced language," a hybrid of the conqueror's tongues (199). But I am arguing here that it is some-thing more than spliced—that (like many translations) it is some-thing new that transcends and exceeds the two languages of which it is comprised.[26] For when translated into English, no matter how effectively, this poem loses some of its linguistic power. This is not because the poem is untranslatable but because the meaning of the poem—its search for voice—lies not in the individual, unsupplemented languages but in their commingling, in their fission and fusion; the poem's meaning can therefore be articulated only as a transmigrated, syncretic, interlingual mode of discourse.

In this poem Moraga also reaches toward something that is perhaps utopian but also extralinguistic. How can a word, after all, "never pass through her lips" but be "utterly heard"? The poem leaves the idea of the extralinguistic voice in tension with the other voice it (and the work as a whole) has marshaled: a reborn, hybridized, mestizaje discourse in which English and Spanish intermix and inmix, enriching each other's meanings. The mestizaje voice presented here is always in the process of transforming itself, of becoming something new, something that finally might escape the constraints of language itself. And so the mestizaje woman's subjectivity and language are always in process. She represents a woman who is constantly "coming out of her mouth" in a continual process of birth and rebirth, of being split open and from this split repairing to a new w/hole.

More than either Rodriguez or Candelaria, Moraga also pushes —indeed, forces—the non-Spanish-speaking reader into the evolving interlingual zone through translative practices. In the first edition of the book (published in 1983), she includes a glossary at the end that translates *some* (but not all) her Mexican Spanish terms. By including the glossary at the end of the book (rather than, for example, translating the words at the bottom of the page), she asks the non-Spanish-speaking reader to flip back and forth (physically) between Spanish and English. Quite literally, a non-Spanish-speaking reader might rewrite the text in his or her own idiom (most probably English), but in so doing this reader might add a number of the Mexican Spanish words that Moraga repeats (such as *mujer*) to his or her vocabulary. And by not including all her words in the glossary, Moraga perhaps prompts her non-Spanish-speaking readers to look them up in a Spanish dictionary or consult a Spanish speaker. In the second edition of the book (2000), she eliminates the glossary entirely, asking the reader to do even more of the arduous work of translation.[27] According to Gary Keller, codeswitches may be unfathomable and even mystifying to monolingual readers but also "beckoning," inspiring us "to travel that extra distance into the writer's home turf, an aesthetic bilingual idiolect" (286). By not translating her Spanish words in the codeswitches, Moraga asks the reader to travel the extra distance in her own mestizaje tongue.[28]

Furthermore, like the writers described by Samia Mehrez in my introduction, Moraga asks her readers to develop a radical bilingual practice of translation that moves back and forth between languages to produce (or "write") the meanings of the text. For example, the book's cover contains the following words: "*Loving in the War Years: Lo que nunca pasó por sus labios.*" Obviously, the English phrase, while being somewhat metaphorical, presents no problem of translation for the reader who speaks only English, but the Spanish phrase does. Even after the English-only reader manages a literal translation of this phrase as "that which never passes through her/our lips," something will be lost in translation unless the reader meditates on the pun Moraga is making in the Spanish subtitle between lips (of the mouth) and labia (lips of the vagina). Here, as elsewhere, Moraga connects voice and sex. Furthermore, since *labia* in Spanish is also a colloquial term meaning something like "glibness," there may be an additional meaning embedded in the subtitle: she writes about what never passes through (is transmitted by) our glibness, about what can never be spoken without serious voice or words. How is this subtitle connected to the dominant title? The reader must mediate on how, during the war years, loving is silent yet present, spoken between the interstices and gaps of words, between the interstices and gaps of language and touches. From Moraga's point of view, the Chicana lesbian feminist is always in the war years, always in danger of having her voice/passion silenced. We cannot be glib about this need for expression, despite the war, despite the silencing. What never seems to pass through our lips *must*, finally, pass through our lips; it must find voice and articulation in some linguistic mode, some discursive zone, and some physical expression. Thus the line in Moraga's text between dominant and disempowered discourses, between reader and writer, and between the translator and the translated text, becomes somewhat permeable. The reader can only actualize Moraga's text if she or he is willing to become (at least temporarily) a bilingual and even interlingual writerly translator. Moreover, both Spanish- and English-speaking readers are encouraged to meditate on language:

on its puns, its interstices, and its plastic possibilities—as well as limits—of expression.

There are two other ways in which Moraga encourages the reader to develop an interlingual translating consciousness. Like Candelaria, she uses contextual translation, as in the following example: "*After months of separation, we are going to visit my mamá in the hospital. Mi tía me dice, 'Whatever you do, no llores Cherríe. It's hard on your mother when you cry.' I nod, taking long deep breathes, trying to control my quivering lip*" (93). It is perfectly obvious from this passage that someone says to Moraga, "Whatever you do, no tears." Words such as "me dice" and "llores," then, can be easily translated contextually by a non-Spanish-speaking reader. But what about "tía"? We have no clues from the passage about whether this is a sister, a grandmother, or a friend—and yet the word is repeated four times in this short journal entry (93–94). And the word is not included in the glossary in the first edition. Once again, Moraga's contextual translations do only part of the work for the reader, the reader-as-translator.

Finally, the hybrid form of *Loving in the War Years*—its collage-like mixture of poetry, prose, and stories—asks the reader to move between different kinds of discourse (the fictional, the autobiographical, the historical, the mythical, the poetic, and so on) to produce meaning. As often as Moraga describes herself as "cracking open" (145), she also cracks open linguistic registers normally kept separate. She includes journal entries (iii), letters (55), and poetry (140) in her essays—fiction, in other words, in her nonfiction. Even within the fictional modes she blurs genres. For example, her short story "The Warbride" ends with a kind of unpoem: "With you, it's supposed to be different and I guess it is when the beat of your hand against my bone / isn't worked against the beat of the water flooding memory / against the walls of my heart beating fast / against the flash of boys beating off, inside me" (88). The slash marks between phrases are in the original text, as if Moraga wanted to end the story with a lesbian love poem but cannot quite reach this juncture, this slash. Which is the poem, which the story? Which the text, which the subtext? The genres merge and blur and evolve together in new directions, and the reader is asked to move between them in a linguistic free-fall zone with few boundaries and markers. "The combining of poetry and essays in this book," Moraga comments, "is the compromise I make in the effort to be understood. In Spanish, 'compromiso' is also used to mean obligation or commitment" (vi). Form itself in this phrase becomes a compromise, a translation, but also an obligation and a commitment. The reader must commit to the formal and linguistic demands this text makes and be willing to move into a new interlinguistic, intergenre zone of meaning through translation practices.

Although Moraga claims at one point that she is "tired of these acts of translation" (125), it should be clear from what I have said that Moraga is fully engaged in a translation struggle. *Loving in the War Years* is a difficult text, one obsessed by language, by voice, by the tongue. But what animates Moraga is a deep and abiding love of language. "I want the language," she cries. "I want . . . [to] feel my tongue rise to the occasion of feeling at home" (141). Finally, however, Moraga does not find a pure Spanish tongue that makes her feel "at home." Instead, she discovers a practice of translation that wraps the Spanish sounds around the English until they cannot be disentangled—a constantly evolving mestizaje discourse that draws the reader into the interlingual zone, into her world of translation.

IN THE THREE WRITERS discussed so far in this chapter, I have explicated a struggle in the second generation to recover Mexican Spanish so that the protagonists can translate between the ethnic tongue and English; I have also argued that readers are asked to participate in this translation struggle, in this recovery and re-creation of voice and self. But Santiago Flores, the poet-activist-hero of Abelardo Delgado's epistolary novel *Letters to Louise*, does not struggle to recover Spanish. He is a balanced bilingual speaker/writer who masters and maintains both English and Mexican Spanish. Flores fluidly and fluently codeswitches between languages, while also teaching the monolingual reader to translate. Moreover, he creates his own unique discourse that transmigrates both Spanish and English and constitutes his mode of voice. The creation of this language is not, as it is in *Loving in the War Years*, a monstrous and frightening process but rather a joyful birth meant to liberate and re-create languages, Spanish and English, as well as the subjects of these languages, the writer and the reader. In the end, the reader becomes a producer not only of a translation of a particular word but also of the translated text itself.

Delgado's novel is set up as a series of letters that Santiago Flores writes to someone named Louise. We never learn who Louise is —we presume she is female, but whether she is Mexican American, Anglo, or anything else is never clear. The letters (written over three summer months) describe Flores's travels, his troubles with his wife and girlfriend, his childhood in Mexico and Texas, and his education. They also explicate his growth as a translator. At the age of twelve Flores moves from Mexico to the United States, where he describes his "gringa" teacher "patiently pumping English into us" (66), into him and his other Chicano *carnales* (brothers, friends). The process of acquiring English is not difficult for Flores ("I began to pick up the language quickly" [69], "school work was a breeze" [86]), and it does not displace his Spanish. Always clever with words, Flores's high school writing is "a source of self-esteem, of pride" (131), and he inflects this English writing with his own brand of Chicano humor (121). But Flores wants to do more than merely inflect English with Mexican Spanish. He compares the letters he writes (as an adult) to Louise with a pregnancy: "I guess my forty-four-year-old pregnancy is showing labor pains. I want to give birth to something, but what is that something?" (11). This birth is then allied with language itself: "Words in English and Spanish rattle their tin cups on the cell bars of my brain, like rioting prisoners. Words that all at once want to scare, to change, to warn, and to form poem-prayer-song" (11). Flores wants to use his languages (Spanish and English) to create an interlingual "poem-prayer-song"—in short, to give birth to a new language.

As his name indicates, Santiago Flores is a kind of savior figure as well as a poet, but an irreverent one. Yet he claims he is *not* a translator. Meeting a Mormon missionary in an airport, for example, Flores is irritated by his insistence on translation:

> "Sir, will you mind translating this for me—"
> "Sir, what does 'te quiero' mean?—"
> "Sir, would you mind answering a million questions I have—"...

I did comply with the translation of a poem called "Artás."
Something I seldom do, translate. (63–64)

Is it true that Flores seldom translates? He does, in fact, translate quite frequently, but his translations are so embedded into the text that at times they go unnoticed. For example, he translates the "many cuentos [tales] my bedridden blind great-grandmother, Andrea Flores, used to tell me" (27) into English, and he also recounts his grandmother's Mexican stories, such as the one she tells about the origins of peyote (96–97). Like Kingston, Flores respects the storytellers who have gone before and the traditions and languages of the earlier generations. Since his grandmother and great-grandmother are dead, he struggles to transmigrate their oral Mexican stories into written English so that they can flourish in a new context.

Before discussing Flores's specific translation strategies, however, it is important to note several aspects of the linguistic matrix he creates, which is not exactly English or Spanish. Like Olivia in Kadohata's *The Floating World* (see Chapter 2), Flores possesses a translating consciousness that sees the world as composed of a multitude of codes, discourses, and languages, all of which are imbricated in each other, and so the novel as a whole actually contains many languages. There is a kind of formal Mexican Spanish, used when his grandmother and mother speak, and a more modernized Americanized Spanish, used when Flores and his friends converse. There is caló (or slang) and "bureaucratic English" (109), which Flores must master to write grants. And there is also a bilingual discourse he uses in his poems (25). Furthermore, codeswitches between Spanish and English and entire sentences or passages written in Spanish occur on almost every page of the novel.[29] Certainly, Delgado's text presents a challenge to the non-Spanish-speaking reader. Can such a reader enter the text's linguistic zone?

But the text draws such a reader into this zone through its translation strategies. I translate Delgado's Spanish in notes rather than in the body of this chapter to demonstrate my claim that even a non-Spanish-speaking reader can translate these passages contextually, at least to some extent. Flores's intrasentential codeswitches are often very smooth and unflagged:

I had a padrino sort of on the crazy side. This was way back in Boquilla. He used to get drunk. Cuando se le pasaban las copas he used to be extra generous with his Godchild Santiago and I would get pesetas and tostones.[30] We had then un escusado de loyo[31] and the paper shortage to wipe our butts with was as I've described it before. Well, the memory I have of my crazy Padrino Julián is that he used to wipe his butt with one and five peso bills, at times even veinte,[32] and throw them out. We would then look for these bills, wash them and iron them, and spend them. He knew we did this and this encouraged him to do it again the next time he got drunk. (49)

These codeswitches are so seamless that a Spanish-speaking reader might not be entirely aware of them. Furthermore, since none of the Spanish words are italicized, the languages flow more easily into each other. The codeswitches present more of a challenge for a non-Spanish-speaking reader, but much of the Spanish in this passage can be contextually understood. For example, "padrino" is not initially translated, but when we learn later that Santiago is this man's "godchild," its meaning as "godfather" becomes clear. Another humorous example of translative codeswitching is provided when Flores recounts how his mother liked to dress him as a girl when he was young and how once "some señoras asked,—es hombrecito o mujercita," whereupon "I raised my dress and showed the inquisitive veijas, who giggled at my daring" (54). Non-Spanish-speaking readers can easily discern that "es hombrecito o mujercita?" means "are you a boy or a girl?" and also comprehend the young boy's daring response. Delgado's novel makes very effective use, then, of intrasentential codeswitching and contextual translations to draw in monolingual readers.

Yet there are times when Delgado also relies on explanative translation, telling readers, for example, "duendes" are the "souls of mischievous children who die as children" (21); "vela" is "a candle which we pasted to the wall with its own melted wax" (4); "arinolina" is "a sort of cow feed" (44); "Te hago un niño" means "I make you a baby" (46); and "culebras" are the "meeting of two storm fronts" (62). "Chavala," he says, is "an old Chicano word now seldom used meaning 'little girl,'" so "Mi chavala" means "My girl"

(127). "Zaguán," on the other hand, is a Mexican word meaning "an entrance to the house with a sort of shelter to each side" (19). Sometimes, too, Flores explains his linguistic puns and jokes and even the meanings of the same word in different dialects of Spanish. When a woman from Caracas explains that the Caraguians use the word "cuchara" (or spoon) as the term for the "female sex organ," he makes a contribution by saying that New Mexicans refer to a sort of cookie as "panocha," while people in Texas or Mexico think of it as the same as "cuchara" (vagina). So Flores is confused in Colorado when he is offered "panocha": "Since I had been without a woman for many months I didn't think her offer was merely a cookie" (40–41). Delgado enlightens the monolingual reader about the various meanings of the Spanish term, but he also demonstrates that even Spanish speakers, using their own tongue, sometimes mistranslate and misunderstand. In other words, both monolingual and bilingual readers have an encounter with interlingualism.

Far more often than he uses contextual or explanative translation, however, Flores uses what I term "storytelling translation": stories that non-Spanish-speaking readers can translate, by their logic and sequence of events, even if they cannot translate all their language. Consider, for example, this early incident:

> [My mother] can giggle and make fun of almost anything, word, or phrase. I didn't think it so funny one morning in Chihuahua. It was in December. She knew I was looking forward to Christmas and Santo Clos, who by then had obviously infiltrated our Mexican culture.
>
> I must have been busy in my fantasy world of paper cutouts, my favorite pasatiempo of my early years, when I heard my mother excitedly call to me.
>
> —Mijo . . . mijo . . . Santiaguito, ven, mira, hay vien Santo Clos. . . .[33]
>
> Down the street a fat Chicano with white hair and white beard herded a couple of burros with some sacks. . . . I ran fast down the half a cuadra that separated me from San Nicols, as he was also called. I stopped him by pulling on his worn chaleco. He seemed very irritated at the little mocosito seeking his attention. His look of anger was ignored in my enthusiasm

in having the unique experience of sharing a word with such an important character.

—¿Usted es Santo Clos?—came the feeble and excited question from my throat.

—Yo soy Guadalupe Jiménez Rodríguez, un arriero. No esté Chingado. (37)[34]

Even if a reader does not understand the exact wording of Guadalupe Jiménez Rodríguez's reply to the pesky "mocosito," he or she will certainly be able to translate the gist of it. This example uses humor and storytelling translation to gently draw the non-Spanish-speaking reader into the Mexican Spanish language and world. A reader's (potential) resistance to translation is undermined by such passages, and we may find, without even quite realizing it, that we have become translators.

At other times, however, the non-Spanish-speaking reader is not treated so gently, and she or he must actively struggle to make sense of the story and its language. The following incident that Flores recounts about his early school days shows the difficulty of this struggle:

This bato would always pester me. Me cantaba por chingazos. I would ignore him. I told him, sí hombre, tú ganas. Ya estuvo, and would walk away. One day I was all dressed up at a party with two or three girls when again he asked me to go y darnos en la madre. Yo le contesté, Pos' aquí está suave, pa' que vamos pa' fuera y le puse dos cambronazos y lo senté. He had a lot of friends and they soon jumped me. My friend Felipe tried to get me out of the mess. Someone le aterrizó un patadón and that brought all his brothers and cuñados into the act. Se armó la bronca. Felipe y yo left very quietly. I knew that guy would try to get me later, so rather than live in fear of that day I sought him out the very next day. I found him y le dije, mira, aquí estoy dame unos fregazos, get it out of your system y ya, que no? To my surprise he said he no longer quería any pedo conimogo y ha murió.—He went on to say how escamado he had been that day but that he would rather face it than live in fear. (112–13)[35]

This passage uses a great deal more codeswitching than the previous one, and more codeswitching than used by any of the other writers discussed. What we have here is a codeswitched, interlingual, syncretic discourse. The passage does, of course, present a challenge to the non-Spanish-speaking reader. It might also present a challenge to some Spanish-speaking readers, since it contains colloquial expressions, slang, and many words that cannot be found in a Spanish-to-English or Mexican Spanish-to-English dictionary. Despite these challenges, Delgado constructs the passage so that readers can follow its action. We know that the narrator has a confrontation with a bully and his friends, and later when he takes on the bully by himself, the bully backs down. How do readers know this? They know not from the literal words of the passage but because they have translated the overall context, the overall story being told. We must actualize this text, actively birth and translate ourselves into this story—into its language and its world. We are enriched, both linguistically and personally, if we do so. If not, the text remains alien, foreign, babble.

Delgado's novel also uses fused linguistic constructions to teach the reader to translate and to push the reader into a mestizaje linguistic matrix. Consider, for example, his description of the readers at school "who struggle and call letters and words but seldom read a sentence straight" as "los slow ones" (67). Is "los slow ones" a Spanish or English term? Certainly it is both, and also more than both, for the humor and aptness of this term comes precisely from its combination of Spanish and English. Similarly, at one point when he reflects on how quickly his life is passing by and his own death, Flores comments, "It takes so much courage to face los condenados tic tics of life" (29). The clock is ticking faster, condemning us all to oblivion. He describes old friends as "ghost carnales I hadn't seen in a chingo of time" (79). The term "carnale" has been used often enough in Delgado's book and in enough contexts that an attentive reader would translate it not literally (as a carnal person) but more metaphorically, as a brother or friend.[36] And so the phrase "ghost carnales" acquires great resonance for someone who understands the meaning of aging, even if she or he does not speak Spanish. Delgado also uses words that have come into Spanish specifically because of its interaction with English, words that therefore could be understood by non-Spanish-speaking readers, such as "lonches" (46) (meaning lunches) and "pasatiempo" (37) (meaning diversion or pastime).

Faced with this challenging text, a non-Spanish-speaking reader has several choices: learn to translate some (although not all) of the words, ignore the words he or she does not understand, or stop reading. Given the compelling nature of Flores's voice, I think most readers will make the choice to translate. But if a reader refuses to translate, does this mean that Delgado's message is lost? Not exactly, because exposure to the world's multilingualism and multiculturalism is also a main goal. As Delgado himself comments in an interview, "to write using natural bilingual style is a very vivid affirmation that we are here, that we are alive and well, thinking and writing in both idiomas [languages], and that there are many like us out there in the mythical Aztlán who also think and talk and write as we do" (101). Furthermore, a certain exposure to "unintelligibility"—to a difficulty of translation—may also be crucial to the text's meaning. In a compelling essay on "unintelligibility" in multicultural literature, Reed Dasenbrock argues that this literature "offers us above all an experience of multiculturalism, in which not everything is likely to be wholly understood by every reader" (12). The work a reader is asked to do when encountering a different mode of expression is crucial to a book's meaning, and the book may actually have been written to make the reader do the work. Discussing Rudolfo Anaya's novel *Bless Me Ultima*, Dasenbrock comments, "The reader is thrown into a world of Spanish without translation or cushioning, and even the monolingual reader moves toward a functional bilingualism, an ability to understand the world of the novel" (16). As the reader moves toward functional bilingualism, however, he or she does not come to understand *everything* about the text's world or language. Thus, the differences of this culture and its language are signaled and left present in the text, even as the monolingual reader moves toward functional bilingualism and biculturalism. I would argue that most readers—even Spanish-speaking ones—when reading Delgado's text (which contains much more Spanish than Anaya's) will struggle to make sense of its languages. And this struggle with multilingualism is crucial to the text's overall themes: the attempt to birth a new mode of language, and the many languages already present in the United States.

A final way Delgado asks readers to translate the novel and construct its meaning is through the mystery surrounding Louise. Flores constantly makes enigmatic comments about Louise, telling us (for example) that she is a figment of his imagination (41), that she is not real (114), but also that she is an address he has picked out of a telephone book (114). At the end of the novel, Flores claims that two of his letters return to him (130). Where are the rest of the letters? How does this text come to be published? Does he actually send these letters, in the first place? If not, how is it that some of them come back to him? And why don't they all come back? Does Louise retype the letters and publish them herself, as Flores suggests that she do at one point in the novel? Or is Louise entirely a fiction?

I would suggest that Delgado embeds questions such as these into his text to make the reader a more active and writerly translator and producer of textual meaning. In a sense, we (the readers) are Louise—the intended audience for the letters. As intended readers we can choose (or not choose) to translate (receive, accept, understand, put forward) these letters. The reader, in a way, must publish the text—decide how it goes from being letters to a book we are holding in our hands. The reader must, then, actualize the text—bring it into being through metaphorical and writerly translation of its ambiguities and its complex language. Like Moraga, Delgado blurs the line between reader and writer, author and character, the translated text and the translator. As we struggle with this text, with the mystery of who Louise is and how the text comes to exist, as well as with its interlingual mestizaje discourse, we ourselves once again take up the task of the translator. We can resist this task, of course, but we cannot fail to be changed by our encounter with the interlinguistic space of translation that Delgado's novel so vividly portrays.

IN DEBATES ABOUT immigrant adaptation to the United States, two metaphors are prevalent: the United States is a "melting pot" where distinct immigrant cultures and languages are melted away (assimilation), or it is a "salad bowl" where individual elements (cucumber, lettuce, tomatoes, and the like) remain distinctive (isolation). But I cannot read Delgado's text—or any of the other texts discussed in this chapter, for that matter—in terms of either of these metaphors. The process these texts describe of languages constantly being brought into dialogue and tension with each other, as well as constantly reshaping each other into new formulations, is much more complex and dialectical than either image suggests. And there are certainly more than two options, both for the characters within the text and for the readers of these works. Translation offers a supple trope that moves beyond this either-or choice, along with a fluid illustration of how languages and cultures can be brought together and fused without losing their distinctive elements. Translation also demonstrates that the concepts of the American and the ethnic can be renovated and transcoded through a creative, interlingual tension between these categories and the tongues they habitually employ. It is precisely this tension that produces a new mode of language that transcends the sum of its parts.

It is not coincidental, then, that each of the texts discussed in this chapter asks readers to also become translators, multilingual and dialogical readers. For it is only "los slow ones"—the readers who can barely call out a sentence—who do not see the multilingualism of the United States. As Arteaga comments, the United States is "the site of polyglossia, where multiple national languages interact. English is neither the sole nor original language." Yet, Arteaga continues, "U.S. American culture presents itself as an English-language culture; it espouses a single-language ethos; it strives very actively to assert a monolingual identity" (72). The books discussed in this chapter, however, insist that readers become aware that the United States is a multilingual, multicultural society. These texts move toward a language of translation, subversion, and re-creation that forces readers into a productive dialogue with the multilinguistic story that constitutes the true history of language struggle in these United—and fortuitously disunited—States of America.

6

Cultural Translation
and Multilingualism in and out
of Textual Worlds

*English has been the most important unifier of our country for the
last 200 years—it's a symbol of being American, right up there with
the flag, "The Star Spangled Banner," the Pledge of Allegiance. . . .
You're free to come here and you're free to make a life for yourself.
. . . You're coming here to be an American. Being an American
means you're going to have to speak English.*—Valerie Rheinstein,
spokeswoman for U.S. English, in Jodi Wilgoren,
"Divided by a Call for a Common Language"

*We are people of the gaps. Only we know the gaps are where
life really is.*—Alfredo Véa, *La Maravilla*

ON 18 JULY 2002, the Brown County Board of Supervisors in Green
Bay, Wisconsin, passed an "English Only" resolution making English the official language of county government. It joined eleven
other Wisconsin counties and twenty-seven states in adopting En-

glish as its "official" language. "Though the movement has gained strength in recent years as part of a backlash against growing numbers of immigrants, it has taken on particular force since Sept. 11, fueled by patriotic fervor and fears about an uncertain economy," reports Jodi Wilgoren in the *New York Times*. The irony of the situation, of course, is that part of the reason CIA and FBI intelligence failed to detect the September 11 plot is that they had few translators who knew both Arabic (a widely spoken language) and English. States have increasingly disbanded university language programs that teach "esoteric" languages, and students in the United States are encouraged to believe that learning a second language is not a useful skill—that English is a lingua franca that will get them by in many, if not all, situations. And it will, up to a point. But the value of learning a second language or maintaining a first one has never been wholly utilitarian, and the importance of keeping ethnic and foreign languages alive in the United States—rather than attempting to eradicate them through English Only legislation or the abandonment of bilingual education—has never been purely a matter of governmental functioning. Complicated ideological issues undergird the attempt to eradicate multilingualism and the possibility of translation. In this chapter I examine how individuals have been able to resist this culture's English Only imperative, and what enables the survival of ethnic tongues and the ability to translate.

As Alfred Arteaga argues, the United States presents itself as aggressively monolingual (72). Consideration of English Only legislation and federal and state support for bilingual and "foreign" language education is one way of assessing the status of multilingualism in the United States, yet another level of multilingualism and translation exists on the personal, performative, and corporate level. I begin this chapter by examining "official" U.S. language policy as represented by support for bilingual education and legal initiatives for and against multilingualism. I then contrast these initiatives with "unofficial" language policy: What people do in their day-to-day lives, how individuals speak or translate (or fail to translate), what languages corporations and companies employ to sell products or explain services, and how performance artists, writers, and novelists preserve multilingualism and the power of cultural and linguistic translation. On the one hand, "official" U.S. language policy implies that, as Valerie Rheinstein suggests, "being an American means you're going to have to speak English" (Wilgoren), but on the other, more and more individuals are "people of the gaps" who create from their multilingualism and translations new forms of language and new ways of life. Perhaps English Only initiatives are futile attempts to stem a rising tide of U.S. multilingualism. What is clear, however, is that the tension between the official and the unofficial realms of language policy and usage animates many of the debates surrounding multilingualism in art, politics, and society, and that a zone of borderized, translated, transcoded, and transmigrated languages and ethnicities persists in spite of, or perhaps precisely because of, this tension.

Official U.S. Language Policy: Language Loss

The first significant area to be assessed is bilingual and foreign language education in the United States today, for without these types of education, the ability to translate is more likely to be imperiled by language loss. The United States has increasingly deemphasized the teaching of "foreign" languages. According to Lucy Tse, only one in six students in U.S. colleges enrolls in more than two years of language study (56); one result is that the CIA has been unable to meet its demands for translators (50). And recent initiatives in some states, such as California and Pennsylvania, have disbanded many long-standing bilingual education programs in favor of English immersion. From a legal standpoint, it is unclear at this juncture whether students who speak a first language other than English—students with Limited English Proficiency, commonly known by the unfortunate name "LEPers"—have a right to instruction in their native tongue. And yet countless studies have shown that bilingual education, when it is carefully planned, long term, and supported by teachers, families, and communities, is the best way to encourage students to learn English while maintaining their mother tongue and the ability to translate.[1] What, then, has led to the abandonment of bilingual education in many school districts? One clear cause is the popular (mis)conception that bilingual education has failed to create individuals fluent in English and the parent tongue and that speaking a first language other than English and preserving the potential to translate will only hamper individuals in their adaptation to U.S. society. For example, a *New York Times* headline on the front page of its 10 February 2003 issue states that "only 16 percent of Hispanic students earn a four-year college degree by age 29, the lowest rate of any group. A study says culture or language often stand [*sic*] in the way" (A1). But Mireya Navarro, author of the article itself (on page A14), which contains the headline "For Hispanics, Language and Culture Barriers Can Further Complicate College," never discusses how language enables or disables college success, instead citing factors such as tight family networks, early pregnancy, the need to contribute to family income, poor secondary schooling, lack of role models, and poverty. The actual report—by Richard Fry of the Pew Hispanic Center (PHC)—only mentions language issues in the context of "foreign born Latinos."[2] Nonetheless, the implication of the *New York Times* headline is clear: bilingualism and lack of fluency in English is a problem for Hispanics, one that "causes" them to be unable to finish college and (by extension) prosper in U.S. society. Articles such as these fuel the popular (mis)conception that bilingual education has been a "failure" and that the ability to translate should not be maintained.

Yet research has shown the converse. Students who have a high degree of literacy in their mother tongue manifest higher levels of literacy in English, as well as greater cognitive functioning; bilingualism has also been shown in numerous studies to enhance metalinguistic awareness, creativity, independent thinking, and concept formation (Soto 3–4). One qualification must be made: bilingual education promotes English literacy skills when it is presented as additive (rather than subtractive) in focus—that is, when it is geared to the maintenance and enhancement of the first tongue while the second is added and when it is phased in over a number of years.[3] The current U.S. policy of English immersion used (for example) in California favors a "subtractive" approach to bilingual education in which the child's mother tongue is displaced as quickly as possible by English; often the capacity to translate is then quickly lost as well. But "additive bilingualism" (also known as "language maintenance") has been shown to increase English literacy and certain metalinguistic abilities. "Subtractive bilingualism," on the other hand, is associated with low self-esteem, parent-child conflict, and the diminishment of literacy. Certainly works such as "Pangs of Love" (discussed in Chapter 1) and *Indian Killer* (discussed in Chapter 3) illustrate that when children displace the mother tongue with English and cannot translate, dire interpersonal consequences result. And these interpersonal consequences can lead to racial and ethnic violence.

The belief that bilingual education does not work, however, has been clearly implanted in the public's mind. One reason for this may have to do with the types of bilingual education advocated. English immersion, which usually asks the students to stop using the mother tongue in schools in one year, sometimes leads to the mastery of English, yet it also often destroys the ability to use the mother tongue and causes other negative consequences. "Quick exit" bilingual education (as it is sometimes called), then, does not work (Cummings 33). A similarly negative effect has been found in "transitional" bilingual education. In these programs, the student is allowed to use the mother tongue for a certain stipulated period of time (usually two or three years) while he or she learns English. But after this time period, the student is expected to transition completely to courses taught only in English. This type of education also has adverse results; the transition to an English Only curriculum is jarring, and the mastery of English is no better than with English immersion programs. Furthermore, since in most cases it takes at least six years to master a new language thoroughly, the students involved in this type of program may become what Pérez Firmat characterizes as *nilingües*: individuals with fluency in neither English nor the mother tongue (*Life* 46), people who are "homeless in two languages" (*Life* 47). The public and the media may tend to confuse these two types of bilingual education— immersion and transitional—and conclude that bilingual education does not work. And both methods do fail. Therefore, immersion is usually chosen, since it is cheaper and requires less teacher training.[4]

Yet there is a third type of bilingual education that is more effective: language maintenance. In this type of learning, the curriculum is typically divided between English and the mother tongue at first in something like a 20/80 percent or 30/70 percent split (i.e., 20 percent of the subject material is taught in English, while 80 percent is taught in Spanish). Gradually, over time (six years or more), the proportion of classes taught exclusively in English is increased but the second language is always part of the curriculum. With such an approach a student who enters school speaking (but not writing) Spanish would eventually learn to write it, while also mastering English. In other words, the ability to translate would be maintained. In some programs, English-speaking students are also encouraged to become bilingual; these "two-way" programs in which all students have instruction in two languages and sometimes even in the process of translation have excellent educational results. Many studies demonstrate that maintenance bilingual education is the most effective form of bilingual education.[5] In addition, certain immigrant communities throughout the history of the United States have maintained schools of their own (either during the day or after school) to teach the native tongue. Hebrew schools, Chinese schools, and (more recently) Korean schools have attempted to impart the values and language of the parent culture and the ability to engage in linguistic or cultural translation, with no dire educational consequences to the students' learning of English.

If bilingual education and bilingual literacy enables, rather than disables, learning English, why has it been such a contentious subject? As noted above, some individuals may compare immersion bilingual education with transitional bilingual education and conclude that they are both equal, but the third alternative—language maintenance bilingual education—is not considered. Of course, these programs are costly, but is this the reason for the dislike? In fact, the reasons may be more ideological than economic. As Marc Shell comments, language is often a test for race (116), and when people speak of abolishing bilingual education, they are trying to eradicate the presence of something they perceive as foreign, alien, other, and racialized. Language minority populations are often viewed negatively (Soto 25), particularly when they are not from European countries. And since their language is viewed negatively, as something to be eradicated, preserving the language or the capability for translation is not seen as an important or vital goal.

In the course of my research I spent some time observing a community of Russian Jewish immigrants who live in Cleveland. Most spoke English relatively well and used it in public, but they clearly preferred to use Russian in private. The children of this immigrant group—who were either born here or arrived before the age of five—were bilingual, and the expectation of the parents was that they would remain so. In some cases the children acted as translators for the parents. The oldest generation—most of whom had immigrated in their 70s—spoke no English. Yet the multilingualism and translative ability of this community of affluent, highly educated, and (it needs to be stated) Caucasian immigrants was never challenged. In *Hunger of Memory*, Richard Rodriguez reports that nuns came to his house and demanded that his parents speak only English at home; his parents, who had only a high school education, quickly obeyed. I cannot imagine this happening to this highly educated and literate group of Russian immigrants, and if it had they would likely not have complied. Immigrant groups from Europe have generally had more control over the preservation of the mother tongue, while the bilingualism or multilingualism of immigrant groups who are racialized is perceived as more problematic, more disruptive of the social fabric of the United States. Of course, education levels and class influence the treatment of "minority" languages, but race is always a salient and crucial characteristic that impinges on which languages are valued and deemed to be worthy of preservation and translation.

One reason for the dislike of bilingual education, then, is certainly race, along with the fact that the largest immigrant groups currently speak a language that is not viewed as having high social prestige—Spanish. As Lourdes Diaz Soto comments, bilingualism can be viewed as a national "problem" or a cultural resource (8–9), yet Americans currently fear bilingualism and bilingual education (xvii). Political and economic uncertainty also typically have contributed to fear of multilingualism, as Susan Dicker argues: "At moments in U.S. history in which economic and/or political insecurity plague the nation, immigrants and American-born minority-language speakers serve as targets for the fear and anger felt by English-speaking Americans. Allowing non-English languages to flourish appears to jeopardize the status quo of the dominance of

English and those who speak it" (17). Thus the fear exists that the "alien" other will rip the social and economic fabric of the United States with a foreign and disruptive babble that the dominant society cannot translate. Yet most immigrants do quickly adapt to the linguistic situation of the United States and master English. Often the mother tongue is forgotten in three generations and sometimes even two: typically the first generation speaks primarily in the mother tongue, the second is bilingual, and the third speaks mainly English. Ninety-seven percent of the people in the United States, according to Geoffrey Nunberg, speak English well, "a level of linguistic homogeneity unsurpassed by any other large nation in history" (121). And many can no longer translate or even function in a multilingual context (Nunberg 121). The United States has no need to fear becoming, in Theodore Roosevelt's words, a heteroglot boardinghouse, and yet it does fear this. And so it attempts to eradicate minority languages.

The reality of the situation is that good bilingual schools can create literate, intelligent, multilingual citizens whose translative skills help them function efficiently in a transnational world community—a world community that is itself most often multilingual. Lily Wong Fillmore, a noted expert on bilingual education, argues that "second language learning does not result in the loss of the primary language everywhere. But it does often enough in societies like the United States and Canada where linguistic or ethnic diversity is not especially valued. Despite our considerable pride in our diverse multicultural origins, Americans are not comfortable with either kind of diversity in our society" ("When Learning" 341). A good bilingual education policy focused on maintenance could lead the United States into the new millennium (Soto xvii). Such a policy would give students additional channels for voice (Wiley, *Literacy* 3) and additional cognitive resources (Kwong 46). Bilingualism and translation enable cognitive growth and should be encouraged and valued.

It might seem that the English Only movement takes the United States in the wrong direction in terms of preservation of multilingualism and the capacity for translation, yet the debates surrounding these initiatives and the formation of a countermovement known as "English Plus" have perhaps served a positive social function in that they have forced individuals, communities, government groups, teachers, and others to reflect on the value of multilingualism in the United States.[6] Nunberg argues that English Only initiatives have functioned primarily as a way of registering symbolic displeasure with immigrants and multiculturalism (123), and it is perhaps no coincidence that one prominent English Only founder has expressed racist views against Hispanics. The ideological underpinnings of the English Only movement are indeed insidious. Languages rights are part of human rights, and the genocide of a language is often allied with the genocide of a people (Rhydwen 132).[7] English Only initiatives attempt to kill "foreign" languages and cultural and linguistic translation capabilities; with this loss, a way of life and a symbolic means of identity construction for many ethnic peoples may also be destroyed.

Furthermore, there are certainly many instances in the past when languages have been lost. James Crawford's statistics demonstrate that today, most "Native American languages are becoming endangered species" (154); 89 percent of indigenous languages are now considered "moribund." Language loss in the United States has occurred within *all* ethnic groups. In an extensive study of language shift in the United States, well-known sociologist Calvin Veltman argues that "all American language minorities in all regions of the United States exhibit high levels of anglicisation . . . [and] strong willingness to accommodate their language behavior to that of the American environment. They are not only disposed to learning the English language, and to learning it well; they are disposed to making English their principal language of use, while many go still further and abandon the use of their mother tongue" (*Language* 90). According to Veltman, the vast majority of the native-born generation eventually "abandons the minority language" (*Language* 212) and, one would postulate, the ability to translate. Some people today claim that Hispanics have been slow to abandon their mother tongue, but that is not precisely the case. Continued immigration from Mexico, Cuba, and other Spanish-speaking countries has made it seem as if these immigrant groups persist in speaking Spanish. However, evidence indicates that native-born Hispanics have adopted English more rapidly, and in greater numbers, than in the past (Veltman, "Mosaic" 63). Most Hispanics can translate between

English and Spanish at this point, but it is very unclear whether this will be the case in the future (Valdés 103). "Spanglish" is also a creative style of communication in which Spanish and English are mixed, but several influential studies have suggested that even Spanglish is abandoned over time and that the third generation of Hispanics will speak mainly English.[8]

It is clear that given the current situation and U.S. policies, multilingualism and the possibility of translation are in danger.[9] Without translation, ethnicity cannot be transcoded, and tongues cannot be transmigrated. According to Crawford, language death does not happen in privileged communities but rather "to the disposed and disempowered, peoples who most need their cultural resources to survive." We should care about preventing language extinction, then, because of the "human costs to those most directly affected" (Crawford 163).[10] But there are also social costs: some studies suggest that multilingual societies are generally more tolerant of diversity and have lower levels of ethnic strife (Varennes 275). The attempt to translate between languages may in and of itself foster an appreciation for how diverse languages function and for how different languages can become powerful social and cultural resources.

The United States now has a choice: to foster linguistic diversity and the ability to translate, or to persist in seeing "foreign" languages as a problem that must be eradicated. In fact, some states have already taken positive steps. Several states have passed legislation requiring foreign language instruction from elementary grades through high school, and some states require foreign language fluency for graduation from secondary schools (Ricento 109). New Mexico and Hawaii have declared themselves officially bilingual, and four states (New Mexico, Washington, Oregon, and Rhode Island) and a multitude of local communities have passed English Plus ordinances. The English Plus movement is dedicated to the idea that first tongues should be preserved as English is added to the linguistic repertoire.[11] The number of states that have passed these ordinances is small, but evidence shows that when English Plus initiatives are presented in response to English Only ones, voters do not favor English Only in as large numbers. This supports a point that Lily Wong Fillmore has also made: at this juncture in U.S. history, we can either emphasize language shift (loss of languages other than English) or language maintenance ("When Learning" 342). Furthermore, at the current moment, English Only has numerous opponents (Edwards 168–69) and little binding legal force, so opportunities to preserve multilingualism and the ability to translate are present.[12]

What interventions have been staged? Some groups have proposed adding to the U.S. Constitution a Cultural Rights Amendment (CRA) that would protect the rights of immigrant and minority groups to engage in their own cultural practices. Perhaps what the United States needs, however, is not a CRA but an LRA—a Language Rights Amendment, modeled on that of other nations and geared to protecting the multilingualism of its citizenry:

> Whereas the genocide of a language eradicates a people's way of conceiving of the world and interacting with each other;
> Whereas language rights have been universally accepted as a human right by the United States and other UN nations;
> Whereas languages should be preserved as an important symbolic and cultural resource, rather than eradicated;
> The United States therefore affirms that linguistic minorities in the United States have the right to keep their first tongues while acquiring English and other languages.
> The United States also resolves to promote bilingualism, multilingualism, and translation skills among all students and the population as a whole by whatever means are available, including English as a Second Language (ESL) programs, maintenance bilingual education, and reinforcement of funding in higher education for language study.
> The United States also resolves to value the linguistic diversity of it population and to protect and enhance linguistic diversity by whatever methods are possible and productive.

Such an amendment might eventually lead to an effective bilingual education program for *all* students that would make bilingualism the norm and increase the ability to value other cultural traditions.[13] Furthermore, as numerous individuals have pointed out, most of the world is multilingual (Dicker 203), so a political reorientation in which multilingualism and translation are valued is worth working for. It is clear, however, that in the official realm of language policy, such a reorientation has not yet occurred.

Unofficial U.S. Language Policy:
Language Maintenance and Translation

Because of the factors listed above, many people give up their multilingualism and become unable (metaphorically and actually) to translate between cultures and languages. Yet other alternatives are present in the subversive and transcultured realm of what I call "unofficial language policy." Unofficially, many parts of the United States are now bilingual or, as Richard Rodriguez points out in *Brown*, trilingual. It is rare these days to call a local or a national business—phone companies, utilities, corporations, nonprofit agencies, and so forth—and not be given the option of hearing information in Spanish. My Puffs tissue box has Family Cold Tip #3 (Conseil anti-rhume #3 / Consejo para los Resfríos Familiares #3) to "strengthen your immune system by getting extra rest, proper nutrition, and moderate exercise" written in three languages: English, French, and Spanish. *The Tonight Show*, with Jay Leno, now has Spanish subtitles which come on automatically and which the viewer must turn *off* if she or he does not wish to see them. Multinational corporations and corporate America appear to be adapting themselves to an unofficial bilingualism in the United States that by its very nature advocates an English Plus stance. Furthermore, the vast majority of the literature I have discussed in this book—both fictional and nonfictional—promotes an English Plus agenda rather than an English Only one and deploys the trope of translation as an actual or metaphorical practice for creating multilingualism. In this section, I focus on specific ethnic communities that have maintained their bilingualism or the capability to translate. They illustrate how the United States can come to value its "native" tongue, which is not English Only but English Plus: Spanglish, Ringlish, Franglais, Portinglês, Yinglish, Italgish, and Konglish.[14]

It is worth noting here that in the past, certain groups, when given the chance, have done an excellent job of preserving or creating bilingualism by unofficial means. As Nessa Wolfson explains, the official policy of the United States in the early part of its history was to destroy all Native American languages and cultures (232).[15] Susan Power illustrates in *The Grass Dancer* (discussed in Chapter 3) that when native individuals were removed from their tribe and educated in missionary schools, they quickly forgot how to translate between English and the native tongue, and studies show that "official" U.S. government policy did have this result. The Cherokee people, however, developed a written form of their language and then, in the early nineteenth century, established a system of bilingual education in Oklahoma. The education led to high levels of literacy in both the Cherokee language *and* English; in fact, the Cherokee educated under this method had a *higher rate of literacy in English* than the English-speaking populations of neighboring Texas and Arkansas (Wolfson 232). Unfortunately, at this point the U.S. government decided to dismantle the bilingual schools and send the students to all-English boarding schools away from their reservations (Dicker 17–18). The literacy rate of the Cherokees in English then declined rapidly, and the mother tongue was almost lost. This example illustrates that bilingualism and translation can be effectively promoted on the grassroots, community level—but only in the face of a benign (rather than adversarial) government policy.

Perhaps such a benign attitude is seen in the current treatment of Chinese Americans. As Xiao-huang Yin points out, since the 1950s there has been a renaissance in the United States of Chinese publications written in Chinese, and Chinese-language journals, newspapers, and works of fiction have proliferated (183). Furthermore, the Chinese immigrant community and Chinese Americans have a very strong history of language maintenance. In 1993, for example, 80 percent of Chinese Americans spoke Chinese at home; this figure includes both immigrants to the United States and the native born (Paisano 5). There are a number of reasons for this: there has been a steady influx of immigrants over the past two hundred years; residential patterns (living in or near immigrant communities) have encouraged language maintenance; and intermarriage has been low. Cultural forces have also contributed to the maintenance of Chinese: "The Chinese culture places high value on group support and interaction; social organizations hold the Chinese together and remind them of their roots. The extended family also works as a unit, with older members caring for the young and passing down knowledge of culture and language" (Dicker 65; see also Wong and Lopéz 288–89 and Xia). Another factor is certainly the rising sociopolitical and socioeconomic status of the Chinese, both in the United States and in the People's Republic of China (PRC). Many studies indicate that Chinese-language maintenance is highest among the most financially successful Chinese Americans. Furthermore, as Sau-Ling Cynthia Wong and M. G. López point out, the business successes of "Greater China" (usually defined as the PRC, Taiwan, and Hong Kong) and of "diasporic Chinese" with their network of transnational capital have created attractive job opportunities for Chinese American bilinguals (288–89). During the 1980s bilingual Chinese Americans sometimes found better job opportunities in Asia than in the United States, and this certainly contributed to maintenance of the Chinese language.

In addition to these social and economic factors, however, over which cultures may have little or no control, there is a final factor: the role of Chinese-language schools. Kingston describes attending these schools in *The Woman Warrior* (discussed in Chapter 1), and perhaps this is how she attains her ability to translate her mother's Chinese language and stories. Chinese schools typically teach Chinese language, history, and culture to American-born children. Wong and López document that enrollment in these schools rose in the 1980s and 1990s and that Chinese-language maintenance appears to have acquired a positive connotation for society, Chinese immigrants, and Chinese American children (288). Like the example of Cherokee bilingualism, it becomes clear that schools run by the community can have a positive impact on language maintenance and translation facility. Similar examples of successful community efforts to preserve the parent tongue and culture through education are found among Korean American second-generation individuals (Min 328), Romanians (Roceric 96–99), and Russian American immigrants (Hinkel 366).

What the Chinese, Russian, Romanian, and Korean American communities appear to possess is social and economic capital; they have the financial ability to set up private schools and send their children there and the basic understanding of how education might protect, rather than destroy, their culture and language. What of impoverished communities who lack this economic or social capital? Several recent studies have indicated that cultural capital—the ability to see the ethnic culture as conveying valuable knowledge and support—is also important in language maintenance and translation skills. A case study in Canada conducted by Bonny Norton, for example, compares women from different communities, some of whom maintained their language and some of whom did not. In particular, she highlights the contrast between Mai (a woman from Vietnam) and Katarina (a woman from Poland). In Mai's family the younger children assimilated rapidly into English monolingualism, while the older generation did not. The older generation, who could not communicate with their children, experienced depression and eventually moved out of the family household to work as live-ins for other families. Finally, the fabric of family life was destroyed: "In Mai's extended family, I observed a breakdown of social relationships and a situation in which parents had difficulty conversing with their children." In Katarina's family, however, the child was "learning English with no loss of her mother tongue" (445).

Norton argues that these differences have less to do with economic or material resources and more to do with cultural and symbolic ones: "Over time, Mai's brother grew to believe that Vietnamese people did not share equality with White Canadians and that the Vietnamese language had little value in Canadian society" (452). Katarina, on the other hand, always felt that it was imperative that her daughter maintain Polish; as Norton explains, "the Polish language meant more to Katarina than a link to the past—it was an essential link to her future and her identity as a mother" (450). Polish was not a denigrated language, and Katarina never felt stigmatized for her ethnic heritage. She also saw the need to engage in acts of linguistic and cultural translation, for without these acts her culture would be lost to her daughter. Certainly, economic factors play into language maintenance, but other factors are equally salient. If a language is denigrated by society or by individual speakers of the language (parents or children), it is unlikely to survive.

A similar finding is presented by Min Zhou and Carl Bankston,

who demonstrate that an ethnic culture and language can be either
a source of "social capital" or a source of shame, depending on how
the dominant culture views the ethnic group *and* on how members
of this group promote or prohibit the ethnic language. Zhou and
Bankston cite a number of studies that indicate that "ethnic group
membership and retention of original culture patterns can create
sources of adaptive advantages . . . ; ethnicity may be utilized as a
distinct form of social capital" (200). They define social capital as
"systems of social networks inherent in the structure of relations
among persons within a collectivity" (200). More important, perhaps, social capital within the family and the community generate
human capital in the second generation. In other words, close family and community relationships within an ethnic group can allow
both the preservation of language and culture and a higher social
status, level of economic wealth, or educational attainment.

To test these ideas, Zhou and Bankston examine the Vietnamese American community of Eastern New Orleans using census
data, newspaper reports, interviews, and a survey of Vietnamese
youth attending a neighborhood public school. In this second-
generation population of high school students, they found that
"Vietnamese students display high levels of ethnic involvement on
all of our indicators. Over 90 percent spoke Vietnamese at home;
55 percent of them reported that they were able to read and write
Vietnamese well; over half of them unequivocally identified as Vietnamese rather than Vietnamese American or American; 80 percent
reported that their close friends were mostly Vietnamese; and 60
percent said that they were likely to marry someone of Vietnamese origin" (212). Despite the low socioeconomic status of this immigrant group, the second generation maintained a high degree of
ethnic involvement and language to form what Zhou and Bankston
term "a coherent complex of immigrant culture" (213). The reasons for this maintenance of language and culture are complex, but
Zhou and Bankston theorize that the ethnic culture provides social capital that facilitates the adaptation of Vietnamese children to
American schools and society. The ethnic culture can foster ideals
such as commitment to a work ethic, to educational success, and to
the ethnic community. Ethnicity and maintenance of ethnic lan-

guage are therefore seen as contributing to success in the United States, rather than inhibiting it, despite external negative views of ethnicity and the Vietnamese tongue.

These studies illustrate a point I have made throughout this book: maintenance of ethnic heritage and language clearly connects to social issues (how particular races are viewed and socioeconomic status), but individual and cultural values are implicated in powerful ways as well. Recall that in some of the literary texts I have discussed, the characters *finally* make a choice to learn to translate, but this choice is made only *after* the characters decide the ethnic heritage is worth transcoding—that it provides important social, cultural, or human capital. Such a decision goes against what Thomas Ricento calls the dominant national language policy in the United States. According to Ricento, "the idea that the maintenance of immigrant and indigenous languages and cultures is intrinsically valuable, let alone that it makes social or economic sense, is a relatively alien notion for most native, and even assimilated, Americans" (90–91). Certainly, negative policies on the part of government or social stigmatization of particular ethnic groups contributes to language loss. But in the unofficial realm of language policy, it is also clear that individuals sometimes choose to resist these negative ideas and to see their ethnic language and culture as valuable, as worthy of translation and transmigration.

What enables this choice? Certainly access to good bilingual education programs and the parents' ability to continue to use the ethnic tongue in the home are crucial, as case studies conducted by Heloisa Souza on Brazilian children indicate. One study done among a very vulnerable population also illustrates that ethnic pride can be crucial in language maintenance. Lourdes Diaz Soto spent nine years observing bilingual Puerto Rican American families in a town in Pennsylvania. She highlights in particular certain "success stories"—families that prospered economically, educationally, or socially. One feature these families shared was a desire to raise bilingual children: "The families described a dialectical relationship between the home language and the home culture. As families faced the challenge of initiating a home learning environment capable of encouraging and enhancing linguistic and cultural learning, they described how they implemented a variety of approaches. The families with a background in education, for example, advocated a 'one parent–one language' approach [in which one parent spoke Spanish to the children at all times while the other spoke English] and initiated this bilingual approach at birth" (27). Language was crucially connected to the ability to be "proud of the Puerto Rican heritage" and aware of "cultural and historical accomplishments" of Puerto Ricans (28). The families also felt that the schools needed to model ways of encouraging linguistic and cultural integrity (36–37). Some of these changes involve financial resources (that is, implementing effective bilingual education programs), but others are cognitive: shifting how the schools think about the children's bilingualism. Spanish speakers in the United States as a whole are extremely vulnerable to language loss; they sometimes lack the socioeconomic resources of other immigrant populations, and Spanish is clearly perceived as a dispreferred language. Yet these success stories indicate that families can sometimes still promote bilingualism and a bicultural identity for the children.

Translation itself is one of the ways that tolerance and respect for linguistic diversity can be encouraged. As argued in the discussion of the Ebonics controversy, in schools translation can be a way teachers ask students to shift between languages without *abandoning* languages and to see languages as distinct resources. Katy Mei-Kuen Kwong, a Cantonese bilingual high school teacher who works in the public school system of Malden, Massachusetts, also uses translation in her classes. She documents a number of pedagogical benefits to the bilingual education program used, in which some subjects (math, science, and social studies) are taught in Cantonese, while students also take English as a Second Language courses: transfer of previous skills, learning English faster, easier student adjustment to the new environment, and students developing a healthy bicultural identity and taking pride in their native language (46). Translation is used by Kwong to promote some of these skills: "My students are also learning special skills, such as translation. The ability to translate from English to Chinese and vice versa improves students' metalinguistic awareness, strengthens their understanding of the structure of both languages, and develops translation skills that they may use in a future career" (47).

Even small interventions that promote translation can have good results. Lucy Tse discusses a program in which librarians at an ethnically diverse school added non-English-language books to the library holdings and encouraged teachers to use them in their classrooms. Some teachers began having their non-English-language students read and translate poems and stories from these books for their monolingual classmates. These translation exercises benefited both groups of speakers; the non-English language was validated, while monolingual children gained access to "a whole world they didn't know about" (65). Tse concludes that "this program not only promoted heritage language development, but also brought about school validation of the students' linguistic and cultural backgrounds" (66). Multiethnic literature, in and of itself, can promote such confidence and pride through translation. When I teach Moraga's *Loving in the War Years* in my ethnic literature classes, I often ask students who speak Spanish to translate phrases for the class. This gives them a source of pride and a level of "expertise" that many of them do not normally experience in their day-to-day interactions with faculty, students, and the general public.

Translation and multilingualism have not, then, been eradicated from U.S. culture; they persist in an unofficial realm of corporations, speakers, parents, educators, and communities that value and promote diverse linguistic backgrounds. Artists also preserve multilingualism through the creation of border zones and border languages and through transmigration of music, art, and discourse. This preservation of multilingualism and the possibilities of translation to remake the dominant discourse are evident in the performance videos and works of the artist/activist Guillermo Gómez-Peña. Indirectly, Gómez-Peña revises the concept of the "native speaker" and the native speaker's voice. I conclude the chapter with a brief assessment of this term as presented and renovated in Chang-rae Lee's novel *Native Speaker* (1995).

Translation and the Performance of the Unofficial Multilingualism of the Border Zone

So far in this chapter I have explicated a tension between the "official" (public, legislative, educational, and governmental) zone of language policy, which favors monolingualism, and the "unofficial" (private, communal, artistic, and social) realm of language usage, which favors multilingualism. These tensions are both embodied and to some extent dismantled in the performance art of Guillermo Gómez-Peña.[16] Gómez-Peña creates texts and videos that unofficially endorse multilingualism, but he also tries to stage at least half of his multilingual performances in public spaces— restrooms, elevators, sidewalks, and even borders themselves (such as the border between Mexico and the United States); he thereby attempts to enter the official (public) zone of language policy with his works and indeed to dismantle the line between the public and the private, the official and the unofficial, the "minority" language and the dominant discourse. Three texts in particular document Gómez-Peña's work as a cultural translator: the collections *Warrior for Gringostroika* (1993) and *The New World Border: Prophecies, Poems and Loqueras for the End of the Century* (1996), and the performance video *Border Brujo* (1990). I will center my discussion of these very diverse and multilayered works around three concepts: the role of art and the artist as a cultural translator, the nature and necessity for a "borderized" future and a border aesthetic, and the role of multilingualism and translation in creating the so-called New World Border.

As I have already hinted, Gómez-Peña's work effectively straddles the line between politics and art, the private and the public, and the language of hegemony and the "disenfranchised" voice of the "minority" artist/cultural translator. In 1979 Gómez-Peña sat on a toilet in a public restroom in California and read "Spanglish poetry" (*New World* 83); he wanted to "bring performance and language into unusual contexts, and to disrupt people's sense of the quotidian" (*New World* 83), as I am sure he did. By introducing Spanglish into a public zone, he embodies but also undermines the tension between public and private spaces and the languages normally utilized in these spaces. Spanglish itself is a hybrid tongue—a mixture of Spanish and English, the minority language and the language of hegemony, the public discourse of the nation and the private discourse of the (Spanish) home. Introducing this hybrid public/private discourse into a space that is both public and private (a bathroom is usually private but a public restroom is not necessarily a "room of one's own") undermines multiple separations "traditionally" made in culture. Such a scene both stages and undermines the tension between "official" language policy and the "unofficial" zone of multilingualism. Gómez-Peña views his performance art as a strategy of "social communication" and "cultural translation" (*Warrior* 16).

In performance pieces such as this, Gómez-Peña in fact creates a border zone between language realms. He also gives artists/activists a central role in political and social change on the linguistic border: "Border artists use experimental techniques and performance-derived practices to intervene directly in the world" (*Warrior* 39); "Thousands of artists of color in the United States, Canada, and Europe are currently crossing different kinds of borders. And as they do it, they are making a new kind of art, an art of fusion and displacement that shatters the distorting mirrors of the 'Western avant-garde'" (*Warrior* 16). Artists and cultural translators create new kinds of art that move toward a future in which the border will not necessarily disappear but will be constantly changing, evolving, and moving. The border, then, is a space of translation, syncretism, critique, and multilingualism, a malleable "intellectual laboratory" (*Warrior* 27). Gómez-Peña also presents the border as a new linguistic and social frontier, or *frontera*: "[Border culture] also means hybrid art forms for new contents-in-gestation . . . ; an art against the monolingües. . . . But it also means to be fluid in English, Spanish, Spanglish, and Ingeñol, 'cause Spanglish is the language of border diplomacy" (*Warrior* 43). Spanglish is "the language of border diplomacy" because it both embodies and undermines tensions between the "dominant" culture and the "marginal" one, the dominant discourse and the "disempowered" one. Later I discuss in more detail the fundamental role translation and multilingualism play in/at the border, especially in terms of the creation of new art forms, but here I want to note that the border is (or rather can be) the space for new art forms and "fluid" languages, new forms of identity, new interactions between the "self" and the "other," and new communications between the various versions of the self that the performance artist and the individual confront and manipulate daily. It is important too that those who watch and engage with Gómez-Peña's works become border crossers themselves and part of border culture and its languages: "The so-called dominant culture is no longer dominant. Today, if there is a dominant culture, it is border culture. And those who still haven't crossed a border will do it very soon. . . . As you read this text, you are crossing a border" (*Warrior* 46–47). Through the text and the performance of the text the reader crosses geographic, cultural, and linguistic borders that parallel the constantly shifting borders of the world outside the text.

As a performer and writer, Gómez-Peña constantly employs multilingualism and translation, speaking or writing in English, Spanish, Spanglais, French, and Nahuatl and in tongues. The video *Border Brujo*, for example, ends (unlike the text published in *Warrior for Gringostroika*) with Gómez-Peña speaking in tongues and then descending into a moody silence. The video itself is often filmed in close-up and makes Gómez-Peña's mobile, multilingual mouth and tongue a strong component and even a character in the narrative or perhaps disnarrative of Border Brujo, the border witch or sorcerer, who "unfolds into fifteen different personae, each speaking a different border language" (*Warrior* 75). So the loss of the voice at film's end disorients the viewer as we confront (in silence) the final persona of the film. What Gómez-Peña attempts to translate and perform in the video is the loss of his "original" language and culture. But out of this loss emerges new, more experimental and multilingual languages and cultures. Out of the loss comes "a proposal for new creative languages" (*Warrior* 38), as he says in another essay—languages that will reflect both the loss and the gain of living on borders and in translation. Like some of the communities discussed in the prior section of this chapter, then, Gómez-Peña remains committed to the possibilities of multilingualism and translation, and like the writers discussed in previous chapters, he is committed to the transmigration and re-creation of both the "mother" tongue and hegemonic discourses.

To embody this renovation and transmigration of language, Gómez-Peña codeswitches and fuses languages to illustrate that new modes of discourse can be created by the interplay of dialects and tongues. Codeswitching is sometimes used for humor and sometimes to draw the (monolingual) reader into the text and teach him or her to translate, as in the following clever multilingual puns:

"Don't worry, be Hopi" and "Selena forever reina" (*New World* 195). Codeswitching and language mixing also create bridges between writer and reader, Chicano/a and Anglo, Chicano/a and Spanish: "Bon soir rrazza. Bienvenue a esta mamada. . . . Such a paradox: A Mexican speaking bad English, and a Chicano speaking awful Spanish, two confused generations onstage, in search of an impossible bridge, an original image, a glimpse of hope . . . c'est dommage!" (*New World* 142–43). This passage, with codeswitches and mixes between Spanish, Spanglish, English, and French, also thematizes the idea that discourse can become "an impossible bridge . . . a glimpse of hope" between different peoples and languages. Gómez-Peña uses translation, codeswitching, Spanglish poetry, and even "Ingleñol," which Gómez-Peña describes as "made-up English" (*Warrior* 17), to create links between the dominant culture and the "suppressed" one. Most radically, *The New World Border* includes a glossary, but it does not translate Spanish to English (or vice versa) but rather borderizes and transmigrates both languages. The "Glossary of Borderismos" contains words such as "gringostroika" (a fusion of Russian and Spanish), defined as "a continental grassroots movement that advocates the complete economic and cultural reform of the U.S. Anarcho-capitalism," and "Funkahuatl" (a combination of English, Spanish, and Nahautl), defined as "the Aztec god of funk and night life" (242). Spanglish or Ingleñol terms such as "el othercide" (*New World* 26) or "waspbacks" (*New World* 27) are also invented by Gómez-Peña, who himself constantly renovates and transmigrates tongues.

The reader or watcher of a Gómez-Peña work of art is constantly forced, then, to translate, to cross borders, and to move toward a multilingual zone. For example, in the performance work "The New World Border," from which Gómez-Peña's later book takes its title, performed with Roberto Sifuentes, Sifuentes's character keeps asking for a translation of Gómez-Peña's Spanish and Spanglish, which Gómez-Peña refuses. Finally, according to the program notes, members of the audience begin to answer in response to Sifuentes's repeated demands for "Translation please!" (35). Audience members become translators and also part of a multilingual society, if but for a moment. In another performance piece from this collection, "The Last Migration: A Spanglish Opera (in progress)," Gómez-Peña also incorporates the process of translation: "Dear audience: / in order to continue this performance, / I demand a translator, de ya! / is there anyone out there in performance limbo / who speaks German with a Mexican accent?" (*New World* 211). After calling for a translator, the persona then asks the audience to become the translator, by saying "out loud" with the performer:

> México es California
> Marruecos es Madrid
> Pakistan es Londres. . . .
> Centroamérica es Los Angeles. . . .
> your house is also mine
> your language mine as well
> & your heart will be mine
> one of these nights. (211–12)

Quite literally, the audience is asked to speak Spanish, but more metaphorically, they are asked to make a number of border crossings as they take on the role of cultural translator: from Spanish to English, from the "new world order" to the "new world border," from the language of the "self" to the language of the "other," from the unofficial realm of multilingualism to the official realm of public discourse. These types of languages and spaces implode into themselves, as they are rendered permeable by the processes of translation.

The audience is also asked, at other times, to take on roles of translation and even coauthorship. Addressing the audience in the performance piece "1992: The Re-Discovery of America," for example, Gómez-Peña asks:

> are you a citizen of this time & place
> or are you still clinging to a dying order?
> are you willing to dialogue?
> or are you going to shoot me after the show?
> are you ready to co-write with me the
> next chapter? (*Warrior* 112)

Elsewhere in this piece, the audience is encouraged to "fuck Official English" (112). In a clever pun, Gómez-Peña implies that the "official" language must be both destroyed and miscegenated (if we interpret "fucking" in its most literal sense as intercourse). In this passage we are also encouraged to join the author/performer in coauthorship and performance of the multilingual, miscegenated self, the multilingual, hybrid, and translating voice, as we "cowrite" the next chapter of the show/our future with Gómez-Peña.

For Gómez-Peña, this multilingual, hybrid, translating voice must also exist on a national level. He believes that the arts can move the United States toward a multilingual future. Gómez-Peña acknowledges that the United States is officially monolingual but unofficially multilingual: "Unlike the images on TV or in commercial cinema depicting a monocultural middle-class world existing outside of international crisis, contemporary U.S. society is fundamentally multiracial, multilingual, and socially polarized. So is its art" (*Warrior* 46). The artists' multilingualism and cultural translations are meant to change the individual and U.S. culture, as this excerpt from "Border Brujo" expresses:

> I speak Spanish therefore you hate me
> I speak in English therefore they hate me
> I speak Spanglish therefore she speaks Ingleñol
> I speak in tongues therefore you desire me
> I speak to you therefore you kill me
> I speak therefore you change. (*Warrior* 78)

Continuing encounters with the unofficial multilingualism of the United States can lead to hate, violence, and even mystification of the "other": "I speak Spanish therefore you hate me." But they can also lead to growth and expansion, not just of the individual but of the "official" culture as well: "I speak therefore you change" (78).

In passages such as these, a process of transcoding has occurred in which both English and Spanish, the dominant culture and the marginalized one, the "other" and the "self" are miscegenated, renovated, and transformed. This concept can be applied to a reader or watcher who encounters a text or performance by Gómez-Peña. Perhaps she or he is transcultured, transcoded, transformed into someone who can appreciate the linguistic diversity of the United States, of its multiple speakers and polyglot tongues. And perhaps she or he is no longer ashamed of the many languages spoken and can engage in acts of cultural translation. Perhaps she or he will move from an English Only to an English Plus ideology.

Given the transcultured and transcoded multilingualism of texts such as those by Gómez-Peña, we must also reconsider what it means to be a native speaker. Does being a "native speaker" mean speaking one language, two, or even three? Is it speaking with or without an accent? Can a native speaker still translate? In Chang-rae Lee's novel *Native Speaker* the main character, Henry, a Korean American, has attempted to perfect his English, to lose all traces of accent that might have been transferred to him by his Korean American first-generation father. Yet Henry finds that the loss of tongue and the loss of the capacity for translation lead not to visibility but to invisibility. In the novel he is a spy (literally) and (less literally) a thief of language, of others' identities and voices, because he has obliterated his own identity and voice. His wife, a speech therapist, accuses him of being "surreptitious," a "B+ student of life," an "illegal alien," a "traitor," and, worst of all, a "false speaker of language" (5–6). Having forgotten his mother tongue and believing that only individuals born in the United States can be "native speakers," Henry is left a *niligüal*—an invisible, barely present presence, trapped in meaningless language that his wife calls "the Henryspeak" (6).

Through a long and painful process of self-scrutiny, however, Henry changes and grows during the course of the novel, and he renovates his attitudes about race, ethnicity, and language. Most important, after the death of his father, Henry comes to accept that "native speakers" are accented, multilingual, and vibrant: "We listen to the earnest attempts of their talk, the bits of their stilted English. I know I would have ridiculed them when I was young: I would cringe and grow ashamed and angry at those funny tones of my father and his workers, all that Konglish, Spanglish, Jive. Just talk right, I wanted to yell, just talk right for once in your sorry lives. But now, I think I would give most anything to hear my father's talk again, the crash and bang and stop of his language, always hurtling by. I will listen for him forever in the streets of the city" (337). Henry grows into an appreciation for the translated, multilinguistic tongue that is the true voice of the United States. In short, the concept of the "native speaker" is transcoded into something that does not exclude ethnicity, and the ethnic tongue is transmigrated to a place within English so that English itself undergoes change. Henry knows that he will listen "forever in the streets of the city" and the nation for this multilingual voice, the unofficial but vibrant voice of the native speaker as it has been redefined and transcultured in the United States.

What I have emphasized in this chapter, as well as in this book, is that although the dominant language policy tries to suppress this transcoded, multilingual voice, authors, artists, activists, and speakers constantly insist on its presence and value. Today there are many "Philomelan members of America's various 'ethnic' and 'racial' groups," as Marc Shell puts it (121), who feel as if they have no tongue. There are also, as Pérez Firmat argues, many "*niligües*"— individuals comfortable in no language (*Life* 46). And, finally, many individuals can no longer translate at all, either on a linguistic or cultural level. But there are also many people who insist on an English Plus ideology and, moreover, people who renovate and transmigrate English *and* their native tongue through their multilingual translation practices. The translator can choose to make English a place of hegemony and monolingualism/monoculturalism, or he or she can attempt to re-create English and in so doing give voice to the many tongues of the United States. The translator can renovate the idea of the "native speaker" and create a future in which languages "divide to conga," free-fall toward (but never quite reach) a new world border.

At this juncture, individuals and institutions in the United States have a choice: to foster the transmigration of tongues and that ability to translate, or to continue destroying first tongues and "foreign" languages in favor of some hegemonic and very unrealistic conception of the perfect "native speaker." As educators, readers, and speakers we can become cultural translators and advocates for the multilingualism of the United States as well as its art forms. Most individuals living in the United States today do not understand its long history of language loss. Works such as *Loving in the War Years* or Gómez-Peña's books and videos allow us to access this history and foster an appreciation for linguistic diversity and transmigrations, while works such as *Native Speaker, Hunger of Memory,* or *Indian Killer* enable an understanding of the personally and socially debilitating consequences of language loss and the alienation of untranscoded ethnicity. Multilingualism in the United States may be wiped out in the next twenty years or it may flourish in a border zone where languages divide to conga, where the fission and fusion between languages in translation produce new ways of speaking and new forms of identity. Finally, then, what I am arguing is that by valuing, speaking, and teaching this history of language loss *and* gain, we may renovate the language of hegemony and become agents in the promotion of multilingualism and the productive possibilities of translation.

Conclusion

Lost and Found in Translation

How many today live in a language that is not their own?
Or no longer, or not yet, even know their own and know
poorly the major language that they are forced to serve? This is
the problem of immigrants, and especially of their children, the
problem of minorities, the problem of a minor literature, but
also a problem for all of us: how to tear a minor literature away
from its own language, allowing it to challenge the language
and making it follow a sober revolutionary path? How to
become a nomad and an immigrant and a gypsy in relation to
one's own language?—Gilles Deleuze and Félix Guattari, *Kafka*

IN SOFIA COPPOLA'S 2003 film *Lost in Translation*, Bill Murray
plays a washed-up and jet-lagged Anglo-American actor named Bob
Harris who travels to Japan to make television commercials pro-
moting a Japanese whiskey called Suntory. In one of the film's most
memorable scenes, the director instructs Bob Harris in Japanese for
several minutes before his first "take" for the commercial. When
the Japanese interpreter translates this speech, however, all she says
is, "He want you to turn and look in camera. Okay?" to which
Harris responds, "Is that all he said?" "He wants you to say it with
intensity" is all that the translator responds, after a long colloquy

with the director. Obviously, something is being lost in translation
—but what? And can it ever be recovered? Should it be recovered?
And what do moments such as these—which appear to signal the
fissures between cultures and languages, the ineffectiveness of
translation—symbolize textually, culturally, and linguistically?[1]

Throughout this book I have argued that the trope of translation is fundamental to ethnic American authors' efforts to transcode ethnicity so that it signifies something positive, an identity
contained within the discourse of Americanness, and also to transmigrate an ethnic tongue so that it is not excluded by the language of hegemony, by English itself. I have contended, then, that
translation as trope often concerns preservation and re-creation—
preservation of ethnic tongues within English so that *both* languages change and evolve together, and re-creation of both ethnic and "American" identities. I have also argued that these texts
frequently gesture simultaneously to gaps in language, to a lacuna
within the text which signifies that something is lost in translation, even while something is gained. Translation does not ame-
liorate cultural and linguistic differences, although at times it may
attempt to move beyond them and create a syncretic new mode of
voice and an interethnic American identity. Nonetheless, in this
conclusion I think it appropriate to investigate what may be lost in
translation, what cannot be recovered, and what the trope of translation may efface by rendering ethnic discourse into English.

"I saw the language shrivel, and though I held out my hands to
catch the words, so many of them slipped away, beyond recall. I am
a talker now and chatter in my people's ears until I grow weary of
my own voice" (Power 282). As argued in Chapter 3, Red Dress's
character in Susan Power's *The Grass Dancer* is an agent of linguistic preservation and translation, but still a great deal of the Dakota
language vanishes. In the last chapter, I cited research suggesting
that the vast majority of native languages are endangered (Crawford 154) and indeed that language loss in the United States has
occurred within *all* ethnic groups (Veltman, *Language* 90). By the
third generation, most ethnic groups have "given up" their mother
tongue. There are exceptions, but perhaps the trope of translation,
by translating these ethnic tongues into English, *promotes* language

loss—and the idea, as seen in Coppola's film, that translation marks and encourages, rather than amends and ameliorates, cultural and linguistic divides.

Through the organization of this book, I have traced an increasingly multilingual approach to the trope of translation on both the lexical and the thematic level. Lexically, the authors of the Chinese American and Japanese American works I discussed in the beginning chapters of the book analyzed how Chinese and Japanese ethnic traditions and terms were translated into English, but the books included very few actual Asian words. The Native American texts discussed in Chapter 3 included more words from tribal languages, but these words were always transcribed and transliterated into English; no actual characters or glyphs from the native language were included. However, the texts I discussed in Chapters 4 and 5 became increasingly multilingual. An author such as A. J. Verdelle shows a character not only fluently codeswitching between African American Vernacular English and Standardized English but also inventing new words that mix these discourses and are her own creations, such as "sliver wigglers" (129) or "beetle bug wig" (139). As I discussed in Chapter 5, authors such as Cherríe Moraga and Abelardo Delgado include a large proportion of Spanish in their texts, thereby forcing the non-Spanish-speaking reader to become a translator. Delgado fuses languages to create new terms, such as "los slow ones," but he also indicates that the remodeling of language he depicts is one in which the "minority" and "majority" language both are changed; both English and Mexican Spanish undergo revision in his text. And, finally, an author such as Gómez-Peña (discussed in Chapter 6) includes a glossary that does not translate Spanish into English but rather borderizes and transmigrates many tongues by introducing terms such as "gringostroika," "Funkahuatl" "el othercide," or "waspbacks."

On a more thematic level, authors of works discussed in this book's first chapters mainly implied that there were two languages being used (English and the ethnic tongue) while those in later chapters illustrated an expansion and amplification of linguistic matrixes and codes. For example, in *House Made of Dawn* Francisco mixes English, Spanish, and several native languages, and in

Tar Baby Son manipulates the various dialects of the vernacular and of Standardized English. Furthermore, the authors I discuss in later sections of this book imply that the more codes and languages one knows and manipulates, the more empowered an individual can become. Birdie Lee in Danzy Senna's *Caucasia*, for example, masters many dialects of English and several different codes of AAVE in order to adapt to, and gain authority within, the various locations she inhabits. There is no pure language of empowerment in these texts and no one language of hegemony. Languages are imbricated and wrapped around each other, and the most powerful speakers move fluently and fluidly in an interlingual and multilingual realm of discourse. Through this book's organization, I have emphasized a movement toward forms of multilingualism that are increasingly complex and challenging to monolingual readers. The writers discussed in the earliest sections of this book, it must be noted as well, do most of the arduous metaphorical work of translation *for* the reader, while writers discussed in Chapters 4, 5, and 6 ask and even force the reader to become a translator, to integrate himself or herself into the text and its translative dilemmas and move toward functional bi- or multilingualism.

Yet even in the texts analyzed in Chapters 4, 5, and 6, Standardized English still constitutes the main linguistic matrix of communication, while ethnic discourses are (quite literally) a minority language in the text; even as multilingual a writer as Abelardo Delgado rarely includes passages where more than a third of the words are in Spanish or Spanglish.[2] Richard Rodriguez insists that American English itself is multilingual, and I will repeat here his thoughts on this subject:

> Americans do not speak "English." Even before our rebellion against England, our tongue tasted of Indian—*succotash, succotash*, we love to say it; *Mississippi*, we love to spell. We speak American. Our tongue is not something slow and mucous that plods like an oyster through its bed in the sea, afearing of taint or blister. Our tongue sticks out; it is a dog's tongue, an organ of curiosity and science. . . . Our lewd tongue partook of everything that washed over it; everything that it washed—even a disreputable history. (*Brown* 111–12)

Our "lewd tongue" is multilingual and curious. It reaches out and sucks up other languages—but at what cost, one must wonder. English has so often been an agent of colonization and domination, as bell hooks and others have pointed out. Anglo-American writers, as I argued in my introduction, employ the trope of translation to focalize this process of language loss and colonization. For ethnic writers, when does conga-ing become conquering? When does the dance of fusion between languages and codes become a dance of destruction or an elegy for what has been lost and cannot be recovered? Has a "Germenglish" identity/voice been achieved in these texts? Or have these writers, through their deployment of the trope of translation, actually facilitated English's ability to absorb the ethnic tongue and undermined the creation of subject positions that could resist this absorption?

I have pointed out that it is imperative to recognize translation's potential both to deconstruct and to reconstruct binarisms, and in this book I have included texts such as Louie's "Pangs of Love," Alexie's *Indian Killer*, and Morrison's *Tar Baby* in which binarisms are not dismantled and translation is ultimately refused or proven to be unviable. Coppola's film functions in a similar way: it marks the limits of translation, the absolute alterity of another culture and language. For the writers I have considered, however, some commonalties exist among translators who can dismantle binarisms and undermine hierarchies between "minority" and "dominant" discourse. Writerly, active, resistant translation is valued in these texts over translation that is readerly, passive, or complicit. The "scandal of translation," as Lawrence Venuti has noted, is that it often effaces itself and attempts to seem politically "neutral" when every act of translation, and every translator, has an ideological agenda (10). The texts discussed in this book emphasize the need to foreground the process of ideological and lexical translation—to render it visible, rather than invisible. The most effective translations are also polyvocal and dialogic, and they allow the voice of the "other" to speak through the voice of the translator. In Sherley Anne Williams's *Dessa Rose*, Dessa translates Ruth's words into her own discourse, but even within this translation she lets Ruth speak—she does not summarize or paraphrase her words but quotes them verbatim in a first-person voice. She therefore allows for the coexistence of multiple voices and modes of discourse. Through an ethics of translation these writers often portray the translated text as a space where a cultural "other" is made manifest and comprehensible. Many of these writers emphasize a mode of translation that is not abrogating and that does not transgress cultural differences.

Successful translators often inhabit a middle space between cultures and languages. They are often interlingual border dwellers, liminal figures who reside literally or metaphorically between ethnic identities. This is a precarious but productive position. In Fae Myenne Ng's *Bone*, Ona (the middle child) cannot negotiate this precarious space and so becomes lost in translation. More positively, in Leslie Marmon Silko's *Ceremony*, Tayo (who calls himself a "half-breed") says he will speak for "both sides" and finds in his mixed-race, mixed linguistic heritage a mode of storytelling and translation that moves beyond his prior linguistic impasse. Individuals with multiple ethnic affiliations and multiple ethnic languages—such as Birdie in *Caucasia*—are often shown to be capable of negotiating the thicket of multilingualism and of preserving and reconfiguring the ethnic language so that it both has a place within, and remodels, Standardized English. Even a text as pessimistic as John Okada's *No-No Boy* insists that hope (such as it is) for a movement beyond binarisms resides in the middle ground, the middle space of language and ethnic identity that Ichiro so uncomfortably inhabits. The middle ground, the border between cultural and linguistic identities, is the space from which the most productive translation practices can emerge. And it is precisely from this middle space that change may occur, as the "American" becomes infused with traditions and ideologies from other cultures, and English becomes a multilingual space of transmigration and translation, of contestation and resistance. In this middle space ethnicity itself also becomes transcoded and transformed into a source of not only cultural capital but also social and human capital, a source of psychological empowerment.

Still, questions remain. Does English absorb the ethnic language? Just how much does English change in this process? When we speak of language loss, is it enough to say these tongues have been "translated" into English? Is the untranslatable remnant preserved within the gap or lacuna in the text, or is it simply lost in translation? Numerous authors have spoken eloquently on this subject, arguing that the de facto use of English does not mean one must succumb to English monolingualism; the "minority" writer can force English to become a multilingual and even nomadic language. "To conquer English may be to complete the process of making ourselves free," argues Salman Rushdie (17). Silko describes her family's use of English as oppositional and positive: "I come from a family which has been doing something that isn't exactly Standard English for a while. I come from a family which, basically, is intent on getting the stories told; and we will get those stories told, and language *will* work for us" ("Language and Literature" 61). Using English against itself, against the grain, and against the standard, changes it and grants authority to the individuals who speak it. Edouard Glissant tellingly argues that "lack" does not reside in the ignorance of a language but in the "nonmastery . . . of an appropriated language" (48). To avoid English might be to exhibit a lack, while mastering and reappropriating it demonstrates a kind of fluency within the "master's" codes, which are no longer precisely the master's. Translation as trope, through its amassment of a series of language skills (bilingualism, intralingual translation, storytelling, codeswitching, and so forth) may be the most incisive way that an individual can exhibit simultaneously both appropriation/mastery of English and also its undermining and reconstruction.

Furthermore, as Rushdie argues, there is ambiguity in the use of English that reflects struggles taking place in the real world, struggles between the cultures within individuals and societies. Through the trope of translation, English can be made to reflect the ongoing struggle between "minority" and "majority" discourses, between the disenfranchised code and the language of hegemony. Formally, as well, the interjection of ethnic language within dominant literary forms (such as the bildungsroman, the coming-of-age story, the epistolary novel, the autobiography, the detective novel) transgresses these forms and both revises and revitalizes them. Michelle Cliff comments that in her writing she uses the forbidden language of her ancestors but that she also must mix in "the forms taught us by the oppressor, undermining his language and co-opting his style, and turning it to our purpose" (59). Translation as trope works formally to allow the introduction of nonstandard speech forms within the "master's texts," the master's pieces, the master's literary forms. Through this practice, the forms themselves are remodeled and remade.

Translation as trope also allows English to be not rejected, not denied, but written and rewritten *from within* through the insertion of an unruly, multilingual, ethnic discursive presence that is both strange and estranging. Lexically, then, as Guillermo Bartelt argues, "non-standard English monolingualism does not necessarily imply total acculturation to mainstream American values" (39) —English can be transgressed or aggressed from within its own linguistic confines. What tribe you are? Do you speak Ebonics? AAVE? SE? Ingleñol? Spanglish? Ringlish? Franglais? Portinglês? Yinglish? Italgish? Konglish? Can English be broken here? Gilles Deleuze and Félix Guattari ask, "How many today live in a language that is not their own? Or no longer, or not yet, even know their own and know poorly the major language that they are forced to serve?" (19). Perhaps the question seems obvious, but they go on to answer it in a way that turns the problem back onto the monolingual reader or speaker: "This is the problem of immigrants, and especially of their children, the problem of minorities, the problem of a minor literature, but also a problem for all of us: how to tear a minor literature away from its own language, allowing it to challenge the language and making it follow a sober revolutionary path? How to become a nomad and an immigrant and a gypsy in relation to one's own language?" (71). The writers I have discussed deploy the trope of translation to challenge English lexically and to force it into a "revolutionary path," a recognition of the multilingualism of our world and our culture. And they also encourage monolingual, Anglo-American readers and speakers to become nomads and immigrants in relation to their own language—whatever that may be. By becoming translators themselves, such speakers may lose an illusionary entity, their "own" tongue—Standardized English, the language of consensus—but gain the poetry and freedom of other tongues, of linguistic innovation and transmigration. Translation, as I argued in Chapter 3, can function as a form of radical bilingualism that encourages the reader to think/speak/read in more than one voice. The reader may come to see "different" systems of signs as open, revisable, and implicated within each other. "Monolingual" readers may come to possess a translating consciousness that sees systems of signs as porous and permeable.

Through translation as trope, readers may also come to sense that "their" language is not really "theirs." In *Monolingualism of the Other*, Derrida argues that it is possible to be monolingual and still speak a language that is not one's own; elsewhere he implies that this is a universal condition, a condition caused by the exile from the mother that creates lack and subjectivity proper. We are always-already alienated from language, from a "mother tongue," even if (or perhaps especially if) we are "monolingual." Translation as trope may force readers to realize that, as Derrida phrases it, "Yes, I have only one language, yet it is not mine" (3). Derrida also argues here that "the master does not possess exclusively, and *naturally*, what he calls his language" (23); rather, through cunning actions of cultural usurpation, colonization, and force, he comes to make others share his belief that the language is his own. Translation as trope often reveals these cunning acts of appropriation and control which naturalize the idea that the dominant language "belongs" to the master.

It is possible, then, to be monolingual and still speak a language that is not one's own, a language of alienation and exile. And translation as trope may force the master to admit that, as Derrida phrases it, "my 'own' language is, for me, a language that cannot be assimilated. My language, the only one I hear myself speak and agree to speak, is the language of the other" (*Monolingualism* 25). Translation puts to question what is the master's language and what is the language of the "other," both for the "minority" discourse speaker and the "majority" one. When translation mixes codes and also undermines them, it illustrates that in the end there is no absolute language of hegemony and no absolute mother tongue; all languages exist in relationship to each other, and all speakers appropriate languages that are not really (nor ever were) their "own." I argued in Chapters 1 and 3 that there is no "pure" or "authentic" mother tongue that can be recovered through translation—that words and songs are always translations of other words and songs, translations of previous verbal and written texts. And in Chapters 4 and 5 I posited that the language of hegemony is not separate or isolatable from the vernacular or ethnic discourse. Finally, then, translation as trope undermines fundamental and much cherished ideological constructs within culture regarding hegemonic language itself: who owns it, who is empowered by it, and whether it exists "apart" from "minority" discourse.

Nevertheless, as Derrida also argues and Coppola's Bob Harris would certainly acknowledge, translation sometimes fails: "The miracle of translation does not take place every day; there is, at times, a desert without a desert crossing" (*Monolingualism* 72). As I have stressed through this book, something may be lost in translation when the "desert crossing" does not occur. And something is also certainly found when translation *does* occur. I mean to signal a pun, here, that has lain buried in my text until this moment, a pun that concerns the lost-and-found space itself. In the English Department at Kent State University where I teach, there is a lost-and-found that functions both as a sort of holding space and an unofficial lending exchange. Sometimes I misplace an umbrella and I think it is gone permanently—I can't find it anywhere in my house or car, the two usual locations in which my umbrella typically resides. But then I recall leaving it in a classroom one day, and when I check the lost-and-found it is there, still, miraculously, several weeks or months after I first lost it. The lost-and-found functions as a temporary way station, a place marker that holds my items until such a point as I choose to reclaim them (or not). Yet this space also allows for exchange and circulation of various items. On one particular sunny day I left my sunglasses at home and had to walk across campus for a meeting with a dean. In the lost-and-found I discovered a pair of lime green wraparound sunglasses with mirrored lenses—the kind typically worn by flashy bicyclists with similarly flashy matching outfits. They looked nothing like mine, nor did they match the black suit I was (as usual) wearing for the meeting with the dean, but I wore them nonetheless. I must have looked like a strange hybrid of a professor/biker as I strolled across campus in my borrowed glasses. When I was done, I returned these glasses to the lost-and-found. I wonder about other individuals who might borrow (or keep) these same sunglasses, who might borrow (or keep) my items or the possessions of others. Pens, sweaters, keys, notebooks, papers, and even toys jam the lost-and-found in my department, a jumble of items that may have once had original owners but that now exist in a sort of permanent limbo of redemption and reclamation, a perpetual cycle of both exchange and loss. Where is the lost-and-found, we ask, if we have left something somewhere? Where, indeed, but in translation? Translation as trope finally constellates a lost-and-found—a locale that holds items/languages until such time as they can be reclaimed, exchanged, or claimed by another user/speaker.[3] The lost-and-found of translation represents a site of simultaneous linguistic loss and gain, of reduction and reimplication of codes, of both the destruction and the resurrection of language. In the end we cannot say whether translation as trope promotes the loss or preservation of ethnic language, for surely it must do both, simultaneously. What we can say is that, as utilized by the writers discussed in this book, translation acts as a lost-and-found for language, for ethnicity, and even for culture. In translation, the characters who have "forgotten" their mother tongue may find or retrieve it, and the culture that has denied its own multilingualism may be forced to acknowledge it. Of course, some items are never reclaimed in the lost-and-found of translation, while others take on new life and new owners, creating hybrid entities like the professor/biker in lime green sunglasses striding across campus on a sunny day. The writers discussed in this book encourage us to situate ourselves as speakers, teachers, and readers within this lost-and-found space of translation. Translation certainly teaches us that what is lost may one day be found and that what is found may one day be lost. Yet translation as trope also may allow the emergence of new configurations of language and new constructions of American identity—configurations in which we are each implicated in a perpetual cycle of debit and exchange, of redemption and reclamation, of being lost and found in translation.

Notes

INTRODUCTION

1. Of course, as Pérez Firmat also points out through the examples of Desi Arnaz and Gloria Estefan, the conga can also degenerate into an art form that merely reproduces stereotypes about Cuban culture and makes it palatable for an American audience. See *Life on the Hyphen* 53–56, 127–33.

2. Throughout this book I use the term "American" (in quotes) to refer to a person who predominantly identifies himself or herself with a white, Anglo-Saxon, monolingual culture. I use American (without quotes) to refer to people who inhabit the United States.

3. Support for translation as producing a new work of art can be found in Gress 55 and Barnstone 10–11. G. N. Devy also discusses this idea in "Translation Theory: An Indian Perspective" (68). Benjamin dissents (76–77).

4. In translation theory, "source text" refers to the text to be translated and "target text" refers to the translation.

5. As Monica Heller observes, codeswitching sometimes works to maintain "the separation of languages in different domains" (Introduction 6). This is not to deny that codeswitching can dismantle the boundaries between languages in some circumstances. In this book, however, I have used "translation" rather than "codeswitching" because I see it as a more capacious term for the attempt to find a *new* mode of language and identity that goes beyond dualism and "either/ or" paradigms. When characters codeswitch in such a way that they combine elements of both languages in a syncretic fashion, I have used the term "translation." For example, in Chapter 5 I argue that Cherríe Moraga codeswitches in order to create a syncretic third language which is made up of both English and Spanish but which also exceeds these two languages. I examine the topic of codeswitching in more detail in Chapters 4 and 5.

6. Willis Barnstone speaks of "writerly" translations (230), borrowing this term from Roland Barthes. I will discuss the concept of "writerly" translation more extensively in Chapter 1.

7. For discussion of translation in American and Chinese American literature, see Huang. The only author Huang discusses that I consider is Kingston, and he reaches very different conclusions from mine (see Chapter 1), mainly because Huang consistently argues that "translation involves . . . a process in which multiple readings of the 'original' text are reduced to a version that foregrounds the translator's own agenda" (4). But see my comments later in the introduction, following Venuti's line of argument, on how translation can either affirm or transgress differences.

8. One notable exception to the paucity of criticism on translation has been Jewish American literature, which has been discussed more extensively in terms of this topic. See, for example, the essays by Taubenfeld and Wirth-Nesher. There have also been studies that deal mainly with translation in Anglo-American and British literature, such as Eric Cheyfitz's *The Poetics of Imperialism: Translation and Colonization from* The Tempest *to* Tarzan (1997).

9. For literal discussions of the translation of Native American literature, see the essays in *On the Translation of Native American Literatures*, edited by Brian Swann. Closest to my discussion of translation in Native American literature is David Murray's book *Forked Tongues: Speech, Writing, and Representation in North American Indian Texts*, which examines "the complex and various ways in which the process of translation, cultural as well as linguistic, is obscured or effaced in a wide variety of texts which claim to be representing or describing Indians" (1). However, Murray's excellent and wide-ranging study contains only brief discussions of contemporary Native American fiction, such as works by Silko and Momaday. See also Arnold Krupat's *The Voice in the Margin* and "Postcoloniality and Native American Literature" for discussions of translation in Native American literature.

10. For discussion of the impossibility of literal translation, see Biguenet and Schulte x, Rabassa 1, and Barnstone 16. For support for translation as a process of finding metaphors, see Barnstone 16. On the subject of choice and freedom of interpretation in translation, see Rabassa 7. Barnstone (230) and Honig (3) both discuss translation as coauthorship.

11. For an excellent essay on the translation of *Yekl*, see Taubenfeld.

12. For examples of translation as an exercise in the conscious and

controlled usurpation of a culture's authority, see Lefevere's essay. For discussion of translation as a weapon, see Bassnett 46.

13. Venuti does not discuss "Pokémon."

14. I discuss Mehrez's ideas in more detail in Chapter 3.

15. Theorists who have discussed the role of gender in translation include Chamberlain, Díaz-Diocaretz, Godard, Levine, and Maier and Massardier-Kenney.

16. In this book, I generally use the term "Chicano/a" (rather than Mexican American) to connote the formation of a new political, social, linguistic, and literary identity that is more than the sum of its parts. For more on this term, see Chapter 5.

CHAPTER ONE

1. In *Robert Frost: A Backward Look*, Louis Untermeyer quotes Frost as stating, "You've often heard me say—perhaps too often—that poetry is what is lost in translation" (18). Also, in an unpublished notebook from 1950 to 1955, Frost defines poetry as "that which tends to evaporate from both prose and verse when translated" (Dartmouth, MS 001728).

2. Unless otherwise noted, all references to these authors are to these texts and will be cited parenthetically within the chapter hereafter.

3. My usage of "Chinese American" follows Bonnie TuSmith, who defines it not as "a 'bicultural' dualism of either/or possibilities" but rather "a *new entity* which is neither Chinese nor European" ("Literary Tricksterism" 284). Nonetheless, I would also emphasize, as several critics have before me, that Chinese American identity, like all identities, is always in process, changing, and evolving. This new identity does not dissolve or homogenize differences between the Chinese and the American but allows them to remain in tension with each other in the new syncretic construction.

4. Hereafter, I use "Kingston" as shorthand for the protagonist of *The Woman Warrior*. The protagonist of the text is a semiautobiographical character who has some relationship to the author's own life but who should not be equated with the author.

5. As Cheng Lok Chua notes, the Chinese "I" is a very assertive word, having its etymology in the radicals meaning "human being" and "sword"; therefore, "to say 'I' in Chinese is to imply that one is a human being with a sword, hence a swordsman or swordswoman"

(57). However, Chua does not discuss why Kingston makes this statement about the equation of woman and slave in the feminine "I."

6. Both Cheung (*Articulate Silences* 96–97) and Li (511) mention translation with reference to the ending of "A Song for a Barbarian Reed Pipe," but neither discuss it in the novel as a whole.

7. These are only some of the binary oppositions that Kingston breaks down in her text. Cheung argues that the text upsets "the opposition between women and men, East and West, fable and fact, orality and chirography, talking and listening, (re)vision and history" (*Articulate Silences* 74), to which might be added self and "other," univocal and multivocal, past and present, and autobiography and fiction.

8. Kingston's translations (or "mistranslations") of specific words such as "kuei" have been attacked by critics such as Benjamin Tong and defended by others such as Sau-ling Cynthia Wong (see "Autobiography"). See Huang and Dong and Hom on this subject as well.

9. For more on the subject of Kingston's transformations of this myth, see Sau-ling Cynthia Wong's essay "Kingston's Handling of Traditional Chinese Sources."

10. Barnstone also calls translation a double art because of the "collaboration of two (three, four) artists, who have joined their arts" (88). Since Kingston's mother probably retells a story that was told to her, we can see this concept of the interplay of two (or three, or four) artists at work. Indeed, by the end of the work, Kingston's voice is multivocal and cannot be distinguished explicitly from the voices she translates (her mother's, Ts'ai Yen's, No Name Woman's, etc.). For other critics who have discussed the double-voiced or multivocal discourse of the novel, see King-Kok Cheung, who argues that "many chapters of her autobiography are in a sense collaborations between mother and daughter" ("'Don't Tell'" 171).

CHAPTER TWO

1. A secret government investigation, headed by the journalist Curtis B. Munson before Pearl Harbor, found that "there is no Japanese 'problem' on the Coast. There will be no armed uprising of Japanese. . . . For the most part the local Japanese are loyal to the United States or, at worst, hope that by remaining quiet they can avoid concentration camps or irresponsible mobs. We do not believe that they would be at the least any more disloyal than any other racial group in the United States with whom we went to war" (quoted in Weglyn 45–47).

2. Throughout this chapter, I will use the following traditional terms to designate the different generations of Japanese Americans: "Issei," who are born in Japan and move to the United States; "Nisei," individuals who are second-generation Japanese Americans (born in the United States); and "Sansei," the children of Nisei, third-generation Japanese Americans.

3. See, for example, Hisaye Yamamoto's "The Legend of Miss Sasagawara," Toshio Mori's "The Travelers," Valerie Matsumoto's "Two Deserts," and Lonny Kaneko's "The Shoyu Kid." All these stories are set during the period of the internment or shortly thereafter yet deal with it in oblique, metaphorical ways. For discussions of the silence surrounding internment, see Takaki 484 and Streamas 125–27.

4. For other Japanese American writers who detail the problems of identity caused by the internment, see Yoshiko Uchida, *Desert Exile: The Uprooting of a Japanese American Family*; Hisaye Yamamoto, *Seventeen Syllables*; and Monica Sone, *Nisei Daughter*. For an analysis of this subject, see Lawson Inada's statement that "in the turmoil and uncertainty of the camps, the very strength of a people—their sense of identity and community, their sense of worth—was called into question. . . . It was as if the term 'Japanese-American' no longer signified a viable whole but denoted an either/or situation, a double bind" (260).

5. Lefevere's argument can be found in Bassnett and Lefevere, *Constructing Cultures* 44. John Guillory similarly defines cultural capital as "*linguistic* capital, the means by which one attains to a socially credentialed and therefore valued speech" (ix).

6. I do not discuss Kadohata's next novel, *In the Heart of the Valley of Love*, a dystopia set in the year 2052 that traces the movements of Francine, a nineteen-year-old part Japanese American woman. I do want to note, however, that although this novel is set in the future, the events seem suspiciously similar to those which occurred on or around December 7, 1941 (after the bombing of Pearl Harbor): people disappearing mysteriously, random violence, businesses taken over by the government, the rationing of supplies, paranoia, a fear of anyone alien (especially the Japanese), and a sense that the government is no longer conducting itself in a rational manner.

7. Matsukawa, telephone conversation, October 1992.

8. For a vivid description of how internment affected children's sense of home, see Yoshiko Uchida's comment that "whenever the children [in Tanforan, a relocation center] played house, they always stood in line to eat at make-believe mess halls rather than cooking and

setting tables as they would have done at home. It was sad to see how quickly the concept of home had changed for them" (88).

9. For other views of the novel as assimilationist, see Sumida and McDonald. But for more sympathetic views, see Inada and Yogi.

10. Ling also comments that "the ending reflects the conflicting concerns of the author, the reader, and the cultural establishment, concerns that imply the author's conscious use of literary strategies in order to be heard—and perhaps also his unconscious conformity to the cultural conventions of his time" (374).

11. None of these words are italicized, which also makes for a smoother transition between English and Japanese, graphically and lexically implying that these languages are not entirely separate or "different" from each other.

12. A small number of Japanese in Hawaii were interned, but the majority were kept under scrutiny but not relocated. For more on this subject see Ogawa and Fox.

CHAPTER THREE

1. For a critique of Benjamin's ideas, see de Man.

2. For a discussion of the power of language in Native American culture, see Schubnell 46–50.

3. For positive readings of Abel's struggle for voice, see Schubnell 117, 133–34; Scarberry-García 10; Evers 320; and Waniek 24. Scarberry-García, in particular, argues that Abel is fulfilling a ceremony that will allow him to find his "inner wind" or breath or *nilch'i* (10). Yet if Abel has found his nilch'i, why is he described as singing "under his breath" at the novel's end? Harold McAllister, on the other hand, argues that Abel is just on the verge of finding voice; when Abel joins the runners, this "signifies not a resurrection, not a completed assimilation into his culture, but the beginning of forty days of penance" (124). See also Bernard Selinger's argument that Abel is "not quite speaking" (59) and Robert Nelson's statement that Abel has not yet succeeded in "converting healing vision into a verbal version of it" (89).

4. There has been little discussion of the subject of translation in *House Made of Dawn*. Guillermo Bartelt considers the text's presentation of American Indian English (spoken or written dialects of English inflected by Native American speech patterns), arguing that "Momaday is certainly aware of the potential of non-standard English in his fiction and seems to have a sophisticated knowledge of linguistic

details of Indian English varieties" (49). James Ruppert briefly mentions translation, contending that Momaday translates oral and tribal discourse into the form of the novel so that they can interrogate the dominant system of language (*Mediation* 38). Momaday himself has discussed his ideas on translation; see "The Man Made of Words" (58, 59) and the interview with Charles Woodard titled "Wordwalker."

5. Tanoan is a family of Native American languages including those of the Kiowa and other tribes in New Mexico and Arizona.

6. For a more detailed discussion of hybridity, see Young. Michael Raymond argues that *House Made of Dawn* depicts a "pervasive cultural diversity" and that "meaning in contemporary life comes when one finds his sense of place by recognizing and living within that large and diverse context" (61). Alan Velie also discusses the positive value of cultural pluralism (62–63). However, neither Velie nor Raymond discusses linguistic pluralism and its power.

7. Louis Owens makes a similar point about Francisco, arguing that "he subverts the language of the Church by assimilating it into his indigenous cosmology" (*Other Destinies* 103). Bernard Selinger contends that Francisco is a better model for Abel than Tosamah or Benally because Francisco continues to practice both Native American and Christian rituals while "gently subverting both orders" (55).

8. The ending of *House Made of Dawn* has excited great controversy. For positive readings, see Evers 320; Hogan 134; Owens, *Other Destinies* 115–17; Raymond 69–71; Trimmer 88; McAllister 123; Ruppert, *Mediation* 54–55; and Velie 62. For readings that focus on the novel's negative or ambivalent overtones, see Kroeber 18; Hanson 203; Larson 91; and Selinger 62. My reading is closest to that of Selinger, who argues that Abel remains in an in-between space by "not quite running with the runners at the end, [and] by not quite speaking" (59). However, I do not believe that Abel has yet realized the power of this in-between space, so I disagree with Selinger's statement that Abel becomes "a menace to authority and control" (59).

9. Momaday's grandmother was Kiowan, as was his father, and both spoke the tribal tongue. His mother was Cherokee and Anglo-American. Momaday was born among the Kiowas in Mountain View, Oklahoma, but grew up on various Navajo reservations in New Mexico and Arizona. Given this familial and geographic background, it should come as no surprise that *House Made of Dawn* values linguistic and cultural hybridity rather than "purity" in racial, linguistic, or cultural identity.

10. Several critics have touched on the subject of translation in *Ceremony*. See Taylor's "Silko's Reappropriation of Secrecy" (32–33) and "Repetition as Cure" (233); see also Ruppert's "Dialogism" (132). Ellen Arnold discusses Silko's translation of the oral tradition into written words that are simultaneously re-created (88). Silko herself has discussed her translation of oral stories into written texts, using the broad meaning of translation that I have been discussing: "Obviously, some things will be lost because you're going from one medium to another. And I use *translate* in the broadest sense" (Silko, "Background" 50).

11. As Silko explains, among the twenty Pueblo groups there are at least six distinct languages; this may be the reason why "what particular language was being used wasn't as important as what a speaker was trying to say" ("Language and Literature" 56).

12. Since numerous critics have discussed Silko's adaptation of oral traditions in the form and themes of *Ceremony*, I will not dwell on this point. For discussion of this topic, see Brill de Ramírez and Zamir.

13. For discussions of the "mixed-blood" or hybrid individual/culture in *Ceremony*, see Sequoya 464–66; Zamir 397–400; Owens, *Mixedblood Messages* 35; and Arnold 78–79. John Peacock discusses "inter-tribalism," arguing that the novel includes syncretic "inter-tribal, Laguna-Navajo" solutions to conflicts (305). Silko describes her own familial background as hybridized: "Laguna, Mexican, white. . . . All those languages, all those ways of living are combined, and we live somewhere on the fringes of all three" (quoted in Rosen 230).

14. Several critics have argued that Ts'eh is an embodiment of Ts'its'tsi'nako, Thought Woman, Grandmother Spider. As Paula Gunn Allen explains, "All tales are born in the mind of Spider Woman, and all creation exists as a result of her naming" (233). Tayo's encounter with Ts'eh may represent, then, an encounter with language itself—with its powers of creation and rejuvenation. Still, it is crucial that Silko does not indicate that this is an original or uncorrupted or even pure Native tongue. Apparently, Ts'eh and Tayo converse in English (although this is never made clear), again illustrating Silko's idea that the telling, not the language per se, is crucial.

15. Paul Taylor makes a similar point about *Ceremony* as a whole: "It is clear that in the translation of Indian cultural experience into the English literary idiom two ontologies as well as two cosmologies exist, and that the Indian writer conjoins received images and meanings of English words with his own distinct image and word-making tradi-

tions" ("Silko's Reappropriation" 32–33). See also Ellen Arnold's argument that in the course of *Ceremony*, "the word, language itself, passes through the same processes of deconstruction and reconstruction, deterritorialization and reterritorialization, as Tayo himself" (86).

16. See also Paul Taylor's argument that the almanac notebooks are quite literally palimpsests that "'write over' the almanac that steered the European destroyer to the plunder and rape of the 'New World'" ("Silko's Reappropriation" 45). For a brief discussion of "anti-imperial translation" in *Almanac of the Dead*, see Krupat's "Postcoloniality and Native American Literature" (174–76).

17. In this sense, Power's text parallels developments in actual Native American language communities. According to Bartelt, there is now a well-documented trend toward the use of nonstandardized English within Native American communities; this language functions as a marker of ethnicity and bridges "the gap between traditional and mainstream cultures" (39).

18. An ability to fathom the language of the alien "other" was crucial to the Euro-American process of colonization, as James Axtell explains (35–36). Rather than learning the native tongues, the colonizers often relied on translators, and it was crucial to find a reliable one. Many native translators foiled incursions into Native American–controlled territories; however, colonization was sometimes enabled by a Native American convert/translator (Axtell 37).

19. Pérez Firmat explicates and expands the meaning of *transculturación* in the writing of Fernando Ortiz. See also Pérez Firmat's discussion of "critical criollism," which is a translational enterprise in which the translator wants to "inflect, rather than efface, European culture" (*Cuban Condition* 12). Mary Louise Pratt also discusses transculturation in *Imperial Eyes* (6–7).

20. But for a different perspective, see Neil Wright's assertion that Red Dress's speaking in two languages in the contemporary moment represents "mere accommodation to a present and perhaps temporary reality" (42).

21. Red Dress's bilingual discourse creates a "contact zone" by depicting relations of interaction rather than separation. Mary Louise Pratt argues that "a 'contact' perspective emphasizes how subjects are constituted in and by their relations to each other. It treats the relations among colonizers and colonized . . . [in terms of] copresence, interaction, [and] interlocking understandings and practices" (7).

22. There are complicated reasons for Lydia's silence; she believes

that her voice has actually caused the death of her adopted son and husband, so she will not unleash "the killing voice" (216). However, Power makes clear that the drunk driver who kills her husband and son emblematizes white dislike for Native Americans: "He could hear voices mixing with the wind, mocking voices speaking a language unfamiliar to him. *Sioux,* he guessed. . . . It was the old enemy rising up to challenge him. *These goddamn Indians, they never quit*" (6). Metaphorically, if not actually, then, Lydia's silence is engendered by racism and an almost apocalyptic war against Native Americans.

23. Transliteration involves writing a word in a foreign language into English without translating it. For example, in many temples Hebrew prayers and songs are transliterated into English so that people who do not read the Hebrew alphabet can still participate in the services by singing the transliterated songs, written in English.

24. There has been no critical discussion of translation and its failure in either *Reservation Blues* or *Indian Killer*. However, an issue of *Studies in American Indian Literatures* (9.4 [1997]) devoted to Alexie's fiction contains an article by P. Jane Hafen discussing music in *Reservation Blues* and an article by James Cox discussing the novel's subversion of popular cultural narratives.

25. Several critics argue that Alexie's writing perpetuates stereotypes of Native Americans and presents no critique of the dominant culture. Louis Owens, for example, claims that Alexie "reinforces all of the stereotypes desired by white readers" and that non-Indian readers come away from his novels believing that "no one is really to blame but Indians" for Native American self-destructiveness (*Mixedblood Messages* 79–80). Gloria Bird argues that alcoholism and drinking are "sensationalized" (51) in *Reservation Blues* while "the core of native community" (49) is omitted. Elizabeth Cook-Lynn believes that *Reservation Blues* does not present "art as an ethical endeavor or the artist as [a] responsible social critic" (69). However, this passage from Thomas's journal clearly *does* blame Euro-American culture for cultural and linguistic genocide against Native Americans. Furthermore, in both the novels I discuss, Alexie illustrates that current problems of the Spokane and other Native American groups (rage, alcoholism, poverty, and despair) must be connected to the long and bloody history of the colonization of indigenous peoples in the United States.

26. For more on the role of blues music, see Hafen 73.

27. Alexie has said in an interview that Big Mom is modeled on his maternal grandmother, Etta Adams, who died when he was eight. "She

was one of the great spiritual leaders of the Spokane tribe; . . . in her last days thousands came to pay their respects" (Marx 2). This hardly sounds "cartoonish" to me, nor do I think that she is represented as such in the text. Of course, as with many of Alexie's characters, there is a degree of humor in her depiction. See also Hafen's comment that Big Mom is "genetic memory" (75). Unlike Owens and Cook-Lynn, Hafen provides a positive reading of *Reservation Blues*, as does James Cox.

28. It seems clear that John Smith is not the Indian Killer, for the killer is seen leaving Seattle *after* John Smith's death. Any number of other individuals could be the Indian Killer: Jack Wilson, Reggie Polatkin, Harley Tate (who disappears), or even Father Duncan. The Indian Killer could also be a mythical figure from the past—a ghost dancer, for example, or even Wovoka, the leader of the ghost dance movement, who was also known as Jack Wilson.

29. John's silence is mentioned repeatedly; see, for example, pages 6, 14, 17, 19, 35, 36, 40, 41, 145, and 377.

CHAPTER FOUR

1. Throughout this chapter I use the term "Standardized English" rather than the more common term "Standard English" to denote that something has been done to this language to make it the standard, to make it "proper." "Standardized English" (or SE), as I use this term, is the grammatically correct language of "consensus" normally taught in schools. For a discussion of some of the features of SE, see Walt Wolfram's *Dialects and American English*. African American Vernacular English (AAVE) is also a rule-governed, fully formed, learned system of communication, but it is generally not taught in schools. Although AAVE is generally a "dispreferred" language, in this chapter I show that many African American writers indicate that it has a crucial role to play in formulations of voice and identity. For a detailed and nontechnical discussion of some of the features of AAVE, see Fasold and Wolfram, "Some Linguistic Features of Negro Dialect"; see also Smitherman, *Talkin That Talk* (20–40), and Wolfram's *Dialects and American English*.

2. "Ebonics" as a term was created by a group of African American scholars at a conference in 1973; these scholars wanted to define black language from a black perspective and so created the term from "ebony" and "phonics." According to Geneva Smitherman, the term

"U.S. Ebonics" is used interchangeably with Black/African American Vernacular English. For more on this term and its history, see Smitherman's *Talkin That Talk* (28–29) and Robert Williams's *Ebonics: The True Language of Black Folks*.

3. For a longer discussion of this controversy and its political and ideological meanings, see Collins.

4. A codeswitch can occur in one sentence ("I left my umbrella at home and it rained but c'est la vie in Ohio") or between sentences, as is often the case with bilingual Spanish-English speakers, who may move between Spanish and English at various points in a conversation. For a general discussion of the linguistic and political significance of codeswitching, see Heller, "The Politics of Codeswitching and Language Choice." Heller argues that codeswitching can either "acquiesce to or resist relations of power" (126) and that it can be part of a "process of ethnic mobilization which is characterized less by social transformation than by a realignment of the relations of power between ethnic groups" (138).

5. For a brief discussion of what a dialect is and whether AAVE should be considered a dialect of English or a separate and different language, see Rickford. This is a complex question which I can summarize here only by saying that even among linguists there is no accepted definition of what a dialect is and that most definitions turn out to have a more political than pragmatic meaning. Smitherman argues that whether AAVE is considered a dialect or a language depends on how language is defined: "If one considers only words, grammar, and sound as the essence of language, then Black speech data might tend to look more like a dialect of white English. If one also considers the history and social rules that govern the use, production, and interpretation of the words, grammar, and sound, then Black speech data more nearly resembles a different language" ("Black Language" 106).

There are two reasons that I describe AAVE as a language in this chapter. First, as Smitherman also points out, in the popular mind, languages have high social status and dialects do not. Second, I believe, like Smitherman, that AAVE is not just related to specific features of syntax but is also an expression of African American ideology ("Black Language" 114). Smitherman also defines Ebonics or AAVE as "an oppositional way of speaking," a "counterlanguage" (*Talkin That Talk* 19). It is also worth noting that AAVE is not a bastardized or corrupted version of English but probably the result of contact between African and European language systems; during this contact European words were grafted onto African language patterns and vice versa, so that both the European and African languages were transformed. For a good discussion of the origins and history of AAVE, see Dillard; see also Davis and Dalby.

6. The most famous example of this is Frederick Douglass's 1845 *Narrative of the Life of Frederick Douglass, an American Slave, Written by Himself,* in which Douglass states: "You have seen how a man was made a slave; you shall see how a slave was made a man" (75). In *Dessa Rose,* Sherley Anne Williams quotes part of this statement directly, which suggests that she is in dialogue with the often male-centered slave narrative tradition.

7. Jadine's fondness for money versus Son's poverty raises the issue of what relationship class differences play in linguistic conflicts. I do not mean to imply here that class plays no role in who does (or does not) speak the vernacular and has no impact on language conflicts. Most linguists who have studied this issue, however, conclude that race, rather than class, is a stronger determinant of whether an individual speaks AAVE or another tongue influenced by an ethnic language. William Labov's research, for example, demonstrates that "there are discontinuities between middle class and working class speech in the American sociolinguistic pattern. But the chief breaks are between ethnic groups in our large cities. The English of Puerto Rican and Mexican Americans clearly shows the effect of the Spanish substratum and is certainly a different subsystem from others. The language of Negro speakers in ghetto areas is much more different from that of the surrounding white community than we normally find in dialect-contact situations" (40).

8. Furthermore, AAVE is not static but changes over time. For discussion of these changes, see Stewart.

9. For more on the trope of the Signifying Monkey, see Gates and Kochman. This figure also comes up in *Caucasia.* For information and tales featuring Anansi, the spider trickster, see Abrahams's *Afro-American Folktales.*

10. In discussing Jadine and Son, Morrison herself comments that both these characters are "sort of wrong" in their views ("Interview" 128). Although such critics as James Coleman and Evelyn Hawthorne tend to see Son as a source of value in the novel, others such as John Duvall argue that Jadine is right to reject his demands.

11. For a good discussion of the novel's ending and its use of the Tar Baby myth, see Werner.

12. Accents are one aspect of dialect, but certainly not the only one. For more on the differences between accents and dialects, see J. C. Wells, who argues that a difference between varieties of English (or dialects) may involve "syntax, morphology, lexicon, and pronunciation," while a difference of accent "involves only pronunciation" (3). It is sometimes difficult to separate accents from dialects, but my point here is that Birdie knows that "English" is not monolithic but composed of many discourses, accents, and dialects.

13. For discussions of patterns of pronunciation of AAVE, see Smitherman, *Talkin and Testifyin* 16–18; Fasold and Wolfram, "Some Linguistic Features" 51–62; and Labov.

14. According to Gates, this trickster figure has different names in different geographic regions: he is called Esu-Elegbara in Nigeria, Legba in Benin, Exú in Brazil, Echu-Elegua in Cuba, and Papa Legba in Haiti (5). Birdie consistently uses the Afro-Brazilian spelling, "Exu-Elegba."

15. See especially in this regard James Weldon Johnson's *The Autobiography of an Ex-Colored Man* (1912), Jessie Fauset's *Plum Bun* (1928), and Nella Larsen's *Passing* (1929).

16. See Smitherman ("Black Language" 104–5) for a discussion of the value and uses of signifying. Smitherman defines signifying as "indirect language used to tease, admonish, or disparage" (104). See also Gates and Kochman.

17. For discussion of differences between African American Vernacular English and a southern dialect, see Fasold ("The Relation between Black and White Speech in the South") and Wolfram ("The Relationship of White Southern Speech to Vernacular Black English"). Both argue that although there is overlap, AAVE has some unique features not possessed by southern, white vernacular English. Fasold, however, believes these differences are "relatively few and rather subtle" (185), while Wolfram argues that there are considerable differences, especially in the use of the variant "be."

18. See also Ashraf Rushdy's point that conflicting theories of "reading" are employed in *Dessa Rose*—that there is a mode of reading "in which an individual attempts to master another" and "a form of reading in which two individuals come to a mutual understanding of each other; this is reading as dialogue" (365). I would argue that in this passage Dessa and Ruth engage in the second form of reading—reading as dialogue.

19. For a longer discussion of clues that Dessa tells the entire story,

NOTES TO PAGES 164–77 269

see Marta Sánchez 21–23. As I do, Sánchez believes that "although two-thirds of the story is told in third person, at novel's end readers discover that Dessa has been telling her story all along. . . . Dessa is 'author' of the book" (22).

20. For discussion of the value of oral communication in African American communities, see Kochman and Smitherman (especially *Talkin and Testifyin*, chap. 4).

21. See also Marta Sánchez's argument that Williams undermines strict boundaries between "writing" and "orality" (34). Mae Henderson and Nicole King also discuss the role of the oral and the vernacular in *Dessa Rose*.

22. See also Catherine Snow, whose research demonstrates that metalinguistic skills such as "recognizing that words have no intrinsic connection to the objects they refer to" typically emerge several years earlier in bilingual children when compared with monolingual ones. Thus bilingual children are more likely to be aware of "formal aspects of the linguistic system" and "the arbitrariness of the linguistic code" (65).

23. This is a quote from a poem by Adrienne Rich called "The Burning of Paper Instead of Children." See also *Teaching to Transgress*, in which hooks clarifies that it is not English per se that she finds oppressive: "I know that it is not the English language that hurts me, but what the oppressors do with it, how they shape it to become a territory that limits and defines, how they make it a weapon that can shame, humiliate, colonize" (168).

CHAPTER FIVE

1. I use the term Chicano/a rather than Mexican American to indicate the formation of a new political, social, linguistic, and literary identity that is more than the sum of its parts. The term has roots in political movements that emphasize the reclaiming of Mexican and Indian heritages, an awareness of exploitation and marginalization, and the use of linguistic reservoirs in English, Spanish, and other languages, as well as bilingualism (Rebolledo 94).

2. It could be argued that some dialects of African American Vernacular English are interlingual as well, because they incorporate "foreign" words. In a 1930s study, for example, linguist Lorenzo Turner demonstrated that over four thousand words from many different African languages were discovered in Gullah. Yet the AAVE presented in

most texts by African American writers on the whole does not include African words but rather synthesizes AAVE with SE, as I argued in the previous chapter.

3. The most extensive study of the use of Spanish and English in the works of Chicano/a writers is Ernst Rudin's *Tender Accents of Sound: Spanish in the Chicano Novel in English.* Rudin reaches some conclusions similar to mine, arguing that the "Chicano author [is] a translator between cultures" (x) and that the Spanish-language elements in texts "constitute one of the most salient and revealing markers of these processes of translation" (xi; see also 60). However, Rudin aims more than I do to catalogue and describe the use of Spanish in a wide variety of Chicano/a novels, and he rarely considers how these Spanish-language elements affect reading practices or force the reader to become a translator. For other critics who have discussed Chicano/a literature's bilingualism, multilingualism, or interlingualism, see Arteaga, Bruce-Novoa, Gingerich, and Keller. None of these critics, however, focus on the texts I write about here or reach the same conclusions regarding the status and use of practices and metaphors of translation.

4. For example, Tomás Rivera writes his early work "*. . . y no se lo tragó la tierra /. . . and the earth did not part*" (1971) in Mexican Spanish and then collaborates on its translation and presentation in a bilingual text that contains side-by-side translations. Another early Chicano writer, Rolando Hinojosa, begins writing his novels in the 1970s in Mexican Spanish and then changes to English in the 1980s, even retranslating some of his earlier works.

5. Codeswitching is the use of two different languages within one communicative episode. For more definition and discussion of codeswitching, see the introduction and Chapter 4.

6. I have only a limited reading knowledge of Spanish, yet I have been consistently drawn into the interlingual zone of the text. I argue throughout this chapter that one aim of many Chicano/a texts is to teach the reader to become a translator who understands the interrelationship between different languages. With this goal in mind, all translations of Mexican Spanish words in this chapter are my own unless otherwise noted and are based on my rudimentary reading knowledge of Spanish, as well as my use of several different Spanish-language dictionaries. Translations are set off in brackets from the texts themselves.

7. As I explained in the introduction and in Chapter 1, a "writerly translator" actively participates with the ethnic culture and language,

struggles to understand its complexities, and refuses to take a passive and literal approach to its meaning. Such a translator does not deny contradictions between languages and cultures but uses them in his or her translation practices to create new formulations of identity and voice.

8. Lora Romero argues, for example, that Rodriguez isolates himself from his community (122–23), and Ramón Saldívar contends that *Hunger of Memory* presents "an uncritical celebration of the autonomous individual" (169). Rosaura Sánchez calls *Days of Obligation* convoluted, inane, and circular (162); solipsistic (157); nonsensical and condescending (165); and reactionary, frivolous, disingenuous, and cliché ridden (171). Sánchez's main concern centers on her belief that Rodriguez constructs essentialistic binaries in which America is constantly elevated over Mexico (160) and that he sees assimilation as inevitable (157). Jerzy Durczak similarly faults Rodriguez for having fully acclimated to English (112–13, 124) and assented to assimilation (124). Several critics have presented more neutral or positive readings of Rodriguez. Laura Fine argues that Rodriguez's autobiographies "enact a simultaneous and paradoxical drama of self-assertion—the claiming of multiple identities—and self concealment" (120), while Norma Alarcón argues that his work demonstrates, perhaps unwittingly, that "totalizing self-construction is elusive" ("Tropology" 150–51). For other essays that persuasively argue that Rodriguez subverts the process of Americanization, see Hunsaker and Browdy de Hernandez.

9. In Rodriguez's and Moraga's works there is a construction of an autobiographical persona who may or may not be the same as the author of the text. Rather than constantly using the term "autobiographical persona," I will simply use the author's last name, but I do not mean to imply that the persona presented in the writing is unconstructed or is necessarily the same as the "real person" who writes the text.

10. Browdy de Hernandez also argues that *Hunger of Memory* "represents a double-voiced response to the dilemma of the marginal postcolonial subject" (152). However, she believes that Rodriguez fails "to recognize the significance of the ambivalence that comes across so clearly in *Hunger of Memory*" (152).

11. According to Norma Alarcón, Rodriguez "plays here with a Mexican idiom applied to those who look too directly at another: 'Comérselo con los ojos'" ("Tropology" 146).

12. In a 1994 interview, Rodriguez states this even more bluntly:

"Maybe what is happening in the Americas right now is that the Indian is very much alive. I represent someone who has swallowed English and now claims it as my language, your books as my books, your religion as my religion—maybe this is the most subversive element of the colonial adventure" ("New, New World" 13).

13. There is much controversy about why Marina helped Cortés colonize the people of Mexico. She may have believed him to be Quetzalcoatl, the feathered serpent god, and she may also have been sold into slavery by her own mother and eventually given to one of Cortés's soldiers. What is clear is that with Cortés she had a son and that this child and other mestizos, rather than the children of the indigenous population, were allowed to flourish. In *Days of Obligation* Rodriguez aligns himself with Malinche, with the translator-as-betrayer, while in *Loving in the War Years* Moraga (like numerous other Chicana feminists) attempts to rethink this legacy of woman-as-betrayer. Malinche also makes a brief appearance in Candelaria's *Memories of the Alhambra* (173), suggesting that the figure of the translator-as-betrayer haunts the consciousness of the interlingual Chicano/a writer.

14. As Steven Hunsaker comments, "Rodriguez forms identity not by accepting wholesale any one world view but through the slow accretion of influence from disparate and often contradictory sources" (124).

15. For more on how the population became miscegenated, see Arteaga (24–43), who explains that the "conquistador father" destroyed "the native culture and native body" so that he could "infuse his own" (26). This conquest began with the mass slaying of Indian men, the elimination of Native children, and the rape of Indian women (26). Within the first century of colonization, disease and deliberate destruction reduced the indigenous population from 25 million to 1 million (82).

16. In 1848 the Treaty of Guadalupe Hidalgo ended twenty-two months of warfare between Mexico and the United States. In the treaty, Mexico gave almost half of its territory to the United States. Given the choice of becoming a citizen of the United States or migrating south, most Mexicans accepted U.S. domination and so became, in the most literal sense, Mexican Americans (Paredes 36).

17. It is certainly not true, then, that Joe opts for assimilation and "carries the idea of being American to its extreme" (57), as Marvin Lewis claims. But for a different point of view, see Lattin 285–86.

18. Here is a partial list of Spanish phrases in *Memories of the Alham-*

bra: velorio (8); que lastima, su padre (10); muy barato, joven, hombre (14); chula, ranchitos, Frijoles Flats (16); posole, momentito, mexicatessen, a sus ordenes (19); senor (20, 33, 42, 46, 146); Mejico (20); policia, gato, "Paso por aqui," "Pues no.

No mas paso por aqui" (22); Museo Nacional De Antropologia, raza suffrida (32); Norteamericano (33, 145); Mejicano, raza, frijoles (35); tortillas and frijoles (36); bolillo (38); "Soy raza, campadres! Soy raza," loco, gringo, que loco (39); "La tursta es muy malo," "que tal" (40); cantina, pulque, chinga, Hijos de la chingada (42); gringo (43); viejitas, centavo (44); manana, cantina (45); cerveza, hombres, pistola, "mi cabeza," la politica, loco (46); "Mi cabeza!," "Que dolor!," aspirina (47); senor Headache, postola, policia, Hijos de la chingada (48); baille, patrona (51); frijoles, tortilla, gatittos (52); "Pelea!" (55); madrina y padrino (59); sanctuario (73); raza suffrida (77); a la chingada (79); "Es verdad que no puedes hablar espanol?," "no puedes" (80); "no puedes" (81); "Hasta la vista," politicos (88); "Eres Mejicano?," "Si" (92); tienda, momento (93); si, primo, abrazzo, mi hijo, "No habla espanol. Es agringado," padrino (94); abrazzo (95); raza (96, 185); ranchito (98); tus naglas, tus pechos (99); "Hablas espanol?" (106); "Catolicos? Si. Somos Catolicos" (108); tia (117); posole, sopaipillas (120); policia, los chotas (121); chota (123); Surumatos, Mejicanos, Chingados (124); corazon (125); pobres (126); que demonio (133); si senor (143, 144); siesta, numero cinco, baso profundo, adios (146); churros, numero cinco, Calle de Los Libreros (147); Recuerdos de la Alhambra (157); morisco (159); barrio, mi vida (161); serapes (163); Mejico (172, 173); parador (174); No soy Mejicano, Biblioteca Nacional (177); no soy Mejicano (180); biscochitos (189); babosa (191).

19. All page numbers refer to the first edition (1983) of *Loving in the War Years*. In 2000 Moraga published an expanded edition of this text that added four new essays to the end of the text but left the first 150 pages of the original virtually unchanged. Since most readers are familiar with the 1983 edition, I have chosen to use the pagination from the first edition rather than that of the second.

20. If, as Norma Alarcón argues, in Chicana women's writing "women may have a voice on the condition that they speak as mothers" ("Making *Familia*" 148), this image becomes even more interesting. See also Arteaga's argument that for Moraga reproduction occurs in an act of the tongue, not the phallus (36).

21. For discussion of La Malinche's presentation in "A Long Line of Vendidas," see Yarbro-Bejarano 33–34 and Sternbach.

22. See, for example, Romero 139 n. 23 or Allatson 117.

23. Several linguistic studies have demonstrated that Spanish-to-English codeswitchers do not have two separate language grammars but one in which the grammars of the two different languages are functionally integrated; see Lipski; Pfaff; and Poplack, "Sometimes I'll Start." These studies have also shown that intrasentential codeswitching is not random but rule-governed behavior with syntactic constraints. Poplack goes so far as to argue that "speakers with the greatest degree of bilingual ability ('true' bilinguals) most favor intra-sentential code-switching" ("Sometimes I'll Start" 254).

24. See, for example, Swigart.

25. Translation of this stanza is taken from Yarbro-Bejarano 162 n. 15.

26. But for a different point of view, see Paul Allatson's argument that in this poem, "an emphatic, authoritative coming to voice in Spanish of lesbian desire is proclaimed, although the effect is muted by the English of the last lines" (117).

27. Most major elements of the first edition remain unchanged, with the exception of the removal of the glossary and the addition of the four new essays and some new footnotes. However, there are some changes in wording. For example, instead of the English word "cunt," used several times in the first edition, in the second edition Moraga substitutes the Spanish word "chocha" (82, 132) or "vagina" (133), which means roughly the same thing in Spanish and English. Since Moraga usually allies her sexuality with her Spanish identity, the change from "cunt" to "chocha" seems logical, but the change to the more technical term "vagina" ("It's as if la boca had lodged itself en el centro del corazón. . . . The same place where the vagina beats" [133, second edition]) seems jarring in this passionate conclusion to "A Long Line of Vendidas." See *Loving in the War Years* (Cambridge, Mass.: South End Press, 2000).

28. There has been some controversy about the audience for codeswitched and interlingual discourse. While some literary critics argue that codeswitching draws the monolingual reader into dialogue with the multilingual text (Arteaga 73) and encourages the monocultural reader to develop a bicultural sensitivity (Dasenbrock 16), one linguistic analysis of codeswitching states that it is intended "for a bilingual audience, an audience more typical of the majority of Chicano communities" (Penfield and Ornstein-Galicia 89). My view is that codeswitched, interlingual Chicano/a literary texts generally are

intended to speak to bilingual audiences *and* to monolingual readers/
speakers.

29. Ernst Rudin identifies Abelardo Delgado and Raymond Barrio
as the authors of Chicano novels in English "who use Spanish most extensively and with many different functions" (132). For an interesting
discussion of the divided self/divided language in Delgado's poetry,
see Bruce-Novoa, Introduction 11–14.

30. [When he was drinking] he used to be extra generous with his
Godchild Santiago and I would get [small change; dimes and quar-
ters].

31. "Escusado de loyo," according to Walter Corbella, is a spoken
representation of a Spanish phrase, "escusado del hoyo," which means
a hole in the ground used for a bathroom, or an outhouse. According
to Corbella, in spoken Spanish there is a tendency to move the final
"l" in "del" to the next word when it begins with a vowel, so that "escusado del hoyo" becomes "escusado de loyo" (the *h* in "hoyo" is silent)
(written communication, 10 December 2004). This is an example of
how Delgado creates a language not only in between Spanish and English but also in between the spoken and the written—he represents
oral language's speech patterns within the written text, as a writer such
as Verdelle does as well (see Chapter 4).

32. "Veinte" means "twenty."

33. "Little one . . . little one . . . Santiaguito, see, look, here comes
Santa Claus!"

34. "Are you Santa Claus? . . . / I am Guadalupe Jiménez Rodríguez, a mule driver. I'm not that fucker."

35. My nonliteral translation of this paragraph is as follows: "This
idiot would always pester me. He loved to seek me out to go at it
[fight]. I would ignore him. I told him, OK, man, you win. I get it already and would walk away. One day I was all dressed up at a party
with two or three girls when again he asked me to go fight outside in
a ditch. I replied to him, Since you are a smooth one, I know if I go
out there I'll have to fight a lot of your asshole brothers, for sure. He
had a lot of friends and they soon jumped me. My friend Felipe tried
to get me out of the mess. Someone landed a good kick on that guy
and that brought all his brothers and relatives into the act. He fought
very wildly. Felipe and I left very quietly. I knew that guy would try
to get me later, so rather than live in fear of that day I sought him out
the very next day. I found him and I said, look, here I am, without
any other business, get it out of your system right now, why don't you?

To my surprise he said he no longer wished any conflict with me and wanted it to end. He went on to say how frightened he had been that day but that he would rather face it than live in fear." 36. María Herrera-Sobek states that "carnal" is a term meaning "brother" and belongs to the pachuco argot (220).

CHAPTER SIX

1. Bilingual education programs need community support to be effective (Brisk 214), as well as support at all other levels—from teachers, administration, and family (McKay 395).

2. Richard Fry's report "Latinos in Higher Education: Many Enroll, Too Few Graduate" actually states that "the PHC report shows that . . . by some measures a greater share of Latinos are attending college classes than non-Hispanic whites. However, most are pursuing paths associated with lower chances of attaining a bachelor's degree. Many are enrolled in community colleges, many also only attend school part time, and others delay or prolong their education but fail to earn a degree."

3. For bilingual education "success stories," see Ricento's discussion of the Oyster Bilingual School in Washington, D.C., and public schools in Brooklyn, New York, and San Diego, California.

4. Bilingual education programs often fail because they are poorly planned, unsupported by the teachers or the community, or lacking in economic resources (Dicker 23–24). Lily Wong Fillmore argues as well that "a close examination of bilingual education where it has performed poorly will often show the extent to which it has been sabotaged from within by people who were supposed to make it work" ("Against" 369–70).

5. According to numerous experts in this field, maintenance bilingual education is the best method for increasing literacy in both English and the mother tongue (see Dicker 24, 103, 108–9; McKay 399–401; Varennes 193–95; Thomas and Collier; and Ramirez, Yuen, and Ramey). Research also demonstrates that there are ways to create good bilingual schools (Brisk 214, 218) and that when bilingual education is well planned it is highly effective (Wiley, *Literacy* 153). For summaries of these studies see Wiley's *Literacy and Language* and Varennes. According to Varennes, most studies conclude that a refusal to educate students in the mother tongue leads to poor educational results, a sense of psychological inferiority, and ethnic conflict (194).

6. See also James Crawford's argument that "the English Only movement sounded the alarm bells that energized Indian leaders in the 1980s to adopt policies designed to promote the use of ancestral tongues in government and schools" (159); eventually Congress passed laws (in 1990 and 1992) to protect indigenous languages and authorized grants for this purpose (160).

7. For more discussion of language rights in international treaties and charters, see Varennes.

8. In a 2001 *Los Angeles Times* news report, Robin Fields comments that "nationally, those between 5 and 17 years old who speak Spanish at home are almost 12% less likely than they were in 1990 to speak little or no English. The drop was nearly 25% in California, where the portion of bilingual children almost drew level with the national rate. Similarly, the portion of Asian school-age children who spoke little or no English dropped 38% nationally and 44% in California. . . . 'People worry about Latinization of America, but this shows the Americanization of Latinos' said Dowell Myers, director of the Demographic Futures Project at USC."

9. See Terrence Wiley's statement that "English has been the dominant language of the United States since its founding, and there appears to be little reason to assume that its status will be eclipsed in the foreseeable future. U.S. Census data indicate that, in 1990, there were approximately 32 million speakers of languages other than English in this country—13.8% of the total population. Only 1.8 million (less than 6%) of this group did not speak any English at all. Based on these data, it is clear that English is overwhelmingly the majority language" ("Myths").

10. For more on the consequences of language loss, see Fishman.

11. For more on the English Plus movement, see Vickie Lewelling's article and the core statement of beliefs at <<http://www.cal.org/resources/digest/lewello1.html>>.

12. On the legal implications of the "Official English" movement, see Miner.

13. See Ricento 109–10 for more on the idea of a national bilingual language policy.

14. In some sense the United States has always been multilingual, as Werner Sollors points out: "For much of multilingual America has used the 'hybrid tongues,' or, as one could also say, the 'melting glots' of Franglais, Portinglês, Yinglish, Italgish, Spanglish, and so forth" ("How German Is It?" 149). See also Heinz Kloss, *The American Bi-*

lingual Tradition, in which the author documents that in the United States there has always been legal freedom to cultivate languages and long-standing bilingual communities. Nonetheless, Kloss argues that while there have only been isolated cases of oppressive state language policy, many instances have occurred in which "individuals (including public school teachers) and groups exerted unofficial moral pressure upon members of the minority groups, especially children, so as to make them feel that to stick to a 'foreign' tongue meant being backward or even un-American" (370). Social attitudes, then, play a strong role in language maintenance or language shift, as well as in the continuing presence of bilingualism in the United States.

15. For example, in 1868 one report on Indian affairs argued that peace with plains Indians could be achieved by linguistic genocide: "In the difference of language to-day lies two-thirds of our trouble. . . . Schools should be established, which children should be required to attend; their barbarous dialects should be blotted out and the English language substituted" (Atkins 48).

16. Gómez-Peña has received fame and won numerous awards for his work, including the prestigious MacArthur Foundation Fellowship in 1991.

CONCLUSION

1. There are several other scenes in Coppola's film where Bob Harris tries and fails to understand Japanese or to translate between English and Japanese. In a hospital he attempts to have a conversation in Japanese with an elderly woman but only amuses her when he repeats her gestures. In a bar he ends up conversing with a Japanese man who is speaking in French, which Bob Harris translates into English. Ironically, when Charlotte (Scarlett Johansson) asks him what he is doing, he says, "My Japanese is getting better and better"—even though he never speaks a word of it in the entire film. Overall, the film seems to mark the alienness of the Japanese language, as well as the alterity of Japanese culture for American individuals like Bob.

2. For example, even the extremely multilingual passage from Delgado's *Letters to Louise* quoted in Chapter 5—the passage that describes the fight after the party when the narrator is young—contains approximately 204 words, but only 68 of them are in Spanish, which means that only a third of the text is in Spanish or Spanglish. In most other passages the percentage of Spanish-language words is much lower.

3. I will give one example of how languages can exist in a lost-and-found that allows the (eventual) reclamation of a "dead" language. For many years, Hebrew was considered a dead language. However, in the 1880s and the 1890s, Eliezer ben Yehudah almost single-handedly brought about a rebirth of the language and made it the language of Israel. Most crucial to his attempts was his dictionary, the first volume of which was published in 1910, in which he created the words necessary to have a modern, living language. Hebrew thus existed for many years in a lost-and-found space, until ben Yehudah reclaimed it.

Works Cited

Aaronson, Doris, and Steven Ferres. "Sentence Processing in Chinese-American Bilinguals." *Journal of Memory and Language* 25 (1986): 136–62.

Abrahams, Roger D. *Deep Down in the Jungle . . . ; Negro Narrative Folklore from the Streets of Philadelphia*. Hatboro, Pa.: Folklore Associates, 1964.

———, ed. *Afro-American Folktales: Stories from Black Traditions in the New World*. New York: Pantheon, 1985.

Acosta, Oscar Zeta. *The Autobiography of a Brown Buffalo*. San Francisco: Straight Arrow, 1972.

Alarcón, Norma. "Making *Familia* from Scratch: Split Subjectivities in the Work of Helena María Viramontes and Cherríe Moraga." *Chicana Creativity and Criticism: Charting New Frontiers in American Literature*. Ed. María Herrera-Sobek and Helena María Viramontes. Houston: Arte Publico Press, 1988. 147–59.

———. "Tropology of Hunger: The 'Miseducation' of Richard Rodriguez." *The Ethnic Canon: Histories, Institutions, and Interventions*. Ed. David Palumbo-Liu. Minneapolis: University of Minnesota Press, 1995. 140–52.

Alexie, Sherman. *Indian Killer*. New York: Warner, 1996.

———. *Reservation Blues*. New York: Warner, 1995.

Allatson, Paul. "'I May Create a Monster': Cherríe Moraga's Transcultural Conundrum." *Antípodas: Journal of Hispanic and Galician Studies* 11/12 (1999/2000): 103–21.

Allen, Paula Gunn. "The Feminine Landscape of Leslie Marmon Silko's *Ceremony*." *Critical Perspectives on Native American Fiction*. Ed. Richard F. Fleck. Washington, D.C.: Three Continents Press, 1993. 233–39.

Ang, Ien. "On Not Speaking Chinese: Postmodern Ethnicity and the Politics of Diaspora." *Feminism and Cultural Studies*. Ed. Morag Shiach. New York: Oxford University Press, 1999. 540–64.

Anzaldúa, Gloria. *Borderlands/La Frontera: The New Mestiza.* 1987. San Francisco: Aunt Lute, 1999.

Arnold, Ellen. "An Ear for the Story, an Eye for the Pattern: Rereading *Ceremony.*" *Modern Fiction Studies* 45 (1999): 69–92.

Arteaga, Alfred. *Chicano Poetics: Heterotexts and Hybridities.* New York: Cambridge University Press, 1997.

Atkins, J. D. C. *Report of the Commissioner of Indian Affairs.* 50th Cong., 1st sess., House Exec. Doc. 1, pt. 5. Washington, D.C.: Government Printing Office, 1887. Rpt. as "Barbarous Dialects Should Be Blotted Out. . . ." *Language Loyalties: A Source Book on the Official English Controversy.* Ed. James Crawford. Chicago: University of Chicago Press, 1992. 47–51.

Axtell, James. *Imagining the Other: First Encounters in North America.* Washington, D.C.: American Historical Association, 1991.

Bakhtin, Mikhail. *The Dialogic Imagination: Four Essays.* Ed. Michael Holquist. Trans. Caryl Emerson and Michael Holquist. Austin: University of Texas Press, 1981.

Barnstone, Willis. *The Poetics of Translation: History, Theory, Practice.* New Haven: Yale University Press, 1993.

Bartelt, Guillermo. "American Indian English in Momaday's *House Made of Dawn.*" *Language and Literature* 19 (1994): 37–53.

Bassnett[-McGuire], Susan. *Translation Studies.* New York: Routledge, 1991.

Bassnett, Susan, and André Lefevere. *Constructing Cultures: Essays on Literary Translation.* Clevedon, UK: Multilingual Matters, 1998.

Benjamin, Walter. "The Task of the Translator." 1923. Trans. Harry Zohn. *Theories of Translation: An Anthology of Essays from Dryden to Derrida.* Ed. Rainer Schulte and John Biguenet. Chicago: University of Chicago Press, 1992. 71–82.

Bhabha, Homi K. *The Location of Culture.* London: Routledge, 1994.

———. "Signs Taken for Wonders: Questions of Ambivalence and Authority under a Tree Outside Delhi, May 1817." *"Race," Writing, and Difference.* Ed. Henry Louis Gates Jr. Chicago: University of Chicago Press, 1986. 163–84.

Bierhorst, John, ed. and comp. *Four Masterworks of American Indian Literature.* New York: Farrar, Straus and Giroux, 1974.

Biguenet, John, and Rainer Schulte, eds. *The Craft of Translation.* Chicago: University of Chicago Press, 1989.

Bird, Gloria. "The Exaggeration of Despair in Sherman Alexie's *Reservation Blues.*" *Wicazo Sa Review* 11.2 (1995): 47–52.

Blanchot, Maurice. "Translating." 1967. Trans. Richard Sieburth. *Sulfur* 26 (1990): 82–86.

Bonnefoy, Yves. "Translating Poetry." Trans. John Alexander and Clive Wilmer. *Theories of Translation: An Anthology of Essays from Dryden to Derrida.* Ed. Rainer Schulte and John Biguenet. Chicago: University of Chicago Press, 1992. 186–92.

Brill de Ramírez, Susan Berry. *Contemporary American Indian Literatures and the Oral Tradition.* Tucson: University of Arizona Press, 1999.

Brisk, Maria Estela. "Good Schools for Bilingual Students: Essential Conditions." *Lifting Every Voice: Pedagogy and Politics of Bilingualism.* Ed. Zeynep F. Beykont. Cambridge, Mass.: Harvard Education Publishing Group, 2000. 209–20.

Browdy de Hernandez, Jennifer. "Postcolonial Blues: Ambivalence and Alienation in the Autobiographies of Richard Rodriguez and V. S. Naipaul." *A/B: Auto/biography Studies* 12.2 (1997): 151–65.

Bruce-Novoa, Juan. "Dialogical Strategies, Monological Goals: Chicano Literature." *An Other Tongue: Nation and Ethnicity in the Linguistic Borderlands.* Ed. Alfred Arteaga. Durham: Duke University Press, 1994. 225–45.

———. Introduction. *Chicano Authors: Inquiry by Interviews.* By Bruce-Novoa. Austin: University of Texas Press, 1980. 3–33.

Candelaria, Nash. *Memories of the Alhambra.* Tempe, Ariz.: Bilingual Press/Editorial Bilingüe, 1977.

Chamberlain, Lori. "Gender and the Metaphorics of Translation." *Rethinking Translation: Discourse, Subjectivity, Ideology.* Ed. Lawrence Venuti. London: Routledge, 1992. 57–74.

Chen, Shih-Hsiang. "Re-creation of the Chinese Image." *The World of Translation.* New York: PEN American Center, 1987. 253–66.

Cheung, King-Kok. *Articulate Silences: Hisaye Yamamoto, Maxine Hong Kingston, Joy Kogawa.* Ithaca: Cornell University Press, 1993.

———. "'Don't Tell': Imposed Silences in *The Color Purple* and *The Woman Warrior*." *PMLA* 103 (1988): 162–74.

Cheyfitz, Eric. *The Poetics of Imperialism: Translation and Colonization from* The Tempest *to* Tarzan. Expanded ed. Philadelphia: University of Pennsylvania Press, 1997.

Chua, Cheng Lok. "Golden Mountain: Chinese Versions of the American Dream in Lin Yutang, Louis Chu, and Maxine Hong Kingston." *Ethnic Groups* 4 (1982): 33–59.

Cliff, Michelle. "A Journey into Speech." *The Graywolf Annual 5: Multi-cultural Literacy*. Ed. Rick Simonson and Scott Walker. St. Paul: Graywolf Press, 1988. 57–62.

Coleman, James. "The Quest for Wholeness in Toni Morrison's *Tar Baby*." *Black American Literature Forum* 20 (1986): 63–73.

Collins, James. "The Ebonics Controversy in Context: Literacies, Subjectivities, and Language Ideologies in the United States." *Language Ideological Debates*. Ed. Jan Blommaert. New York: Mouton de Gruyter, 1999. 201–33.

Cook-Lynn, Elizabeth. "American Indian Intellectualism and the New Indian Story." *American Indian Quarterly* 20.1 (1996): 57–76.

Coppola, Sofia, dir. *Lost in Translation*. Perf. Scarlett Johansson and Bill Murray. 2003. DVD. Universal Studios, 2004.

Cox, James. "Muting White Noise: The Subversion of Popular Culture Narratives of Conquest in Sherman Alexie's Fiction." *Studies in American Indian Literatures* 9.4 (1997): 52–70.

Crawford, James. "Endangered Native American Languages: What Is to Be Done, and Why?" *Language and Politics in the United States and Canada*. Ed. Thomas Ricento and Barbara Burnaby. Mahwah, N.J.: Lawrence Erlbaum Associates, 1998. 151–65.

Cummings, Jim. "Bilingual Education and Politics." *Education Digest* 53.3 (1987): 30–33.

Dalby, David. "Black through White: Patterns of Communication in Africa and the New World." *Black-White Speech Relationships*. Ed. Walt Wolfram and Nona H. Clarke. Washington, D.C.: Center for Applied Linguistics, 1971. 99–138.

Dalji, Hafeezah AdamaDavia. "'Listen to Your Students': An Interview with Oakland High School English Teacher Hafeezah AdamaDavia Dalji." *The Real Ebonics Debate: Power, Language, and the Education of African-American Children*. Ed. Theresa Perry and Lisa Delpit. Boston: Beacon Press, 1998. 105–15.

Daniels, Roger. "Relocation, Redress, and the Report: A Historical Appraisal." *Japanese Americans: From Relocation to Redress*. Ed. Roger Daniels, Sandra C. Taylor, and Harry H. L. Kitano. Rev. ed. Seattle: University of Washington Press, 1991. 3–9.

Dasenbrock, Reed Way. "Intelligibility and Meaningfulness in Multicultural Literature in English." *PMLA* 102 (1987): 10–19.

Davis, Lawrence M. "Dialect Research: Mythology and Reality." *Black-White Speech Relationships*. Ed. Walt Wolfram and Nona H.

Clarke. Washington, D.C.: Center for Applied Linguistics, 1971. 90–98.

Dearborn, Mary V. *Pocahontas's Daughters: Gender and Ethnicity in American Culture.* New York: Oxford University Press, 1986.

Deleuze, Gilles, and Félix Guattari. *Kafka: Toward a Minor Literature.* Trans. D. Polan. Minneapolis: University of Minnesota Press, 1986.

Delgado, Abelardo B. Interview. *Chicano Authors: Inquiry by Interviews.* By Juan Bruce-Novoa. Austin: University of Texas Press, 1980. 95–114.

————. *Letters to Louise, via Air Mail.* Berkeley, Calif.: Tonatiuh-Quinto Sol International, 1982.

de Man, Paul. "Walter Benjamin's 'The Task of the Translator.'" *The Resistance to Theory.* Minneapolis: University of Minnesota Press, 1986. 73–105.

Derrida, Jacques. *The Ear of the Other: Otobiography, Transference, Translation: Texts and Discussions with Jacques Derrida.* Ed. Christie V. McDonald. Trans. Peggy Kamuf. New York: Schocken, 1985.

————. "Living On/Border Lines." Trans. James Hulbert. *Deconstruction and Criticism.* Ed. Harold Bloom et al. New York: Continuum, 1986. 75–176.

————. *Monolingualism of the Other; or, The Prosthesis of Origin.* 1996. Trans. Patrick Mensah. Stanford: Stanford University Press, 1998.

Devy, G. N. "Translation and Literary History: An Indian View." *Post-colonial Translation: Theory and Practice.* Ed. Susan Bassnett and Harish Trivedi. London: Routledge, 1999. 182–88.

————. "Translation Theory: An Indian Perspective." *Bombay Literary Review* 1 (1990): 64–74.

Díaz-Diocaretz, Myriam. *Translating Poetic Discourse: Questions on Feminist Strategies in Adrienne Rich.* Amsterdam: Benjamins, 1985.

Dicker, Susan J. *Languages in America: A Pluralist View.* Clevedon, U.K.: Multilingual Matters, 1996.

Dillard, J. L. "A Sketch of the History of Black English." *Black American English: Its Background and Its Usage in the Schools and in Literature.* Ed. Paul Stoller. New York: Dell, 1975. 19–48.

Dingwaney, Anuradha. "Introduction: Translating 'Third World' Cultures." *Between Languages and Cultures: Translation and*

Cross-Cultural Texts. Ed. Anuradha Dingwaney and Carol Maier. Pittsburgh: University of Pittsburgh Press, 1995. 3–20.

Dong, Lorraine, and Marlon K. Hom. "Chinatown Chinese: The San Francisco Dialect." *Amerasia Journal* 7 (1980): 1–29.

Douglass, Frederick. *Narrative of the Life of Frederick Douglass, an American Slave, Written by Himself.* Ed. David W. Blight. Boston: St. Martin's, Bedford Books, 1993.

Durczak, Jerzy. *Selves between Cultures: Contemporary American Bicultural Autobiography.* San Francisco: International Scholars Publications, 1999.

Duvall, John. "Descent in the 'House of Chloe': Race, Rape, and Identity in Toni Morrison's *Tar Baby.*" *Contemporary Literature* 38.2 (1997): 325–49.

Edwards, John. *Multilingualism.* London: Routledge, 1994.

Evers, Lawrence J. "Words and Place: A Reading of *House Made of Dawn.*" *Western American Literature* 11 (1977): 297–320.

Fanon, Frantz. *Black Skin, White Masks.* Trans. C. L. Markmann. New York: Grove Press, 1967.

Fasold, Ralph. "The Relation between Black and White Speech in the South." *American Speech* 56 (1981): 163–89.

Fasold, Ralph, and Walt Wolfram. "Some Linguistic Features of Negro Dialect." *Black American English: Its Background and Its Usage in the Schools and in Literature.* Ed. Paul Stoller. New York: Delta, 1975. 49–83.

Felstiner, John. "'*Ziv*, that light': Translation and Tradition in Paul Celan." *The Craft of Translation.* Ed. John Biguenet and Rainer Schulte. Chicago: University of Chicago Press, 1989. 93–116.

Fields, Robin. "Foreign-Born Population Reaches 30 Million." *Los Angeles Times.* 6 August 2001. <<http://archives.his.com/population-news/msg02279.html>>. 12 November 2004.

Fillmore, Lily Wong. "Against Our Best Interest: The Attempt to Sabotage Bilingual Education." *Language Loyalties: A Source Book on the Official English Controversy.* Ed. James Crawford. Chicago: University of Chicago Press, 1992. 367–76.

———. "When Learning a Second Language Means Losing the First." *Early Childhood Research Quarterly* 6 (1991): 323–46.

Fine, Laura. "Claiming Personas and Rejecting Other-Imposed Identities: Self-Writing as Self-Righting in the Autobiographies of Richard Rodriguez." *Biography* 19 (1996): 119–36.

Fishman, Joshua. *Reversing Language Shift: Theoretical and Empirical Foundations of Assistance to Threatened Languages*. Clevedon, U.K.: Multilingual Matters, 1991.

Flores, Lauro. "Chicano Autobiography: Culture, Ideology and the Self." *Americas Review* 18.2 (1990): 80–91.

Flotow-Evans, Luise von. *Translation and Gender: Translating in the "Era of Feminism."* Manchester, U.K.: St. Jerome Publishing, 1997.

Frost, Robert. Unpublished notebook, 1950–55. MS 001728. Robert Frost Collection. Dartmouth College, Hanover, N.H.

Fry, Richard. "Latinos in Higher Education: Many Enroll, Too Few Graduate." 5 September 2002. The Pew Hispanic Center. <<http://www.pewhispanic.org/page.jsp?page=reports>>. 14 December 2004.

Fusco, Coco. *English Is Broken Here: Notes on Cultural Fusion in the Americas*. New York: New Press, 1995.

Gates, Henry Louis, Jr. *The Signifying Monkey: A Theory of African-American Literary Criticism*. New York: Oxford University Press, 1988.

Gingerich, Willard. "Aspects of Prose Style in Three Chicano Novels: *Pocho*; *Bless Me, Ultima*; and *The Road to Tamazunchale*." *Form and Function in Chicano English*. Ed. Jacob Ornstein-Galicia. Rowley, Mass.: Newbury, 1984. 206–28.

Glissant, Edouard. *Caribbean Discourse: Selected Essays*. Trans. J. Michael Dash. Charlottesville: University Press of Virginia, 1989.

Godard, Barbara. "Therorizing Feminist Discourse/Translation." *Translation, History, and Culture*. Ed. Susan Bassnett and André Lefevere. London: Pinter, 1990. 87–96.

Gómez-Peña, Guillermo. *The New World Border: Prophecies, Poems, and Loqueras for the End of the Century*. San Francisco: City Lights Press, 1996.

———. *Warrior for Gringostroika: Essays, Performance Texts, and Poetry*. St. Paul: Graywolf Press, 1993.

———, perf. *Border Brujo*. Video. Dir. Issac Artenstein. Cinewest, 1990.

Gress, Elsa. "The Art of Translation." *The World of Translation*. New York: PEN American Center, 1987. 53–63.

Guillory, John. *Cultural Capital: The Problem of Literary Canon Formation*. Chicago: University of Chicago Press, 1993.

Hafen, P. Jane. "Rock and Roll, Redskins, and Blues in Sherman

Alexie's Work." *Studies in American Indian Literatures* 9.4 (1997): 71–78.

Hakuta, Kenji. "Language and Cognition in Bilingual Children." *Bilingual Education: Issues and Strategies.* Ed. Amado Padilla, Halford Fairchild, and Concepción Valadez. Newbury Park, Calif.: Sage, 1990. 47–59.

Hall, Stuart. "The New Ethnicities." *Ethnicity.* Ed. John Hutchinson and Anthony D. Smith. New York: Oxford University Press, 1996. 161–63.

Hanson, Elizabeth I. "N. Scott Momaday: Evocations of Disruption and Defeat." *American Literature in Belgium.* Ed. Gilbert Debusscher. Amsterdam: Rodopi, 1988. 197–204.

Haraway, Donna. "A Manifesto for Cyborgs: Science, Technology, and Socialist Feminism in the 1980s." *Coming to Terms: Feminism, Theory, Politics.* Ed. Elizabeth Weed. New York: Routledge, 1989. 173–205.

Hawthorne, Evelyn. "On Gaining the Double-Vision: *Tar Baby* as Diasporean Novel." *Black American Literature Forum* 22 (1988): 97–107.

Heller, Monica. Introduction. *Codeswitching: Anthropological and Sociological Perspectives.* Ed. Monica Heller. Berlin: Mouton de Gruyter, 1988. 1–24.

———. "The Politics of Codeswitching and Language Choice." *Codeswitching.* Ed. Carol M. Eastman. Clevedon, U.K.: Multilingual Matters, 1992. 123–42.

Henderson, Mae G. "(W)riting *The Work* and Working the Rites." *Black American Literature Forum* 23 (1989): 631–60.

Herrera-Sobek, María. "Mexican American Oral Traditions." *Teaching Oral Traditions.* Ed. John Miles Foley. New York: MLA, 1998. 216–23.

Hinkel, Eli. "Soviet Immigrants in the Unites States: Issues in Adjustment." *New Immigrants in the United States: Readings for Second Language Educators.* Ed. Sandra Lee McKay and Sau-ling Cynthia Wong. Cambridge, U.K.: Cambridge University Press, 2000. 352–68.

Hoffman, Eva. *Lost in Translation: A Life in a New Language.* New York: E. P. Dutton, 1989.

Hogan, Linda. "Who Puts Together." *Critical Perspectives on Native American Fiction.* Ed. Richard F. Fleck. Washington, D.C.: Three Continents Press, 1993. 134–44.

Honig, Edwin. Introduction. *The Poet's Other Voice: Conversations on Literary Translation*. Ed. Edwin Honig. Amherst: University of Massachusetts Press, 1985. 1–8.

hooks, bell. *Teaching to Transgress: Education as the Practice of Freedom*. New York: Routledge, 1994.

————. "'this is the oppressor's language / yet I need it to talk to you': Language, a place of struggle." *Between Languages and Cultures: Translation and Cross-Cultural Texts*. Ed. Anuradha Dingwaney and Carol Maier. Pittsburgh: University of Pittsburgh Press, 1995. 295–301.

Huang, Yunte. *Transpacific Displacement: Ethnography, Translation, and Intertextual Travel in Twentieth-Century American Literature*. Berkeley: University of California Press, 2002.

Humboldt, Wilhelm Von. "Introduction to His Translation of *Agamemnon*." 1816. Trans. Sharon Sloan. *Theories of Translation: An Anthology of Essays from Dryden to Derrida*. Ed. Rainer Schulte and John Biguenet. Chicago: University of Chicago Press, 1992. 55–59.

Hunsaker, Steven. *Autobiography and National Identity in the Americas*. Charlottesville: University Press of Virginia, 1999.

Inada, Lawson Fusao. "Of Place and Displacement: The Range of Japanese-American Literature." *Three American Literatures: Essays in Chicano, Native American, and Asian-American Literature for Teachers of American Literature*. Ed. Houston Baker Jr. New York: MLA, 1982. 254–65.

Jakobson, Roman. "On Linguistic Aspects of Translation." 1959. *Theories of Translation: An Anthology of Essays from Dryden to Derrida*. Ed. Rainer Schulte and John Biguenet. Chicago: University of Chicago Press, 1992. 144–51.

Johnson, Barbara. *The Critical Difference: Essays in the Contemporary Rhetoric of Reading*. Baltimore: Johns Hopkins University Press, 1980.

————. "Taking Fidelity Philosophically." *Difference in Translation*. Ed. Joseph Graham. Ithaca: Cornell University Press, 1985. 142–48.

Johnson, Charles. *Middle Passage*. 1990. New York: Scribner, 1998.

Kadohata, Cynthia. *The Floating World*. New York: Ballantine, 1989.

————. *In the Heart of the Valley of Love*. New York: Penguin, 1992.

Karlgren, Bernhard. *Sound and Symbol in Chinese*. Hong Kong: Hong Kong University Press, 1962.

Kekeh, Andrée-Anne. "Sherley Anne Williams' *Dessa Rose*: History and the Disruptive Power of Memory." *History and Memory in African-American Culture.* Ed. Geneviève Fabre and Robert O'Meally. New York: Oxford University Press, 1994. 219–27.

Keller, Gary D. "The Literary Stratagems Available to the Bilingual Chicano Writer." *The Identification and Analysis of Chicano Literature.* Ed. Francisco Jiménez. New York: Bilingual Press/ Editorial Bilingüe, 1979. 263–316.

King, Nicole R. "Meditations and Mediations: Issues of History and Fiction in *Dessa Rose.*" *Soundings* 76.2–3 (1993): 351–68.

Kingston, Maxine Hong. *China Men.* 1980. New York: Random, 1989.

———. "Personal Statement." *Approaches to Teaching Kingston's* The Woman Warrior. Ed. Shirley Geok-lin Lim. New York: MLA, 1991. 23–25.

———. *The Woman Warrior: Memoirs of a Girlhood among Ghosts.* 1976. New York: Random, 1989.

Kloss, Heinz. *The American Bilingual Tradition.* 1977. Washington, D.C.: Center for Applied Linguistics; McHenry, Ill.: Delta Systems, 1998.

Kochman, Thomas. "Toward an Ethnography of Black American Speech Behavior." *Afro-American Anthropology: Contemporary Perspectives.* Ed. N. E. Whitten and J. F. Szwed. New York: Free Press, 1970. 145–62.

Kroeber, Karl. "Technology and Tribal Tradition." *Narrative Chance: Postmodern Discourse on Native American Indian Literatures.* Ed. Gerald Vizenor. Albuquerque: University of New Mexico Press, 1989. 11–37.

Krupat, Arnold. "Postcoloniality and Native American Literature." *Yale Journal of Criticism* 7 (1994): 163–80.

———. *The Voice in the Margin: Native American Literature and the Canon.* Berkeley: University of California Press, 1989.

Kwong, Katy Mei-Kuen. "Bilingualism Equals Access: The Case of Chinese High School Students." *Lifting Every Voice: Pedagogy and Politics of Bilingualism.* Ed. Zeynep F. Beykont. Cambridge, Mass.: Harvard Education Publishing Group, 2000. 43–51.

Labov, William. *The Study of Nonstandard English.* Washington, D.C.: National Council of Teachers of English, 1969.

Larson, Charles. *American Indian Fiction.* Albuquerque: University of New Mexico Press, 1978.

Lattin, Vernon E. "Time and History in Candelaria's *Memories of the Alhambra.*" *Contemporary Chicano Fiction: A Critical Survey.* Ed.

Vernon E. Lattin. Binghamton, N.Y.: Bilingual Press/Editorial Bilingüe, 1986. 278–88.

Lee, A. Robert. "*Chicanismo* as Memory: The Fictions of Rudolfo Anaya, Nash Candelaria, Sandra Cisneros, and Ron Arias." *Memory and Cultural Politics: New Approaches to American Ethnic Literature.* Ed. Amritjit Singh, Joseph Skerrett, and Robert Hogan. Boston: Northeastern University Press, 1996. 320–39.

Lee, Chang-rae. *Native Speaker.* New York: Riverhead, 1995.

Lefevere, André. "Translation: Its Genealogy in the West." *Translation, History, and Culture.* Ed. Susan Bassnett and André Lefevere. London: Pinter Press, 1990. 14–28.

Lévesque, Claude. "The Exile in Language." *The Ear of the Other: Otobiography, Transference, Translation; Texts and Discussions with Jacques Derrida.* Ed. Christie V. McDonald. Trans. Peggy Kamuf. New York: Schocken, 1985. 142–45.

Levine, Suzanne Jill. "Translation as (Sub)version: On Translating *Infante's Inferno.*" *Rethinking Translation: Discourse, Subjectivity, Ideology.* Ed. Lawrence Venuti. London: Routledge, 1992. 75–85.

Lewelling, Vickie. "Official English and English Plus: An Update." *ERIC Digest.* ERIC Clearinghouse on Languages and Linguistics. May 1997. EDO-FL-97-07. 1–5. <<http://www.cal.org/resources/digest/lewello1.html>>. 9 December 2004.

Lewis, Marvin A. "The Urban Experience in Selected Chicano Fiction." *Contemporary Chicano Fiction: A Critical Survey.* Ed. Vernon E. Lattin. Binghamton, N.Y.: Bilingual Press/Editorial Bilingüe, 1986. 46–61.

Lewis, Philip E. "The Measure of Translation Effects." *Difference in Translation.* Ed. Joseph Graham. Ithaca: Cornell University Press, 1985. 31–62.

Li, David Leiwei. "The Naming of a Chinese American 'I': Cross-Cultural Sign/ifications in *The Woman Warrior.*" *Criticism* 30 (1988): 497–515.

Ling, Jinqi. "Race, Power, and Cultural Politics in John Okada's *No-No Boy.*" *American Literature* 67 (1995): 359–81.

Lipski, John M. *Linguistic Aspects of Spanish-English Language Switching.* Tempe: Center for Latin American Studies, Arizona State University, 1985.

Louie, David Wong. *Pangs of Love: Stories.* New York: Plume, 1992.

Lubiano, Wahneema. "The Postmodern Rag: Political Identity and the Vernacular in *Song of Solomon.*" *New Essays on Song*

of Solomon. Ed. Valerie Smith. Cambridge, Eng.: Cambridge
University Press, 1995. 93–116.

Magnet, Joseph. "Language Rights as Collective Rights." *Perspectives
on Official English: The Campaign for English as the Official
Language of the USA*. Ed. Karen Adams and Daniel Brink. Berlin:
Mouton de Gruyter, 1990. 293–99.

Maier, Carol S. "A Woman in Translation, Reflecting." *Translation
Review* 17 (1985): 4–8.

Maier, Carol S., and Françoise Massardier-Kenney. "Gender in/and
Literary Translation." *Translation Horizons: Beyond the Boundaries
of Translation Spectrum*. Ed. Marilyn Gaddis Rose. Binghamton,
N.Y.: Center for Research in Translation, 1996.

Marx, Doug. "Sherman Alexie." *Writing for Your Life #3*. Ed. Sybil
Steinberg and Jonathan Bing. Wainscott, N.Y.: Pushcart Press,
1997. 1–5.

Mass, Amy Iwasaki. "Psychological Effects of the Camps on Japanese
Americans." *Japanese Americans: From Relocation to Redress*. Ed.
Roger Daniels, Sandra Taylor, and Harry Kitano. Rev. ed. Seattle:
University of Washington Press, 1991. 159–62.

McAllister, Harold S. "Incarnate Grace and the Paths of Salvation
in *House Made of Dawn*." *South Dakota Review* 12.4 (1974):
115–25.

McDonald, Dorothy Ritsuko. "After Imprisonment: Ichiro's Search
for Redemption in *No-No Boy*." *MELUS* 6.3 (1979): 19–26.

McKay, Sandra Lee. "English Language Learners and Educational
Investments." *New Immigrants in the United States: Readings for
Second Language Educators*. Ed. Sandra Lee McKay and Sau-ling
Cynthia Wong. Cambridge, U.K.: Cambridge University Press,
2000. 395–420.

Mehrez, Samia. "The Subversive Poetics of Radical Bilingualism:
Postcolonial Francophone North African Literature." *The Bounds
of Race: Perspectives on Hegemony and Resistance*. Ed. Dominick
LaCapra. Ithaca: Cornell University Press, 1991. 255–77.

———. "Translation and the Postcolonial Experience: The
Francophone North African Text." *Rethinking Translation:
Discourse, Subjectivity, Ideology*. Ed. Lawrence Venuti. London:
Routledge, 1992. 120–38.

Milroy, Lesley, and Li Wei. "A Social Network Approach to Code-
Switching: The Example of a Bilingual Community in Britain."
One Speaker, Two Languages: Cross-Disciplinary Perspectives on

Code-Switching. Ed. Lesley Milroy and Pieter Muysken. New York: Cambridge University Press, 1995. 136–57.

Min, Pyong Gap. "Korean Americans' Language Use." *New Immigrants in the United States: Readings for Second Language Educators.* Ed. Sandra Lee McKay and Sau-ling Cynthia Wong. Cambridge, U.K.: Cambridge University Press, 2000. 306–32.

Miner, Susan. "Legal Implications of the Official English Declaration." *Language and Politics in the United States and Canada: Myths and Realities.* Ed. Thomas Ricento and Barbara Burnaby. Mahwah, N.J.: Lawrence Erlbaum Associates, 1998. 171–84.

Momaday, N. Scott. *House Made of Dawn.* 1968. New York: Harper, 1989.

———. "The Man Made of Words." *Indian Voices: The Native American Today; Convocation of American Indian Scholars.* San Francisco: Indian Historian Press, 1970. 49–84.

———. *The Way to Rainy Mountain.* Albuquerque: University of New Mexico Press, 1969.

———. "Wordwalker." Interview. *Ancestral Voice: Conversations with N. Scott Momaday.* By Charles L. Woodard. Lincoln: University of Nebraska Press, 1989. 75–149.

Moraga, Cherríe. *Loving in the War Years: Lo que nunca pasó sus labios.* Boston: South End Press, 1983.

Mori, Toshio. "The Travelers." *"The Chauvinist" and Other Stories.* Los Angeles: Asian American Studies Center, 1979. 127–32.

Morrison, Toni. *Beloved.* New York: Plume, 1987.

———. "An Interview with Toni Morrison." By Bessie W. Jones and Audrey Vinson. *The World of Toni Morrison: Explorations in Literary Criticism.* Dubuque, Iowa: Kendall Hunt, 1985. 127–51.

———. *Tar Baby.* New York: Plume, 1981.

Murray, David. *Forked Tongues: Speech, Writing, and Representation in North American Indian Texts.* Bloomington: Indiana University Press, 1991.

Nabokov, Vladimir. "Problems of Translation: *Onegin* in English." *Theories of Translation: An Anthology of Essays from Dryden to Derrida.* Ed. Rainer Schulte and John Biguenet. Chicago: University of Chicago Press, 1992. 127–43.

Nancy, Jean-Luc. "Cut Throat Sun." *An Other Tongue: Nation and Ethnicity in the Linguistic Borderlands.* Ed. Alfred Arteaga. Durham: Duke University Press, 1994. 113–23.

Navarro, Mireya. "For Hispanics, Language and Culture Barriers Can Further Complicate College." *New York Times*, 10 February 2003, A14.

Nelson, Robert. *Place and Vision: The Function of Landscape in Native American Fiction*. New York: Peter Lang, 1993.

Neubert, Albrecht, and Gregory M. Shreve. *Translation as Text*. Kent, Ohio: Kent State University Press, 1992.

Ng, Fae Myenne. *Bone*. New York: Harper Collins, 1993.

Niranjana, Tejaswini. *Siting Translation: History, Post-structuralism, and the Colonial Context*. Berkeley: University of California Press, 1992.

Norton, Bonny. "Investment, Acculturation, and Language Loss." *New Immigrants in the United States: Readings for Second Language Educators*. Ed. Sandra Lee McKay and Sau-ling Cynthia Wong. Cambridge, U.K.: Cambridge University Press, 2000. 443–63.

Nunberg, Geoffrey. "Speaking of America: Why English-Only is a Bad Idea." *The Workings of Language: From Prescriptions to Perspectives*. Ed. Rebecca S. Wheeler. Westport, Conn.: Praeger, 1999. 117–28.

Ogawa, Dennis M., and Evarts C. Fox Jr. "Japanese Internment and Relocation: The Hawaii Experience." *Japanese Americans: From Relocation to Redress*. Ed. Roger Daniels, Sandra Taylor, and Harry Kitano. Rev. ed. Seattle: University of Washington Press, 1991. 135–38.

Okada, John. *No-No Boy*. 1957. Seattle: University of Washington Press, 1976.

Owens, Louis. *Mixedblood Messages: Literature, Film, Family, Place*. Norman: University of Oklahoma Press, 1998.

———. *Other Destinies: Understanding the American Indian Novel*. Norman: University of Oklahoma Press, 1992.

Paisano, Edna L., ed. *We the American . . . Asians*. Washington, D.C.: Bureau of the Census, 1993.

Paredes, Raymund. "The Evolution of Chicano Literature." *Three American Literatures: Essays in Chicano, Native American, and Asian-American Literature for Teachers of American Literature*. Ed. Houston Baker. New York: MLA, 1982. 33–79.

Paz, Octavio. Interview. *The Poet's Other Voice: Conversations on Literary Translation*. Ed. Edwin Honig. Amherst: University of Massachusetts Press, 1985. 153–63.

Peacock, John. "Unwriting Empire by Writing Oral Tradition: Leslie Marmon Silko's *Ceremony.*" *(Un)writing Empire.* Ed. Theo D'haen. Amsterdam: Rodopi, 1998. 295–308.

Penfield, Joyce, and Jacob Ornstein-Galicia. *Chicano English: An Ethnic Contact Dialect.* Amsterdam: Jon Benjamins Publishing Company, 1985.

Pérez Firmat, Gustavo. *The Cuban Condition: Translation and Identity in Modern Cuban Literature.* Cambridge, Eng.: Cambridge University Press, 1989.

———. *Life on the Hyphen: The Cuban-American Way.* Austin: University of Texas Press, 1994.

Pfaff, Carol. "Constraints on Language Mixing: Intrasentential Code-Switching and Borrowing in Spanish/English." *Language* 55 (1979): 291–318.

Poplack, Shana. "Contrasting Patterns of Codeswitching in Two Communities." *Codeswitching: Anthropological and Sociolinguistic Perspectives.* Ed. Monica Heller. New York: Mouton de Gruyter, 1988. 215–42.

———. "Sometimes I'll Start a Sentence in Spanish *y termino en español*: Toward a Typology of Code-Switching." 1979. *The Bilingualism Reader.* Ed. Li Wei. New York: Routledge, 2000. 221–56.

Power, Susan. *The Grass Dancer.* 1994. New York: Berkley, 1995.

Pratt, Mary Louise. *Imperial Eyes: Travel Writing and Transculturation.* New York: Routledge, 1992.

Rabassa, Gregory. "No Two Snowflakes Are Alike: Translation as Metaphor." *The Craft of Translation.* Ed. John Biguenet and Rainer Schulte. Chicago: University of Chicago Press, 1989.

Ramanujan, A. K. "On Translating a Tamil Poem." *The Art of Translation: Voices from the Field.* Ed. Rosanna Warren. Boston: Northeastern University Press, 1989. 47–63.

Ramirez, David J., Sandra D. Yuen, and Dena Ramey. *Final Report, Longitudinal Study of Structured English Immersion Strategy, Early-Exit and Late-Exit Transitional Bilingual Education Programs for Language-Minority Children.* San Mateo: Aguirre International, 1991.

Raymond, Michael W. "Tai-me, Christ, and the Machine: Affirmation through Mythic Pluralism in *House Made of Dawn.*" *Studies in American Fiction* 11 (1983): 61–71.

Rebolledo, Tey Diana. *Women Singing in the Snow: A Cultural*

Analysis of Chicana Literature. Tucson: University of Arizona Press, 1995.

Rhydwen, Mari. "Language Loss, Our Loss." *The Workings of Language: From Prescriptions to Perspectives.* Ed. Rebecca S. Wheeler. Westport, Conn.: Praeger, 1999. 129–36.

Rice, Alan. *Radical Narratives of the Black Atlantic.* New York: Continuum, 2003.

Ricento, Thomas. "National Language Policy in the United States." *Language and Politics in the United States and Canada: Myths and Realities.* Ed. Thomas Ricento and Barbara Burnaby. Mahwah, N.J.: Lawrence Erlbaum Associates, 1998. 85–112.

Rickford, John. "Holding on to a Language of Our Own: An Interview with Linguist John Rickford." *The Real Ebonics Debate: Power, Language, and the Education of African-American Children.* Ed. Theresa Perry and Lisa Delpit. Boston: Beacon Press, 1998. 59–65.

Roceric, Alexandra. *Language Maintenance within an American Ethnic Community: The Case of Romanian.* Grass Lake-Jackson, Mich.: Romanian-American Heritage Center, 1982.

Rodriguez, Richard. *Brown: The Last Discovery of America.* New York: Viking, 2002.

———. *Days of Obligation: An Argument with My Mexican Father.* New York: Penguin, 1992.

———. *Hunger of Memory: The Education of Richard Rodriguez.* 1982. New York: Bantam, 1983.

———. "The New, New World: Richard Rodriguez on Culture and Assimilation." Interview with Virginia I. Postrel and Nick Gillespie. 1994. *Reason Magazine Online.* <<http://reason.com/Rodri.shtml>>. 12 December 2004.

Romero, Lora. "'When Something Goes Queer': Familiarity, Formalism, and Minority Intellectuals in the 1980s." *Yale Journal of Criticism* 6 (1993): 121–42.

Rosen, Kenneth, ed. *Voices of the Rainbow: Contemporary Poetry by American Indians.* New York: Viking Press, 1975.

Rubin, Donald, ed. "Introduction: Composing Social Identity." *Composing Social Identity in Written Language.* Hillsdale, N.J.: Lawrence Erlbaum Associates, 1995. 1–30.

Rudin, Ernst. *Tender Accents of Sound: Spanish in the Chicano Novel in English.* Tempe, Ariz.: Bilingual Press/Editorial Bilingüe, 1996.

Ruppert, James. "Dialogism and Mediation in Leslie Silko's *Ceremony.*" *Explicator* 51 (1993): 129–34.

―――. *Mediation in Contemporary Native American Fiction.* Norman: University of Oklahoma Press, 1995.

Rushdie, Salman. *Imaginary Homelands: Essays and Criticism, 1981–1991.* London: Granta, 1991.

Rushdy, Ashraf H. A. "Reading Mammy: The Subject of Relation in Sherley Anne Williams' *Dessa Rose.*" *African American Review* 27 (1993): 365–89.

Saldívar, Ramón. *Chicano Narrative: The Dialectics of Difference.* Madison: University of Wisconsin Press, 1990.

Sánchez, Marta E. "The Estrangement Effect in Sherley Anne Williams' *Dessa Rose.*" *Genders* 15 (1992): 21–36.

Sánchez, Rosaura. "Calculated Musings: Richard Rodriguez's Metaphysics of Difference." *The Ethnic Canon: Histories, Institutions, and Interventions.* Ed. David Palumbo-Liu. Minneapolis: University of Minnesota Press, 1995. 153–73.

Sato, Gayle K. Fujita. "Momotaro's Exile: John Okada's *No-No Boy.*" *Reading the Literatures of Asian America.* Ed. Shirley Geok-lin Lim and Amy Ling. Philadelphia: Temple University Press, 1992. 239–58.

Scarberry-García, Susan. *Landmarks of Healing: A Study of* House Made of Dawn. Albuquerque: University of New Mexico Press, 1990.

Schermerhorn, Richard. *Comparative Ethnic Relations: A Framework for Theory and Research.* New York: Random, 1970.

Schleiermacher, Friedrich. "On the Different Methods of Translating." 1938. Trans. Waltraud Bartscht. *Theories of Translation: An Anthology of Essays from Dryden to Derrida.* Ed. Rainer Schulte and John Biguenet. Chicago: University of Chicago Press, 1992. 36–54.

Schubnell, Matthias. *N. Scott Momaday: The Cultural and Literary Background.* Norman: University of Oklahoma Press, 1985.

Secret, Carrie. "Embracing Ebonics and Teaching Standard English: An Interview with Oakland Teacher Carrie Secret." *The Real Ebonics Debate: Power, Language, and the Education of African-American Children.* Ed. Theresa Perry and Lisa Delpit. Boston: Beacon Press, 1998. 79–88.

Selinger, Bernard. "*House Made of Dawn*: A Positively Ambivalent Bildungsroman." *Modern Fiction Studies* 45.1 (1999): 38–68.

Senna, Danzy. *Caucasia*. New York: Riverhead, 1998.

Sequoya, Jana. "How (!) Is an Indian?: A Contest of Stories." *New Voices in Native American Literary Criticism*. Ed. Arnold Krupat. Washington, D.C.: Smithsonian Institution Press, 1993. 453–73.

Shell, Marc. "Babel in America; or, The Politics of Language Diversity in the United States." *Critical Inquiry* 20 (1993): 103–27.

Silko, Leslie Marmon. *Almanac of the Dead*. 1991. New York: Penguin, 1992.

———. "Background to the Story: A Leslie Marmon Silko Interview." By Kim Barnes. *"Yellow Woman": Leslie Marmon Silko*. Ed. Melody Graulich. New Brunswick: Rutgers University Press, 1993. 47–65.

———. *Ceremony*. New York: Penguin, 1977.

———. "Language and Literature from a Pueblo Indian Perspective." *English Literature: Opening Up the Canon*. Ed. Leslie Fiedler and Houston Baker Jr. Baltimore: Johns Hopkins University Press, 1981. 54–72.

Silverstein, Michael. "Monoglot 'Standard' in America: Standardization and Metaphors of Linguistic Hegemony." *The Matrix of Language: Contemporary Linguistic Anthropology*. Ed. Donald Brenneis and Ronald Macaulay. New York: Harper Collins, 1996. 284–306.

Simon, Sherry. "The Language of Cultural Difference: Figures of Alterity in Canadian Translation." *Rethinking Translation: Discourse, Subjectivity, Ideology*. Ed. Lawrence Venuti. London: Routledge, 1992. 159–76.

Smitherman, Geneva. "Black Language as Power." *Language and Power*. Ed. Cheris Kramarae, Muriel Schulz, and William M. O'Barr. Beverly Hills: Sage, 1984. 101–15.

———. *Talkin and Testifyin: The Language of Black America*. Detroit: Wayne State University Press, 1986.

———. *Talkin That Talk: Language, Culture, and Education in African America*. London: Routledge, 2000.

Snow, Catherine. "Rationales for Native Language Instruction: Evidence from Research." *Bilingual Education: Issues and Strategies*. Ed. Amado Padilla, Halford Fairchild, and Concepción Valadez. Newbury Park, Calif.: Sage, 1990. 60–74.

Sollors, Werner. *Beyond Ethnicity: Consent and Descent in American Culture*. New York: Oxford University Press, 1986.

———. "How German Is It? Multilingual America Reconsidered." *Not English Only: Redefining "American" in American Studies.* Ed. Orm Øverland. Amsterdam: Vrije Universiteit Press, 2001. 148–55.

———. "National Identity and Ethnic Diversity: 'Of Plymouth Rock and Jamestown and Ellis Island'; or, Ethnic Literature and Some Redefinitions of 'America.'" *History and Memory in African-American Culture.* Ed. Geneviève Fabre and Robert O'Meally. New York: Oxford University Press, 1994. 92–121.

———, ed. *Multilingual America: Transnationalism, Ethnicity, and the Languages of American Literature.* New York: New York University Press, 1998.

Soto, Lourdes Diaz. *Language, Culture, and Power: Bilingual Families and the Struggle for Quality Education.* Albany: State University of New York Press, 1997.

Souza, Heloisa. "Language Loss and Language Gain in the Brazilian Community: The Role of Schools and Families." *Lifting Every Voice: Pedagogy and Politics of Bilingualism.* Ed. Zeynep F. Beykont. Cambridge: Harvard Education Publishing Group, 2000. 7–20.

Spellmeyer, Kurt. "'Too Little Care': Language, Politics, and Embodiment in the Life-World." *Rhetoric in an Antifoundational World: Language, Culture, Pedagogy.* Ed. Michael Bernard-Donals and Richard R. Glejzer. New Haven: Yale University Press, 1998. 254–91.

Sternbach, Nancy Saporta. "'A Deep Racial Memory of Love': The Chicana Feminism of Cherríe Moraga." *Breaking Boundaries: Latina Writing and Critical Readings.* Ed. Asunción Horno-Delgado et al. Amherst: University of Massachusetts Press, 1989. 48–61.

Stewart, William A. "Continuity and Change in American Negro Dialects." *Black-White Speech Relationships.* Ed. Walt Wolfram and Nona H. Clarke. Washington, D.C.: Center for Applied Linguistics, 1971. 51–73.

Streamas, John. "The Invention of Normality in Japanese American Internment Narratives." *Ethnicity and the American Short Story.* Ed. Julie Brown. New York: Garland, 1997. 125–40.

Sumida, Stephen. "Japanese American Moral Dilemmas in John Okada's *No-No Boy* and Milton Murayama's *All I Asking for Is My Body.*" *Frontiers of Asian American Studies: Writing, Research, and*

Commentary. Ed. Gail Nomura et al. Pullman: Washington State University Press, 1989. 222–34.

Swann, Brian, ed. *On the Translation of Native American Literatures.* Washington, D.C.: Smithsonian Institution Press, 1992.

Swigart, Leigh. "Two Codes or One? The Insiders' View and the Description of Codeswitching in Dakar." *Codeswitching.* Ed. Carol M. Eastman. Clevedon, U.K.: Multilingual Matters, 1992. 83–102.

Takaki, Ronald. *Strangers from a Different Shore: A History of Asian Americans.* New York: Penguin, 1990.

Taubenfeld, Aviva. "'Only an "L"': Linguistic Borders and the Immigrant Author in Abraham Cahan's *Yekl* and *Yankel der Yankee.*" *Multilingual America: Transnationalism, Ethnicity, and the Languages of American Literature.* Ed. Werner Sollors. New York: New York University Press, 1998. 144–65.

Taylor, Paul Beekman. "Repetition as Cure in Native American Story: Silko's *Ceremony* and Momaday's *The Ancient Child.*" *Repetition.* Ed. Andreas Fischer. Tübingen: Gunter Narr Verlag, 1994. 221–42.

———. "Silko's Reappropriation of Secrecy." *Leslie Marmon Silko: A Collection of Critical Essays.* Ed. Louise K. Barnett and James L. Thorson. Albuquerque: University of New Mexico Press, 1999. 23–62.

Thomas, W. P., and V. P. Collier. "Language-Minority Student Achievement and Program Effectiveness Studies Support Native Language Development." *NABE News* 18.8 (1996): 5, 12.

Tong, Benjamin. "Critic of Admirer Sees Dumb Racist." *San Francisco Journal,* 11 May 1977, 6.

Trimmer, Joseph. "Native Americans and the American Mix: N. Scott Momaday's *House Made of Dawn.*" *Indiana Social Studies Quarterly* 28.2 (1975): 75–91.

Ts'ai Yen. "From 18 Verses Sung to a Tatar Reed Whistle." *Women Poets of China.* Trans. and ed. Kenneth Rexroth and Ling Chung. New York: New Directions, 1972. 4–7.

Tse, Lucy. *"Why Don't They Learn English?": Separating Fact from Fallacy in the U.S. Language Debate.* New York: Teachers College Press, 2001.

Turner, Lorenzo Dow. *Africanisms in the Gullah Dialect.* 1949. Columbia: University of South Carolina Press, 2002.

TuSmith, Bonnie. *All My Relatives: Community in Contemporary*

Ethnic American Literatures. Ann Arbor: University of Michigan Press, 1993.

———. "Literary Tricksterism: Maxine Hong Kingston's *The Woman Warrior: Memoirs of a Girlhood among Ghosts.*" *Anxious Power: Reading, Writing, and Ambivalence in Narrative by Women.* Ed. Carol J. Singley and Susan Elizabeth Sweeney. Albany: State University of New York Press, 1993. 279–94.

Uchida, Yoshiko. *Desert Exile: The Uprooting of a Japanese American Family.* Seattle: University of Washington Press, 1982.

Untermeyer, Louis. *Robert Frost: A Backward Look.* Washington, D.C.: Reference Department, Library of Congress, 1964.

Valdés, Guadalupe. "Bilingualism and Language Use among Mexican Americans." *New Immigrants in the United States: Readings for Second Language Educators.* Ed. Sandra Lee McKay and Sau-ling Cynthia Wong. Cambridge, U.K.: Cambridge University Press, 2000. 99–136.

Varennes, Fernand de. *Language, Minorities and Human Rights.* The Hague: Martinus Nijhoff, 1996.

Véa, Alfredo. *La Maravilla.* New York: Plume, 1994.

Velie, Alan R. *Four American Indian Literary Masters: N. Scott Momaday, James Welch, Leslie Marmon Silko, and Gerald Vizenor.* Norman: University of Oklahoma Press, 1982.

Veltman, Calvin. "The American Linguistic Mosaic: Understanding Language Shift in the United States." *New Immigrants in the United States: Readings for Second Language Educators.* Ed. Sandra Lee McKay and Sau-ling Cynthia Wong. Cambridge, U.K.: Cambridge University Press, 2000. 58–93.

———. *Language Shift in the United States.* Berlin: Mouton Publisher, 1983.

Venuti, Lawrence. Introduction. *Rethinking Translation: Discourse, Subjectivity, Ideology.* Ed. Lawrence Venuti. London: Routledge, 1992. 1–17.

Verdelle, A. J. *The Good Negress.* 1995. New York: Harper, 1996.

Vizenor, Gerald. "Trickster Discourse: Comic Holotropes and Language Games." *Narrative Chance: Postmodern Discourse on Native American Indian Literatures.* Ed. Gerald Vizenor. Albuquerque: University of New Mexico Press, 1989. 187–211.

Walker, Cheryl. *Indian Nation: Native American Literature and Nineteenth-Century Nationalisms.* Durham: Duke University Press, 1997.

Waniek, Marilyn Nelson. "The Power of Language in N. Scott Momaday's *House Made of Dawn.*" *Minority Voices: An Interdisciplinary Journal* 4.1 (1980): 23–28.

Wechsler, Robert. *Performing without a Stage: The Art of Literary Translation.* North Haven, Conn.: Catbird Press, 1998.

Weglyn, Michi. *Years of Infamy: The Untold Story of America's Concentration Camps.* New York: Morrow Quill, 1976.

Weinberger, Eliot, and Octavio Paz. *Nineteen Ways of Looking at Wang Wei: How a Chinese Poem Is Translated.* Wakefield, R.I.: Moyer Bell, 1987.

Wells, J. C. *Accents of English.* Vol. 1. Cambridge, U.K.: Cambridge University Press, 1982.

Werner, Craig. "The Briar Patch as Modernist Myth: Morrison, Barthes and Tar Baby As-Is." *Critical Essays on Toni Morrison.* Comp. Nellie McKay. Boston: G. K. Hall, 1988. 150–67.

Wiley, Terrence G. *Literacy and Language Diversity in the United States.* Washington, D.C.: Center for Applied Linguistics; McHenry, Ill.: Delta Systems, 1996.

———. "Myths about Language Diversity and Literacy in the United States." <<http://www.ericdigests.org/1998-1/myths. htm>>. 9 December 2004.

Wilgoren, Jodi. "Divided by a Call for a Common Language." *New York Times*, 19 July 2002, A8.

Williams, Robert L., ed. *Ebonics: The True Language of Black Folks.* St. Louis: Institute of Black Studies, 1975.

Williams, Sherley Anne. *Dessa Rose.* 1986. New York: Berkley, 1987.

Wirth-Nesher, Hana. "The Languages of Memory: Cynthia Ozick's *The Shawl.*" *Multilingual America: Transnationalism, Ethnicity, and the Languages of American Literature.* Ed. Werner Sollors. New York: New York University Press, 1998. 313–26.

Wittgenstein, Ludwig. *Philosophical Investigations.* Trans. G. E. M. Anscombe. Oxford: Basil Blackwell, 1958.

Wolfram, Walt. *Dialects and American English.* Englewood Cliffs, N.J.: Prentice Hall, 1991.

———. "The Relationship of White Southern Speech to Vernacular Black English." *Language* 50.3 (1974): 498–527.

Wolfson, Nessa. *Perspectives: Sociolinguistics and TESOL.* Cambridge, U.K.: Newbury, 1989.

Wong, Sau-ling Cynthia. "Autobiography as Guided Chinatown Tour? Maxine Hong Kingston's *The Woman Warrior* and the

Chinese-American Autobiographical Controversy." *Multicultural Autobiography: American Lives*. Ed. James Robert Payne. Knoxville: University of Tennessee Press, 1992. 248–79.

———. "Kingston's Handling of Traditional Chinese Sources." *Approaches to Teaching Kingston's* The Woman Warrior. Ed. Shirley Geok-lin Lim. New York: MLA, 1991. 26–36.

Wong, Sau-ling Cynthia, and M. G. López. "English Language Learners of Chinese Background: A Portrait of Diversity." *New Immigrants in the United States: Readings for Second Language Educators*. Ed. Sandra Lee McKay and Sau-ling Cynthia Wong. Cambridge, U.K.: Cambridge University Press, 2000. 263–305.

Wright, Neil. "Visitors from the Spirit Path: Tribal Magic in Susan Power's *The Grass Dancer*." *Kentucky Philological Review* 10 (1995): 39–43.

Xia, Ningsheng. "Maintenance of the Chinese Language in the United States." *Bilingual Review/La Revista Bilingüe* 17.3 (1992): 195–209.

Yamada, Mitsuye. *Camp Notes and Other Writings*. New Brunswick: Rutgers University Press, 1998.

Yarbro-Bejarano, Yvonne. *The Wounded Heart: Writing on Cherríe Moraga*. Austin: University of Texas Press, 2001.

Yin, Xiao-huang. "Redefining Chinese-American Sensibility: A Sociohistorical Study of Chinese Language Literature in America." *Not English Only: Redefining "American" in American Studies*. Ed. Orm Øverland. Amsterdam: Vrije Universiteit Press, 2001. 178–98.

Yogi, Stan. "'You Had to Be One or the Other': Oppositions and Reconciliation in John Okada's *No-No Boy*." *MELUS* 21 (1996): 63–77.

Young, Robert J. C. *Colonial Desire: Hybridity in Theory, Culture and Race*. London: Routledge, 1995.

Zamir, Shamoon. "Literature in a 'National Sacrifice Area': Leslie Silko's *Ceremony*." *New Voices in Native American Literary Criticism*. Ed. Arnold Krupat. Washington, D.C.: Smithsonian Institution Press, 1993. 396–415.

Zhou, Min, and Carl L. Bankston. "Social Capital and the Adaptation of the Second Generation: The Case of Vietnamese Youth in New Orleans." *The New Second Generation*. Ed. Alejandro Portes. New York: Russell Sage Foundation, 1996. 197–220.

Index